WORCESTERSHIRE

WORCESTERSHIRE

PETER NEVILLE HAVINS

EDITED BY ANNE BRADFORD

ROBERT HALE • LONDON

ISBN 978-0-7090-7988-0

Robert Hale Limited
Clerkenwell House
Clerkenwell Green
London EC1R 0HT

www.halebooks.com

2 4 6 8 10 9 7 5 3 1

Typeset by Eurodesign
Printed in India

CONTENTS

ACKNOWLEDGEMENTS

My thanks are due to the following:

Neville Billington, historian and author
Tim Bridges, church historian and author
Hal Dalwood, Worcestershire County Council Archaeology project manager
James Dinn, Archaeology Officer
Paul Harding of Discover History
Brian Haughton, early Medieval author and historian
Ian Hayes, railway historian and writer
Pat Hughes, Worcester historian and tutor
Carole Hodgson, author of Clent Clarion series
Len Holder, retired skipper
Mike Johnson, war historian and author
Val Lewis, historian
David Morrison, Worcester cathedral librarian
Mike Napthan, archaeologist
Caroline Roslington, Archivist of King's School, Worcester
John H. Smith for information on Trevor Nunn May
Melvyn Thompson, Carpet Museum Trust, Kidderminster
Cora Weaver, Malvern historian and author
Martyn Webb, Morgan Motors archivist
Robin Whittaker, Head Archivist, Worcester Record Office
Members of Unitarian Church in Hollywood
Staff of The Evesham Hotel, Bengeworth

Special thanks to John Bradford, photographer

1

THE MAKING OF A HISTORIC COUNTY

Worcestershire is now an unspoilt county of winding lanes and scattered pictur-esque villages, where the steeples and towers of ancient churches rise above the trees. The magnificent ancient cathedral at Worcester towers over the River Severn.

Its bishops were once as powerful as kings and four of them have been canonized, more than from any other city – the saints Dunstan, Egwin, Oswald and Wulstan were all once bishops of Worcester. King John, who died in 1216, loved Worcester so much that he asked to be buried in its cathedral monastery, where he rests between two of its saints. Henry VII (1457–1509) chose its

View of Worcester cathedral from the hill known as Fort Royal –
a remnant of the Battle of Worcester defences

cathedral as the last resting place of his beloved eldest son and heir, Prince Arthur.

Many of the county's towns are tourist attractions – Worcester, Bewdley, Stourport-on-Severn, Pershore and Evesham. Products from industries in the county have been exported all over the world – such as needles from Redditch, carpets from Kidderminster, nails from Bromsgrove, and porcelain from Worcester. The Teme valley was once filled with orchards and hopyards and the Evesham plain is still famous for its fruit and vegetables.

Among the county's famous offspring are Edward Elgar, the composer, and Stanley Baldwin, three times Prime Minister.

The longest river in Great Britain, the River Severn, runs from north to south through the county and during its course is joined by the Stour, the Salwarpe and the Teme. In the south of the county, the Avon runs from east to west, joining the Severn just over the border in Gloucestershire.

However, Worcestershire has not always been the rural haven that it is today. Few counties have had such an eventful history. During the civil war of the 1100s between Empress Matilda and King Stephen, Worcester was burned down twice. Two great battles that changed the whole history of England have been fought in its towns. The Battle of Evesham took place in 1265 and the Battle of

View across the River Severn to the Malvern Hills

Worcester in 1651. The Gunpowder Plot of 1605 was planned in Worcestershire, after which many of the Catholic gentry were hung, drawn and quartered. Two of the Oxford martyrs, Hugh Latimer and John Hooper, who were burned at the stake in the reign of Queen Mary, had been bishops of Worcester.

WORCESTERSHIRE HILLS

Although most of Worcestershire is gently undulating countryside, the county is surrounded on three sides by green and beautiful hills. To the north-east are the Waseley, Lickey and Clent Hills. With Birmingham and the Black Country on their northern edge, this is the playground of the industrial Midlands. The Lickey Hills Country Park was secured for general use in the early twentieth century by the Birmingham Society for Open Spaces, whose members included personnel from the Cadbury family and the Second Earl of Plymouth.

Between 1924 and 1953 a tram service ran from Birmingham to the foot of the Lickeys at Rednal, bringing thousands of Birmingham day trippers at bank holidays and weekends for a scramble up the hills. Among them was a very

*The Waseley, Lickey and Clent Hills were popular
for outings from the Black Country and Birmingham*

The Clent Hills

young editor whose memories are chiefly those of long queues for the trams and searching for a cobbler as her mother, unused to the countryside, always insisted on wearing strappy high heels for the day out, which soon disintegrated.

On the north-eastern slopes of the Clent Hills, just over 1 mile north-west of Romsley, is a tiny Norman church. Much of the church is typical of the 1100s, including the tympanum over the entrance door. In traditional Norman style it shows a seated Christ in a heavily draped robe, wearing a crown and surrounded by angels. The church is dedicated to a Mercian saint, St Kenelm, said to have been murdered here in 819.

Legend states that when Kenulf, king of Mercia, died in 810, he left one son, Kenelm, and two daughters, of whom Quenryda was the elder. Quenryda had her eye on the throne and conspired with her lover to murder Kenelm. The lover slew the young king while he was out riding in the Cowbach valley between Clent and Romsley, cut off his head, and hid the body under a thornbush.

Months later, as the Pope officiated in St Peter's in Rome, a snow-white dove flew in through a window and dropped a scroll from its beak. On the scroll was a message that read:

In Clent, in Cowbach, lyeth under a thorn
His head off-shorn, Kenelm, King born.

St Kenelm's church

Intrigued, the Pope sent messengers to England to investigate. Looking for a buried body in the wild and desolate countryside was like looking for a needle in a haystack, but the searchers were guided to the spot by a shaft of light and the lowing of a milk-white cow. As they disinterred the corpse, a holy spring gushed from the ground.

Divine vengeance had not done with Quenryda. Giraldus Cambrensis in *The Journey through Wales*, written in 1188, tells that when the body of Kenelm was carried out, the crowd shouted, 'He is God's martyr! There is no doubt about it! He is the martyr of God!' Quenryda replied, 'He is indeed God's martyr, as truly as my eyes are resting on this psalter.' By chance she was reading a psalter and at that point her two eyes were torn from her head and fell on the open book. The psalter, with its bloodstains running down the page was, for centuries, a prized possession of Winchcombe Abbey.

No one knows for certain which is the original spring. The official one is a carefully preserved spring a few yards from the church, down a path. However, Sir Nikolaus Pevsner, the learned architect, wrote that below the east end of the church is an undercroft containing the holy spring and a blocked arch in the south wall of the chancel led to the stairway down. John Amphlett, in *A Short History of Clent*, says that 500 yards away in the garden of Spring Farm is a magnificent surge of water. He suggests that this could be the original spring around which the legend grew.

Sadly, there is apparently very little truth in this fascinating legend that has captured the imagination of people from Medieval times to the present day, although there are some facts upon which the legend is based. There was a King Kenelm, but he was not a boy king, but an adult, and his bones seem to have been taken from Clent and deposited by the side of his father at Winchcombe Abbey. As for Quenryda, she entered a monastery and became a virtuous abbess.

To the south of Worcestershire is an outlier of the Cotswold hills, Bredon Hill, the characteristic Cotswold limestone isolated within the Worcestershire boundary. Overlooking Kemerton are the King and Queen stones; these are actually three stones, although only two are celebrated.

For centuries they were believed to have magical healing properties and anyone who passed between them would have their health restored. On the summit are two more huge stones known as the elephant and her calf, a prominent landmark.

West of the River Severn are the Abberley and Suckley Hills, rising to the Malvern Hills in the south. These are all part of a geological chain stretching from north to south. Between Abberley and Woodbury Hill, on a little hill of its own, is the Abberley clock tower, 161 feet high, another well-known landmark.

The King and Queen stones on Bredon Hill

It was built in about 1883 by John Jones, who inherited Abberley Hall and grounds from a cousin. The reasons for building it have been given variously as a memorial to his late cousin, as a retreat for his wife who liked to sew in a room at the top (presumably she was very fit to climb all those stairs regularly), and so that his employees had no excuse for bad time-keeping. There is also a suggestion that it enabled him to overlook the Dudley estate at Witley Court and spy on his neighbour, which no doubt gave him much satisfaction but caused annoyance to the Dudley family. Abberley Hall and grounds were sold in 1916 and it is now a private school.

In the south-west of the county are the impressive Malvern Hills, which will feature many times in this book and which have been an inspiration to so many familiar names – W. H. Auden, C. S. Lewis, J. R. R. Tolkien, and especially Edward Elgar, the composer, who was born in Lower Broadheath in 1857. His birthplace is now a museum.

WORCESTERSHIRE'S PREHISTORIC YEARS – A BRIEF SUMMARY

The Malvern Hills, an outstanding geological chain

Walkers struggling up the Malvern Hills may not be aware that these are some of the oldest and hardest rocks in the United Kingdom, going back nearly 700 million years.

Most of the Lickey Hills are made up of rocks reckoned to be 570 million years old. These hills were formed by numerous convulsive earth movements, both plunging and up-thrusting. Then the earth stabilized, the climate cooled, and glaciers crept across the county, smoothing and rounding the hills. As they melted, great lakes filled the flat Worcestershire plain. Icy waters escaping through the Lickey Hills and Kinver Edge formed the Rivers Severn, Avon and Teme. The whole course of the Teme was altered when melting ice caused torrents of water to force their way through Downton Gorge in Herefordshire, forming the present course of the river on its way to join the Severn at Worcester.

Between 600,000 and 10,000 BC, the climate fluctuated between very cold and very warm. Archeological evidence suggests that the first humans arrived in Worcestershire during the warmer spells. Some of their stone tools have been found along the banks of the River Avon. They rarely settled anywhere and moved from place to place, probably hunting game and gathering berries. England was then joined to Europe, there was no English Channel, and much of the North Sea did not exist, so they may have wandered up from the south or across from the east.

From about 10,000 to 4,000 BC, Worcestershire became a landscape of heavily wooded river valleys with clearer higher ground. As the centuries passed, its inhabitants began chopping down trees and hunting with flint tips attached to spears. They made tiny tools from flints, called microliths, used to barb and top the arrows they used for hunting. Most of those so far discovered come from the Kidderminster area, but they have also occasionally been found elsewhere, at places such as Kemerton on Bredon Hill, nearby Beckford which is 2 miles south-east, and Baginton on Hartlebury Common.

Then lifestyles changed. Between about 4,000 BC and 1,500 BC, communities began to settle, and became more sophisticated. In about 2,000 BC, bronze and copper began to be used. Excavations at Kemerton have confirmed that, between 1,200 and 1,000 BC, people were living in small clusters of round houses with thatched roofs, surrounded by rough tracks. They used water from primitive wells, ate and drank from pottery utensils, wove their clothes on looms, bred pigs, sheep, cows and other domestic animals, grew crops and cleared huge stretches of forests.

Around 2,200 BC, burial mounds or barrows began to appear. The corpse was usually cremated before being placed in an urn and interred, and was probably accompanied by some kind of ritual or religious ceremony. At Castle Farm, Holt, archaeologists discovered an Early Bronze Age body cremated and buried in a large pottery urn.

These burial mounds varied in size and were once dotted around the countryside, but most have now been ploughed out. Aerial photography has revealed many forgotten barrows. There were once five barrows on Clent Heath, but now only two survive. Chaddesley Corbet has a road and a hill named after its prehistoric barrow – Barrow Hill and Barrow Lane. Some of those that survive are marked on Ordnance Survey maps as 'tumuli'.

Burial mounds continued to be built well into the Iron Age. It was the Iron Age people who mainly changed the Worcestershire landscape, by clearing the woodland, settling in villages and cultivating fields. The working and use of iron spread through the region from about 700 BC. Iron-tipped ploughshares meant that they could grow more and better crops, and improved trading routes found them better seeds. They became skilled wheat farmers, using a quern stone for grinding corn, and were skilled woodworkers, using a lathe.

Excavations of an Iron Age village at Beckford revealed clusters of buildings, each surrounded by a ditch and perhaps, originally, a fence. Desirable accommodation for an Iron Age family was a circular house built round a wooden framework. The walls were low and built of wattle and daub, a mix of straw, mud and manure. As anyone who has driven through a farmyard knows, manure can be very hard when dried out. The roofs came up to a point and were thatched. Some buildings were probably used for storing grain; pits had been dug for the same purpose. Outside the village a number of fields were surrounded by ditches.

There was great excitement in 1957 when aerial photography of Bewdley revealed a prehistoric site on Blackstone Rock, a rocky outcrop overlooking the River Severn, where the river could be forded at low tide. The ford was on a main route from Worcester to Wales. Archaeologists were able to excavate the site in the 1970s and 1980s, and the site proved so interesting that it was dug again in 2008. Investigations showed an Iron Age settlement enclosed by a double ditch and although the inhabitants were farmers, they probably augmented their income by providing a resting place for travellers.

The most spectacular way in which Iron Age people have left their mark in the county is in the shape of hill forts. Remnants of several hill forts survive. The Clent Hills have Wychbury Camp, the Bredon Hills have Kemerton and Conderton camps, while to the east, beyond the River Severn, are Midsummer Hill and British Camp in the Malverns, Woodbury and Berrow Hill in the Abberley Hills, Garmsley Camp near Kyre (off the B4214 and about 4 miles south-east of Tenbury) and Gadbury Bank in the south-east of the county. Some of the forts may have been occupied for hundreds of years and changed and developed over time.

Archeologists have been surprised to find that people actually lived in these forts. Excavations on a section of Midsummer Hill revealed tightly packed housing.

The forts vary enormously in size; one could house a small village, while another only has room for one dwelling at its summit. Malvern's British Camp is among the largest at 32 acres, while among the smallest is 9-acre Garmsley Camp.

The latest thinking is that some hill forts may have been built for defence, not so much against invaders but against land-hungry neighbours. The population had grown, there was a hunger for fertile land, and perhaps each settlement needed to protect itself from a rival chieftain. Some archaeologists think they may have only been used during the summer months.

<hr>

THE ROMAN ERA

When the Roman Emperor Claudius invaded Britain in AD 43, people were still living in circular wooden huts with thatched roofs. Only a small number of people occupied what is now Worcestershire and it was mainly a region that was marched through to get to Droitwich or, later, to one of the three Midland Roman towns – Gloucester, Wroxeter and Leicester. There were no Roman towns of this size in Worcester.

Local legends tell of fierce resistance by the Ancient Britons in Worcestershire. There is, for example, the story of Caractacus, leader of the Ancient Britons. The Malvern hill known as the Herefordshire Beacon is often referred to as 'British Camp' and it is said that it was strengthened as a fort under the threat of the Roman invasion. An attack was expected from the east, but the Romans came from the west. After breaching the outer wall, they attacked, shields locked, swords hacking and stabbing. The Britons had neither breast-plates nor helmets to defend themselves and most were killed. The story goes that Caractacus managed to escape and fled to Yorkshire to hide at the home of his stepmother, Cartimandua, Queen of the Brigantes. However, his mother had no desire to upset the Romans, so she put him in chains and handed him over. He was taken to Rome and brought before the Roman Emperor. Caractacus said to the Emperor, 'How is it that you, who dwell in such grand palaces, envy us poor Britons with our thatched cottages?' The Emperor took a liking to Caractacus and ordered that his chains be removed. Caractacus is said to have settled in Rome and remained there until the end of his days.

Another confrontation with the Romans was thought to have taken place at the ancient hill fort on top of Bredon Hill known as Kemerton Camp.

Kemerton ditches, part of the hill fort on Bredon Hill.
Archaeologists found evidence of a massacre here

In the passageway of the inner entrance was a gruesome find. Here were fifty mutilated skeletons, all aged between twenty-five and thirty-five and buried with their weapons. Pottery and other nearby finds suggested that the date was somewhere between the fourth and the first century BC. Bredon Hill was at the forefront of the huge area (west Gloucestershire, Herefordshire, Worcestershire and the West Midlands) occupied by a tribe known as the Dubonni and there were frequent skirmishes between them and neighbouring tribes.

Yet another battle with the Romans is said to have taken place in Clent, where the British gathered on the hills before descending on Clent Heath for the battle.

However, any friction between the local people and the Romans only lasted a few years. The military presence had disappeared by the year 70 and the Romans were here until AD 450, resulting in almost 400 years of peace as the native British became Romanized, embracing Roman customs and patronage. There were hardly any uprisings in this area as there were in the south. Worcestershire was mainly a rural settlement; the same families continued century after century. It was a time of continuity and stability. By the fourth century, people saw themselves as having Roman identity. They considered themselves to be part of the Roman Empire. In the country, the houses had little temples in them and the people were using amphorae. In the towns, the architecture was Roman.

Roman remains have been found right across Worcestershire. By the time *The Victoria History of the Counties of England* was published in 1926, Roman remains had been found in forty-three towns and villages. Perhaps the most valuable find was made in October 1811, when a workman named Thomas Sheppey, while digging stone in a quarry at Cleeve Prior, found two urns that had been carefully buried and protected by stones above and below. One of the urns contained gold coins and the other contained silver coins, the bulk of them belonging to the fourth century. Unfortunately, the hoard soon disappeared. Thomas later stated that there had been about 3,000 coins.

One thing the Romans did was organize a provincial market. Before they arrived, the farmer sold his produce locally; afterwards, he was supplying the large cities with meat and corn. Iron-working and wholesale pottery production were taking place in the towns and supplying markets right across England and even in Roman provinces.

Christianity was introduced into Britain during the Roman occupation (probably during the third century). In Kempsey, a milestone has been found in the present churchyard referring to Constantine I, Roman Emperor from 306 to 337 and the first Christian Roman Emperor. Tradition says that he was converted when, on the eve of a battle, he saw the shape of a cross glowing in the sky with the inscription, 'By this thou shalt conquer'. Christian he may have been, but he lived a most unchristian existence. He killed his son, his second wife, several relatives, friends and various advisers over imagined infringements of his rights. He kept pagans in positions of authority and was not baptized into the Christian faith until he was close to death.

During the fifth or sixth century, two churches, Saint Albans and Saint Helens, were built in Worcester on what appears to have been the old town ditch. Both churches were dedicated to saints who were canonized in Roman times.

THE ROMANS IN WORCESTER

Around AD 50, a Roman settlement was founded on the site of (what is now) Worcester city. It was on the River Severn and on the road between the legionary fortresses at Kingsholm (near Gloucester) and Wroxeter (on the Severn near Shrewsbury).

It so happened that, in about the year 2000, Worcestershire County Council decided to develop 2.5 acres of the centre of Worcester behind the Crowngate shopping area and bus station, an area known as 'The Butts'. It gets its name from an archery target that was known as a 'butt' (see Chapter 8).

The 'Butts Dig'. This site is now occupied by 'The Hive', a huge history, library & archaeology centre

The site was turned over to Worcestershire Historical and Environmental Archaeology Service (WHEAS) for excavation, which began in August 2008 and lasted until 2010, although it will take many years to finish cleaning and identifying all the artefacts. It was decided to get the public involved and 200 volunteers took part.

The results surprised everyone, not only in Worcester but across England. No one had any idea of the huge size and industry of Roman Worcester. The town was known as 'Vertis' and the River Severn was called 'Sabrina'. The Roman town stretched from Britannia Square southwards to Diglis and was much larger than the Medieval town. However, the houses were scattered and there was evidence of large enclosures where people kept their animals, such as cattle, sheep and goats. There was no clear formal street layout; there were simply roads and smaller lanes. Living there were Britons with just a few Romans. The locals had become Romano-British. This was a town of Roman villas, attractive and substantial. The Romano-British appear to have lived very comfortably – there is evidence of hypocausts for underfloor heating, and part of the town had pipework for running water. The walls were painted, the floors were laid with mosaic, and some villas were decorated with ornamental stonework. These splendid houses were not in one small part but were quite widespread, scattered across the town. Pieces of large pots known as amphorae have come to light;

these were usually filled with wine, together with all kinds of exotic foodstuffs, such as grapes, olives, oysters and a fish sauce of which the Romans were very fond.

During the second century AD a major iron-smelting industry developed in Worcester. Some of the houses were close to ironworks so the smoke would have been billowing round them each day; it must have been very unpleasant. The ore for this industry seems to have come from a local source of bog iron. The charcoal fuel would have been produced locally.

One of the first things recognized in the excavations was the amount of slag on the site. In 1651, during the Civil War, the ironmaster, Andrew Yarranton, was stationed in Worcester city, and he noticed the amount of iron slag lying about. He obtained a permit from the city corporation to quarry the slag and shipped hundreds of boat loads up to his quarries (his main furnace was at Astley) to extract the iron.

One Worcester archaeologist has remarked: 'As excavations continue, I expect there will be other surprises. This is one of the things that make archaeology so exciting, it's so unpredictable, you never know what you are going to find. There's always something new.'

Dodderhill church overlooks Vines Park. The Romans lived on the cliff top in luxury

DROITWICH SALT

One of the precious commodities that made Worcestershire so desirable a county was the 'white gold' of Droitwich (see also Chapter 8). Beneath the town is a great salt lake, laid down in prehistoric times. The Romans named the town Salinae, meaning 'salt works' or 'salt workings'. The production of salt (together with iron working) was strictly controlled and regulated by the Romans. By the second century, they were leasing out the mines to wealthy individuals.

In the first century the Romans settled on the escarpment overlooking the town, now known as Dodderhill.

A large fort was built in Bays Meadow, then a second fort was erected near to where St Augustine's church now stands. Droitwich was of such importance that in the second century, the residence of a high-status family, perhaps an imperial administrator in charge of local salt production, was also built in Bays Meadow. It had eighteen rooms, many with colourful mosaics and was centrally heated by a hypocaust system.

In the late third century, the main Bays Meadow building was burned to the

Vines Park in Droitwich is now a picturesque scene but once most of the salt wells were here

ground, possibly during a period of general uprising in the Western Roman Empire. The occupants must have been expecting a rebellion of some kind, because a ditch and rampart defences were thrown around the villa just before disaster struck.

Vines Park is now a pleasant stretch of green running alongside the River Salwarpe, but in past centuries the scene would have been very different.

Here, and along the river, is the old industrial area where the chief brine wells were situated. The sky would have glowed red from furnaces and the air would have been filled with steam.

On the north-east side of Vines Lane, between Bays Meadow Villa and Dodderhill Fort, was a cemetery, either late Roman or used just after the Romans left. In the 1980s, fourteen burials were found here. Other skeletons have been found along Vines Lane, suggesting that the cemetery may have been much larger. A dramatic find came from a prehistoric brine storage tank. In the early Roman period, the tank was abandoned and infilled. In the debris was the body of a fifteen-year-old boy or girl. In his book *Savouring the Past*, J. D. Hurst remarks that this is 'suggestive of some terrible deed being covered up'.

Roman coins dated to *c*. AD 370 were found in an archeological dig at the villa, though occupation continued until the fifth century.

Courtesy of the Church of the Sacred Heart and St Catherine in Alexandria.

The story of St Richard is shown in mosaics in Droitwich's Catholic church

SAINT RICHARD

Seven hundred years later, the salt springs dried up. The town was on the point of ruin. The locals suggested that the wood spirits were annoyed at the amount of wood being used to purify the salt. Fortunately, Richard de la Wyche, later Saint Richard, lived in the area.

Richard was born in Droitwich in 1197, reputedly on the site of The Raven Hotel. A few remnants of his early home, Wyche Manor, still exist in parts of the

Droitwich's St Richard, immortalized in Vines Park

hotel. Richard went to Oxford, but his brother mismanaged the family estate so he returned to Droitwich to restore the family fortunes. This being done, he resumed his studies and joined the priesthood. In 1244, he was elected bishop of Chichester, but Henry III had wanted another member of the clergy to be bishop, and Richard was outlawed. His property was confiscated and an edict was issued, forbidding anyone to help him. He had nowhere to live and had to rely on people giving him food and clothing; it is said that he became a hermit at Droitwich.

Richard was called in, he blessed the wells, and the brine began to flow again. Sir Hugh Frogmore, Lord of Crowle and senior bailiff, cried, 'My Lord, you have saved the town, let this day never be forgotten.' Droitwich still celebrates his feast day in April.

Finally, after three years, the Pope ordered the king to accept Richard or be excommunicated, and so he became bishop of Chichester in 1247. He was canonized in 1262. His life is shown in mosaics in the Church of the Sacred Heart on the Worcester Road, Droitwich (see Chapter 13) while his statue stands in Vines Park.

WORCESTERSHIRE IN THE DARK AGES

By the early fifth century the Roman Empire was in disarray. The Roman legions began to withdraw from Britain and the last was probably gone by AD 410. The effects on Britain were extreme. The market economy was destroyed. The Roman towns declined and their markets disappeared, together with various manufacturers and trades. Rural settlements were abandoned. The coinage had gone. The political power was in the hands of small local units. Not only had the army gone, so also had the basic structure of their society. Christianity almost disappeared, with much of Britain reverting to paganism, though the religion did manage to survive in some western areas. England was plunged into the Dark Ages and the country was left defenceless.

Sometime about 1113, a monk at Worcester Cathedral Priory, Florence of Worcester, attempted to write a history of England. He drew from his own experiences and used the *Anglo-Saxon Chronicle* along with other sources, some of which have since disappeared. Little is known about Florence of Worcester, only that he was a native of the city. He had been working on the book for five years when he died, and the history had to be continued by another monk or perhaps a series of monks.

Florence writes: 'No sooner were the Romans departed than the enemy, landing in boats, levelled, trampled down and swept off whatever came in their way, as if they were reaping corn ripe for the harvest.' He goes on to say that the Britons pleaded for the return of the Romans, who returned and built solid defensive walls of stone and erected watchtowers along the south coast, but as soon as the Romans had left, the Scots and Picts invaded from the north.

The British then asked the Anglo-Saxons for help, who seem to have been successful in keeping the Picts and Scots at bay. However, they found England so agreeable that they began to settle here. Florence reports that in the fifth and sixth centuries more and more Angles, Saxons and Jute tribes left their home-lands in Germany, Denmark and northern Holland and rowed across the North Sea to live in England. They themselves had become the invaders.

Over the next few hundred years England became a country of small king-doms, with changing rulers and boundaries as battles were lost and won.

Matters came to a head in AD 577 at a great battle in south Gloucestershire. A Saxon tribe emerged from obscurity to defeat the last of the British kings. These were the rulers of the small kingdoms based in (what is now) Gloucester, Cirencester and Bath. The Saxon victors assimilated this whole area and formed their own kingdom known as the 'Hwicce'. Their name survives in such place names as 'Wychavon'. The Bishops of Worcester called themselves 'Bishops of the Hwicce' until the tenth century. The whole of England was now under Saxon rule.

The Hwicce were at first pagan, but were converted to Christianity. Mission-aries came from both Rome and Ireland. Saint Augustine arrived in Kent in 597, having been sent from Rome, and in the 600s Lindisfarne in north Northumber-land (sometimes known as 'Holy Island') was a training centre for the Irish and English missionaries who then travelled south.

The Hwicce were only to rule for just over half a century before, in 628, they were overrun by the Saxon chief Penda, king of Mercia, so that they became a sub-Mercian kingdom. Florence of Worcester tells how the battle-hungry warrior Penda had succeeded to the throne in 626, ruling from Tamworth. He terrorized the neighbouring kingdoms, slaying in battle Kings Sigebert, Ecgrig and Anna of the East Angles, as well as Kings Edwin, Oswald and Oswy of the Northumbrians. During the thirty years of his reign, Mercia became the largest and most powerful kingdom in England.

Penda was the last great Pagan king, although he had no objection to Chris-tianity. When Penda died in 655, paganism was brought to an end and the whole of England was ostensibly united under Christianity.

The Irish missionaries soon found themselves in disputes with the hierarchy in Rome – for example, they each calculated the dates of Easter in a different way. When Oswy, the Northumbrian king, was celebrating Easter, his queen, who had been brought up in the south in the Roman Church, was fasting. Something had to be done, so the Synod of Whitby was held in 664, where it was decided to adopt the Roman rather than the Celtic form of Christianity.

By the 600s, Worcester was a great city. Florence of Worcester writes that it had 'fine walls and towering ramparts'. It was the capital of the large area occupied by the Hwicce people that probably included Droitwich, Gloucester and Bath. By the late 600s, the Hwicce had become one of the many subkingdoms of Mercia. Mercia was a huge area, at one time bordered by Northumbria, Powys, the kingdoms of South Wales, Wessex, Sussex and East Anglia. Florence of Worcester's *Chronicle*, under the heading 'Hwiccia', states that in 701 it was ruled by Penda's third son, King Ethelred. The leader of the Hwicce, Oshere, asked King Ethelred if he could have his own bishop. The king consulted the archbishop of Canterbury and it was decided that they should hold a synod at Hatfield (presumably in Hertfordshire). Mercia was divided into five diocese, each with its own bishop. The bishop of the largest diocese, the Hwicce, was given authority over the other four. These were, in order of importance, Litchfield, Mid-Anglia, Lindsey and South Anglia, with bishops at Litchfield, Leicester, Sidnacester (later becoming Lincoln) and Dorchester respectively. Consequently, the Bishop of Worcester was one of the most influential men in (what is now) England with Worcester becoming a major city.

Among his responsibilities were the collection and distribution of tithes, rents and other dues, the provision of men-at-arms for the king's service, and the maintenance of law and order within his See.

The Minster Church of St Mary's, the forerunner of the cathedral, was built on or near the site of the present cathedral in about 680. It was a time of religious enthusiasm. Monasteries and abbeys were founded across the county – Pershore Abbey in about 689, Evesham in about 701, and although Malvern Priory was officially founded in 1085, its origins were much earlier.

But there were clouds on the horizon. Viking raids began on the east coast of Britain in the late 700s and became more and more severe. They reached Mercia in 874. Pershore's early monastery was attacked many times. Worcester cathedral, too, fell victim to pirate Vikings sailing up the River Severn. There is an old story that one of the pirates tried to make off with the great Sanctus bell of Worcester, but it was too heavy for him. He lagged behind his comrades with the result that he was caught by the townsfolk. They flayed him alive and his skin was pinned on to the door of the cathedral to deter other raiders, where it remained for many years. Although there are references to 'tests' that have shown that the skin from the door was human skin from about the right period, there are no records of the flaying of captured Vikings by the English. It seems likely the story is a folktale as the same tale, under the title of the 'Dane's Skin', is told of many churches in Essex and also of Westminster Abbey.

KING ALFRED AND HIS DESCENDANTS

By 877 the situation for the Anglo-Saxons was serious. Vikings had conquered the kingdoms of East Anglia, Northumbria and Mercia and were planning to expand into Wessex, ruled by the twenty-one-year-old King Alfred. At first he was forced into hiding in the Somerset Levels, which is when he was supposed to have famously let the cakes burn. The peasant woman at whose house he sheltered, not knowing he was the king, asked him to mind her cakes cooking on the fire. Alfred was so preoccupied with how he could defeat the enemy that he forgot them and they burned, so that he received the sharp end of her tongue.

Alfred defeated the Viking leader, Guthrum, in Wiltshire in May 878 after which Guthrum not only admitted defeat, but agreed to be baptized as a Christian. The country was again unified under Christianity. Alfred reached an agreement with the Vikings by which England was divided into two, the south and west, where Saxon law would apply, and the north and east, where Danish law ruled. This second territory became known as the Danelaw. Worcestershire came under Saxon law.

Alfred died in 899. His eldest son, Edward, reigned until about 924, and reconquered all the Danish settlements south of the Humber with the result that Mercia became a new and much larger kingdom. This new kingdom needed a fresh title; the name chosen was 'England', an Anglo-Saxon word meaning 'land of the Angles'.

King Alfred's daughter, Aethelflead, married Ethelred, a high-ranking official of Mercia. Although she was known by the genteel title 'The Lady of the Mercians' she was a tough warrior queen. She fought the Vikings and captured parts of Wales and Northumbria and, together with her husband, ordered the fortification of towns. Worcester was their first; the town was already fortified but these fortifications needed to be improved. The relevant charter is still in existence; dated somewhere between 884 and 901, it reads: 'At the request of Bishop Waerfirth, their friend Ealdorman Ethelred and Aethelflead ordered the borough of Worcester to be built for the protection of the people.'

Worcester monastery was chosen for the education of King Alfred's grandson, Athelstan. Consequently, when Athelstan became king of Mercia in 924, he looked to the bishop, Saint Dunstan, for help and advice. The prestige of Worcester was increased.

Athelstan turned the tables on the Vikings who held Northumbria, Cumbria and Scotland. Together with Aethelflead, he launched raids into their territories so that within a few months the Vikings submitted and Athelstan became the first king of a united England, Wales and Scotland.

Around 918, counties such as Worcestershire were established. Unfortunately, the great landowners, usually bishops, wanted the land that they owned included in the county in which they lived. This led to all kinds of strange anomalies. For example, distant Yardley belonged to Pershore Abbey and was therefore in Worcestershire. To make matters worse, landowners from other counties claimed pieces of Worcestershire. Clent belonged to the king, together with Kingswinford, and was therefore annexed to Staffordshire. Until 1544, it was uncertain whether Bewdley belonged to Worcestershire or Shropshire, which was very convenient for criminals. Amazingly, most of these anomalies remained unchanged for 1,000 years, until the twentieth century. Then, in the 1900s a series of Acts took Dudley, Halesowen and Stourbridge from Worcestershire. As the history of each of these three towns could fill a book, it has been necessary to ignore them and concentrate on Worcestershire county as it stands today.

The shires were subdivided into 'Hundreds' – that is, an area of land capable of supporting a hundred families. A Hundred of poor ground would be larger than a Hundred of fertile soil. These divisions were used for assessing taxes and calculating military obligations. Each hide (approximately 30 acres) was to supply one armed man for the defence of the kingdom. The inhabitants of each Hundred were responsible for keeping law and order in their own area. Courts were held once a month, and twice a year the sheriff attended. King Edmund (reigned 939–46) was one of the grandsons of Alfred the Great and he decreed that one of their duties was to round up slaves who had deserted their masters and had become bandits. The leaders were to be hanged and the rest flogged three times, scalped and have their little fingers cut off!

The Victoria County History, an encyclopaedic work compiled in 1926, is divided into Hundreds. By that time, Worcestershire had five Hundreds: Halfshire Hundred to the north-east of the county, Doddingtree Hundred on the western side, Pershore Hundred to the south and south-west, and Blackenhurst occupying the eastern limits. The principal Hundred was Oswaldslow, so called because it had once belonged to Saint Oswald. Gradually, most of the Hundred courts fell under the control of the lords of the manor and from the sixteenth century onwards ceased to have much importance.

A part of the court that dealt with petty law became known as the Court Leet. As late as the eighteenth century, the King and Queen stones on Bredon Hill were still being ceremonially whitewashed for meetings of the Court Leet of the

Oswoldstow Hundred. A Court Leet still meets at Alcester and Bromsgrove, although this is now simply a ceremonial occasion.

In the eleventh century England was a wealthy country. Quite apart from its rich farmland, it held reserves of iron, copper and other minerals and it therefore continued to attract Viking attention. In 1016, faced only by a fragmented army and run-down English navy, Sweyn, the pagan king of Denmark and his son, Canute, were easily able to invade the country. The Severn provided easy access and soon most of Worcestershire found itself behind enemy lines. The king of England, Ethelred, had to flee to exile in Normandy with his wife, Emma, and two sons, Alfred and Edward. Military conflict has always been an expensive business and Sweyn laid heavy taxes upon the whole of England. In order to pay it, nearly all the cathedral ornaments were sold, and the gold and silver tables, crosses and chalices were melted down.

Sweyn died in 1017 and his warrior son, Canute, was chosen to be king of England by the Witanagemot, or Council of Wise Men. The years between 1014 and 1016 saw many struggles between the Danish and the English for the throne of England. In 1016 a peace agreement was made between Canute and Edmund Ironside, younger son of King Ethelred. The latter was given control of Wessex while Canute controlled Mercia and Northumbria. Whoever died first was to give his share of the country to the other. Edmund died somewhat suspiciously in November 1016; consequently, Canute became king of England.

Canute's second son, Harthacanute, succeeded to the throne in 1040. He reinstated and increased a tax system introduced by Alfred the Great. For every hide of land held, the owner was to supply either the work of a man for a year or the financial equivalent in Danegeld. The people of Worcester rebelled and refused to pay. Harthacanute sent two 'housecarls' to enforce payment, but they were attacked by an angry crowd. The two men took refuge in the monastery attached to the cathedral, but the crowd rushed in and killed them. Harthacanute sent an army to Worcester to exact vengeance. The army spent four days burning, plundering and razing the town to the ground. The cathedral was severely damaged, most of the roof was destroyed, and the walls were blackened. It remained so until replaced by Saint Wulstan.

Harthacanute was the last Danish king of England. When he died in 1042, his half brother, Edward, came to the throne. Edward the Confessor was born in 1002 and is said to have acquired his nickname because of his gentle, pious manner. He was especially popular in Worcester as he managed to exist on his official income and dispensed with the Danegeld which had caused so much trouble. Edward was the youngest son of the Anglo-Saxon King Ethelred, but after the unfortunate death of Ethelred, his mother had married the Danish King Canute. Edward had lived in exile in Normandy. It is said that when he became king, he ordered his mother to be bound in chains because of the unhappy child-hood she had inflicted on him.

At his uncle's court, Edward gradually amassed a party of Norman friends and promised various territories to friends and relations. However, when he became King of England, he turned his back on his old allies and married the daughter of the most powerful man in England, Earl Godwin of Wessex. It was not long before Edward's Norman party and an English party, led by Earl Godwin, were at loggerheads. When King Edward granted land to Norman nobles in the Herefordshire borders, the animosity grew. Three Norman great stone castles were built: one at Hereford itself, another at Ewyas Harold and another, known as Richard's Castle (10 miles north of Leominster), which controlled much of the Teme valley. The Anglo-Saxon nobles resented all these castles and the influence of the Normans on the English court. The stage was set for battle between the Anglo-Saxons and the Normans.

Edward the Confessor died in 1066 and was canonized in 1161. Henry II held him in great affection and made him England's patron saint, a post that he held until 1348.

Edward had no children and left no direct heir. The Anglo-Saxons and the Normans, at each other's throats, could not agree who should inherit the throne. It was believed that, while he was in Normandy, Edward had promised the English throne to his uncle's son, William. However, he appears to have compli-cated matters yet further by promising the English succession to Earl Godwin's eldest son, Harold, who was also commander-in-chief of the English field army. Harold was crowned King of England on 6 January 1066, but he had enemies on all sides. Harald Hardrada of Norway, together with Harold's brother, Tostig, had gathered Viking forces and invaded the country at Stamford Bridge, York-shire. Although the ensuing battle was a great triumph for Harold and the Saxons, their strength was sadly depleted, and they were soon to face an even greater enemy. His cousin, Duke William of Normandy, had landed in Sussex to claim the throne that had been promised to him. The weary Saxons turned south once more and marched back as quickly as they had come. They met the Normans at the fateful Battle of Hastings.

After a mere nine months on the throne, King Harold was killed on 14 October 1066, and the Duke of Normandy became William the Conqueror, King of England.

2

WILLIAM THE CONQUEROR

England was now ruled by the Normans, and centuries of Anglo-Saxon influence came to an end. There were tremendous changes in law, customs, taxation, justice and culture. The new lords spoke in Norman French and anyone who did business with them had to speak it too.

William the Conqueror was the illegitimate son of the Duke of Normandy and Herleva, a humble tanner from Falaise, a small town in north-western France. A castle there was formerly the seat of the Dukes of Normandy. Because his mother was not of royal birth, William was often regarded with contempt, but he was the Duke's only son and, despite his illegitimacy, he inherited the title of Duke of Normandy.

In his *Historia Anglorum*, William of Malmesbury (1095–1143) tells us that he was of average height and of 'fierce countenance; his forehead was bare of hair, of such great strength of arm that it was often a matter of surprise, that no-one was able to draw his bow, which himself could bend when his horse was in full gallop; he was majestic whether sitting or standing, although the protuberance of his belly deformed his royal person'.

About 5,000 barons and knights came over from Normandy. The English lords who had taken part in the battles against the Normans saw their homes and their property taken from them and given to Normans. One Anglo-Saxon to lose his property was Brictric, son of Algar, Lord of Tewkesbury, who owned large tracts of land at Malvern Chase and Hanley. He had been a favourite at the court of Edward the Confessor, and was often sent on diplomatic missions. One of these took him to the Count of Flanders in Normandy. The count's daughter, Matilda (see page 74) fell madly in love with him but he rejected her advances. Years later, Matilda married Duke William of Normandy. Unfortunately for Brictric, he became William the Conqueror, and Matilda was crowned queen of England. Legend states that on the day the queen was crowned, her first act was to send soldiers to arrest him; he was dragged out of a church service at Hanley Castle and thrown into prison, where he remained until he died. As for Matilda, she was married to William for sixteen years and bore him nine children.

Site of Homme Castle, near Clifton-upon-Teme. A Medieval motte and bailey was here before 1207, seen here behind the buildings on the left of the picture

William reigned for twenty-one years. To be on good terms with the Church and its leaders, while at the same time exercising military power by utilizing a chain of strategically placed castles, were to be the two keystones to William the Conqueror's continuing success. Land was given by the king to his followers who hastily erected mottes and baileys, later to be rebuilt in stone. In return, the new landowners were required to swear oaths of loyalty to William.

_____

WORCESTER CASTLE

William the Conqueror appointed a new sheriff to Worcester, Urse d'Abitot, a high-ranking French knight. Urse soon constructed a huge motte and bailey castle next to the cathedral on the ground between the school and the river, consequently encroaching on the monk's burial ground and other land belonging to Worcester Priory. This so annoyed the church authorities that the sheriff was cursed by the Archbishop of York (who had once been the bishop of Worcester), a serious matter in those superstitious days. The curse went something like: 'Highest thou Urse, Receive thou this curse.' There is no record that Urse was particularly alarmed.

The castle was burned down in 1113, the same year that the monk, Florence of Worcester, began writing a history of the county. A terrible fire razed Worcester to the ground, spreading rapidly through the houses with their wooden chimneys and thatched roofs, and sixteen people died in the blaze. The castle was then replaced by a stone structure. A century later, a tower was added.

By the 1500s the castle had disappeared; it had long been used as a county court and prison. In 1653 a house of correction was built within its precincts, a terrible place which, in 1783, suffered an outbreak of the dreaded gaol fever, a kind of typhus. Thirteen years later eighteen new cells were added for solitary confinement; they measured 10 feet by 7 feet. It remained a house of correction until a new prison was built in 1809 in Castle Street – the street was named after the castellated towers. The motte remained and was not levelled until somewhere between 1829 and 1840. Some of the stonework of the old castle still survives in the walls of King's School.

WILLIAM THE CONQUEROR AND SAINT WULSTAN

One personality stands out during the days of William the Conqueror – that of Bishop Wulstan, also written as Wulfstan or Wostan.

Since Alfred the Great, the diocese of Worcester had been one of the most important in England, and the bishop had advised the king not only in spiritual affairs but also in civil and government matters. The tradition had continued and the Anglo-Saxon Bishop Wulstan was therefore one of the most important men in England. He had been friend and adviser to both Edward the Confessor and King Harold. He is said to have restored the sight of Gunhild, daughter of King Harold, whose eyes had been attacked by a malignant tumour. Apparently he made the sign of a cross and 'straightaway she was able to … receive the light of day'.

Bishop Wulstan was born in about 1008. When he was a young man his parents moved to Worcester where his mother became a nun and his father a monk; he was therefore encouraged by his family to become a priest.

He was educated at Evesham monastery, became Prior of Worcester when he was about forty-two, and was chosen to be bishop of Worcester twelve years later. Tales of his holiness spread throughout Christendom; it was said that he fasted for three days every week and spent that time in silence.

William the Conqueror slowly replaced any Anglo-Saxons holding high office with Normans, and this included bishops. The Saxon Wulstan was summoned to Westminster by the Archbishop of Canterbury who ordered him to surrender his bishop's staff and ring. The tale is told that Wulstan laid his staff on the tomb of Edward the Confessor and said that he would only surrender the staff and ring to the person who gave it to him (that is, Edward the Confessor). Although everyone tried to lift the staff from the tomb it was stuck fast. Wulstan removed it with ease. Be that as it may, William the Conqueror allowed him to stay in his post, and he was the only Saxon bishop in England.

We read in Florence of Worcester's *Chronicle* that Bishop Wulstan had a curious and entertaining quirk. He hated long hair, and whenever a long-haired individual bowed his head to receive the Episcopal blessing, 'before he gave it, the bishop would cut off a lock of his hair with the sharp knife that he carried

Courtesy of the Church of the Sacred Heart and St Catherine in Alexandria at Droitwich Spa

St Wulstan in mosaics

about him and commanded him by way of penance that he should cut off the rest of his hair in the same manner, denouncing dreadful judgments against such as disobeyed the injunction'.

Bishop Wulstan was involved in a quarrel with the Prior of Evesham over ownership of Bengeworth. The matter went to the brother of William the Conqueror to be settled. For his evidence, the Abbot of Evesham produced the bones of Saint Egwin while Bishop Wulstan supplied a forged charter. Judgement was given in favour of the bishop and appropriate documentation was made out by the sheriff. However, the sheriff had built a castle in Bengeworth and, when he was off on a crusade, the monks of Evesham Abbey burned down his castle in spite.

He was an old man when, in 1084, Wulstan began his life's work – the building of a cathedral to replace the fire-damaged St Oswald's. Norman architects and builders were far superior to those in England. The

French had become experts in stonework and so masons came over from Normandy to fulfil Wulstan's dream. His cathedral was built of perfectly dressed stone, with sturdy pillars and thick walls. Arches were rounded in the Romanesque (that is, similar to Roman arches) style. The Normans introduced stone vaulting, a tremendous step forward as roofs could be made of stone instead of wood and were much stronger and higher. A crypt was built to house the shrine of Saint Oswald. The cathedral was completed in 1089 and was one of the most outstanding religious buildings in England, whitewashed inside and outside, and situated in an impressive position above a sweeping curve of the River Severn. Those entering these splendid buildings must have believed that they were indeed in God's house. Bishop Wulstan's cathedral was so well built that the crypt has survived to this day and now contains a model of Saint Wulstan's cathedral.

A miracle is said to have been performed during the building of the cathedral. A workman fell 40 feet off the roof of the building, but Saint Wulstan saw him fall, made the sign of the cross, and the man was unhurt.

According to Florence of Worcester, in 1088 Wulstan was the hero of a battle fought in fields on the opposite side of the Severn to the cathedral. The previous year William the Conqueror had died and his second son, William Rufus, had

A few remnants of St Wulstan's building remain in the cathedral. The crypt was built by St Wulstan

been crowned king. Although Wulstan was then seventy-nine, he was one of the officiating clergy at the coronation. Unfortunately William Rufus proved to be a ruthless tyrant, and consequently three powerful lords, led by the Earl of Shrewsbury, rose against him. They assembled a great army of Normans and Welshmen and marched on Worcester. The citizens refused to join them, remaining loyal to the king. The three lords declared that they would burn down the city of Worcester and, with it, the cathedral, and 'take heavy vengeance on the loyal inhabitants'. The garrison, the bishop's household and all the citizens assembled and nervously prepared for battle, but Wulstan assured them that God would help them. Florence continues:

> He [Bishop Wulstan] declared: 'Go my children, go in peace, go in security, with the blessing of God and mine. Trusting in the Lord, I promise you this day no sword shall injure you, no mishap, no adversary. Be firm in your allegiance to the King, manfully fighting for the safety of the people and the city.' With these words, they eagerly crossed the bridge and beheld the enemy approaching rapidly at a distance. Among the enemy already raged the madness of war, for, despising the commands of the bishop, they had burnt many portions of his territory.
>
> On this day, however, a wonderful thing, proclaiming the power of God and the goodness of the man, came to pass, for immediately the enemy, who were wandering scattered over the fields, were stricken with so great a weakness in their limbs and enfeebled by such blindness of the outward eye, that they were hardly able to bear their arms. They could neither recognise their friends, nor distinguish those who were attacking them from the opposite party. While blindness deceived them, confidence in God and the Bishop's benediction comforted our men. So stupefied were the enemy that they knew not how to escape, neither did they seek any means of defence but, by the will of God, fell easy prey. The footmen were slain and the horsemen captured – English, Norman and Welshmen – the rest just escaping by a feeble fight.

Saint Wulstan lived to the ripe old age of eighty-seven. He died in 1095 and was buried in a golden shrine within his beautiful cathedral. Miracles were witnessed at his tomb and he was canonized in 1203.

The cathedral suffered another severe fire in 1202; fortunately, Saint Wulstan's shrine was unharmed (another miracle) and the revenue from his shrine paid chiefly for the rebuilding. However, his reputation for working miracles did not deter the Earl of Hereford from plundering the cathedral in 1216 and demanding protection money. Wulstan's tomb had to be melted down to extract the gold. King John came to visit and commuted a fine that was due to him so

Today's view across the River Severn to Worcester Cathedral.
The exterior has been subject to Victorian renovation

that the cathedral authorities could afford to repair the damage. The new shrine and the renovated cathedral were completed by 1218 and dedicated in a grand ceremony to St Mary, St Peter, St Oswald and St Wulstan.

The young Henry III, five English bishops, four Welsh bishops, seventeen abbots and a large number of noblemen were present at the event. *The Victoria County History* states:

> To the bishop [Bishop Sylvester] it was an unfortunate day. A new and very gorgeous shrine had been repaired for St Wulstan (his body), since the precious metals on the old one had been melted down to pay the fine placed on the monastery for submitting to Prince Louis and the French. There was some difficulty in getting St Wulstan to fit into his new shrine, which was not long enough for him. The bishop thought that if all the bones were placed within it the mode in which they were placed did not very much matter; so 'with his own hand', says the chronicler, 'he cut them up, placed them in the shrine, and praised himself for the deed'. This impious act took place on 6 June; on 16 July the bishop was dead; St Wulfstan had avenged himself!

The Commandery

Another building associated with Wulstan is the Commandery, across the road from the cathedral.

The present building is of the late fifteenth century, but it is believed to have been founded in 1085 for a master chaplain and four brethren. It ministered to the sick, relieved the poor, and sheltered the isolated traveller arriving after the gates of the city were closed. It was named after one of its masters who assumed the name of 'Commander'. We know that it was flourishing in 1221 because of the story of Thomas, who was blinded and castrated after a duel. Florence of Worcester tells us that Thomas's sight and virility were restored after prayers to Saint Wulstan. He was nursed back to health in the Commandery by the nurse Ysobel, who usually spent her days praying over dead paupers and laying them out.

_____

WILLIAM THE CONQUEROR AND WORCESTERSHIRE CHURCHES

The Normans were devout Christians and William the Conqueror always maintained that his invasion was a Christian crusade. The splendid abbey build-

St Martin's at Holt, one of Worcestershire's most richly decorated Norman churches

ings of Pershore, Evesham, and perhaps Malvern Priory were all begun during his reign. He went even further by replacing most of the small wooden churches with stone ones. Most of these were simple, squat stone buildings, rendered and whitewashed on the outside, but in some of the churches, when the peasant opened the door he would be met by a blaze of colour. The carvings, tombs and other ornamentation would be covered in paintwork while the walls would be festooned with paintings.

Many of William's friends were given a piece of land on condition that they built a church there and endowed a priest. Once the priest was installed, he became the sole responsibility of the bishop. A priest was therefore appointed by the lord of the manor but could not be dismissed by him. In this way William the Conqueror could reward his allies without making the Church too powerful. The repercussions of this arrangement are still being felt today!

By 1068 there were sixty priests in Worcestershire in fifty-seven places. Nikolaus Pevsner writes, 'As regards Norman work in parish churches, Worcestershire is one of the richest of all counties.' Norman stonework still exists today, especially in the area around Tenbury Wells, such as Rochford, Eastham,

Ridge and furrow near Bredon Hill

Knighton-on-Teme and Bockleton. The largest Norman churches are at Bredon, Broadway, Kempsey, Powick, Ripple and Rock. Both Rock and Holt have a wealth of fine Norman carving and are well worth a visit.

THE CONQUEROR'S ENGLAND

In William the Conqueror's time, Worcestershire was very different in appearance from today. Some estimates of the population put it as low as about 23,000, about the same as the present town of Evesham. Roughly, one-third of Worcestershire was thought to be a wild and desolate place of impenetrable forest, heath, wasteland and marsh to trap the unwary traveller. Wolves, snakes, wild boars and wild cats made the forests their home. Worst of all were the thieves, castle rustlers and vagabonds, living rough in the woods or raiding from Wales.

Where the land had been cleared, fields were huge, and divided into long strips. Farming was basic, ploughing was by a team of oxen, usually eight harnessed in pairs, and seeds were scattered by hand. The ploughing threw up the soil at the side of the strips and accumulated into ridges and furrows.

A typical strip would be the width of two oxen side by side, and 220 yards long. The outline of these strips can still be seen in fields today, especially in the Vale of Evesham. Crops were rotated to improve the soil then, on the fourth year, usually left fallow.

By this time, people were chiefly living in villages or towns. Each large village usually had a church, an inn, a mill, a blacksmith and a baker and was mostly self-sufficient. The staple diet was beer and coarse black bread. Even children drank weak beer, known as 'small beer', which was safer than the local water. The majority of the population spent their lives working on the land. Planting was done according to the phases of the moon – for example, root crops like carrots, beets, radishes and potatoes had to be sown during a waning moon. Animals played a large part in the people's lives – pigs and hens for food, cows for milk, oxen for ploughing, horses for transport, sheep for food and for wool. Very few people could read, but this was of no consequence as a peasant had neither books nor newspapers and there were no signs or signposts.

Houses were still thatched and made of wattle and daub, but the walls were higher and the shape had become rectangular, long and narrow. They were known as 'longhouses'. The people lived at one end and the animals at the other, sometimes divided by a passageway. A well-known example is The Fleece Inn at Bretforton.

The Fleece Inn at Bretforton. As the layout suggests, it was once a longhouse

The building was originally a longhouse dating back to the 1300s and, although altered considerably, the basic outline of such a dwelling can still be seen. The Byrd family had owned the building since the fifteenth century, the last descendant being the formidable Lola Taplin. Almost nothing has been changed either inside or outside since the 1600s, even the white lines painted over any cracks to keep out the witches are still in place. Lola left it to the National Trust when she died in 1977, aged eighty-three. She would not allow any food to be eaten in The Fleece Inn and the tale is told that, after her death, a few workmen were called in to make some minor alterations. When lunchtime arrived, the workmen decided to take advantage of the fine weather and go for a short walk. They stacked their sandwich boxes against the bar wall, and carefully locked up the cottage. When they returned, their lunch boxes had been opened and their sandwiches were strewn across the floor!

The Fleece Inn was badly burned in 2004, but has been carefully restored.

THE DOMESDAY BOOK

William the Conqueror has left us with a magnificent description of the whole of England, including Worcestershire. He commanded that a list of all his assets should be made, possibly to check on the book-keeping. Known as 'The Domesday Book', it contains information about almost every village. No other country in the world has such a detailed record of life at that time. Today, anyone living in an old town or village can look it up in one of the Domesday Book's translations to find information about it as it was around 1068.

Before looking at the Domesday Book the non-historian needs to know a little about the manorial system. This had been developing through the centuries, whereby every man's place in society was known from birth. At the head of the hierarchy were the landowners, the lords of the manor. Under them were the freemen, or knights, usually professional soldiers and necessary with all the Medieval wars. Next were the villeins, or peasants, who 'rented' several long strips of land from the lord of the manor. In return, the villein and his family not only had to work on the lord's land for one or two days each week, but they also had to give him a percentage of their produce. They belonged to the lord and could not marry, pass on land to their children, etc. without his permission. Below the villeins were the borders and cottars. They owned a little ground and, in addition, usually worked for others. These three categories – villeins, borders and cottars – are thought to have made up one-third of the Medieval population.

On the bottom rung of the ladder was the poor slave who had no posses-sions and no rights. There is an interesting document dating back to the 880s which illustrates the position of the slave. Two estates in Oxfordshire were being transferred to an estate at Pirton, west of Great Malvern, owned by the bishop of Worcester. Included in the lists of goods and farming equipment are the names of six men: Almund, Tidulf, Tidheh, Lull, another Lull, and Gadwolf – all slaves.

From the Domesday Book we learn, for example, that Bromsgrove belonged to the king, the royal demesne extending to some 300 hides supporting a steward, bailiff, priest, twenty villeins and ninety-two bordarii. Items that were of no financial interest, such as women and children, were omitted, so the figure of a population of 104 would have been a great deal larger.

One of the poorest villages was Little Witley, with a priest, two smallholders with one plough, and woodland. Part of the revenue was paid in honey. Chad-desley Corbett is interesting in that it was held by a woman, Edeva, from the king. It had thirty-three villeins, twenty cottars, and two priests with four cottars; between them they had twenty-five ploughs and eight slaves male and female. At Droitwich, the great salt town, no fewer than sixty-eight manors and estates had the right to receive salt, including Princes Risborough, 70 miles distant in Buck-inghamshire. The Bishop of Worcester owned an extraordinary eighty-five manors across Worcestershire! Westminster Church owned twenty-eight, all in the Pershore area. For Kidderminster, the Domesday Book reports that, 'The whole of this manor was waste.'

There are examples of the way in which the king disliked any lord having too much land and property in any one area. It would be difficult for anyone in authority to organize a rebellion against the king if his tenants were scattered here and there. The village of Bellum was taken from the Saxon lord and split into two. One part was called 'Broctum' (Broughton) and given to Urse d'Abitot, sheriff of Worcester, while the other half kept the name of Bellum and was given to Dudley's William Fitz Ansculf. Thus the village of Belbroughton was created.

The manorial system was still in existence in the late 1300s when William Langland wrote his vision of Piers Plowman on the Malvern Hills (see Chapter 13). Langland remarks: 'Some spent their lives ploughing, seeding and sowing and working hard to gather what the greed of wastrels would scatter again. Some spent their lives dressing in fine clothes, while others passed their days in prayers and penitence.'

Castlemorton Common, below the Malvern Hills, is a rare survival of Medieval 'forest' terrain

WILLIAM THE CONQUEROR AND THE FORESTS

William of Malmesbury, writing in the 1100s, reports that William the Conqueror was 'so given to the pleasures of the chase, that … ejecting the inhabitants, he let a space of many miles grow desolate that, when at liberty from other vocations, he might there pursue his pleasures'.

King William created huge 'forests' – that, is, areas where landowners and commoners could be prosecuted for stealing both his timber and his game animals: deer, hares, pigs, rabbits, pheasants, partridges and so on.

Forests have changed in size and in name but, to summarize, in Worcestershire the following were probably the major forests.

The Wyre was in the north-west of the county; this remained in the hands of the king until the end of the 1800s. Large areas have survived to this day.

To the south-west of the county, on the western side of the Severn, up to the River Teme and into Gloucestershire, was another forest, sometimes known as the Forest of Dean. Part of it later became Malvern Chase. Malvern Chase was the subject of a great lawsuit in 1278 between the Earl of Gloucester and the Bishop of Hereford. The earl claimed that the bishop had encroached on his land in Colwall and Eastnor, where the bishop held manors. The court decided in favour of the bishop and the earl cut a long ditch across the top of the Malverns to mark the boundaries, traces of which still remain today. However, in so doing, he infringed on the rights of the bishop. The matter was settled by the earl agreeing to pay to the bishop and his successors two deer and two does every year. Recent tests have revealed that parts of the ditch go back to prehistoric times.

East of the Severn was another great forest, usually known as Feckenham Forest, which followed the line of the Severn from Worcester to Bewdley, then spread across the Lickey and Clent Hills. Charles I sold the forest rights of both the Dean and Feckenham Forests.

When William first established his forests, people were moved out and their homes destroyed. This caused so much antagonism that laws were established so that people could live within the forest limits, but were subject to strict rules. For example, anyone passing through the forest had to carry their bow with the arrows tied to the bowstring. Any hunting dogs had to be tied together in twos. If you owned a mastiff, the dog's claws had to be cut off. A whole team of officials looked after each forest, ranging from the most important warden of the forest, to the forester who looked after a certain area, tending and pollarding the trees and vegetation, and keeping his eye open for poachers.

The penalties for breaking the forest laws were at first severe. Under William you could have an eye taken out simply for disturbing the deer. Killing the king's deer was punishable by death. Later these punishments were replaced by fines. Offences against forest laws were heard by special courts. One of these special courts was in the village of Feckenham, which gave its name to the surrounding forest and became the administrative centre.

A royal hunting lodge was located here, and on the south-west side of the church are the remains of a ditch that once surrounded the prison where offenders against the forest laws were housed.

The number and range of people coming before the courts at this time is astonishing; they ranged from the poor peasant selling a bit of brushwood, to the lord of the manor who could not resist hunting the king's deer. Among them were Sir Walter Beauchamp who was fined £30 in about 1281 for hunting, and several church officials including Ivo, the rector of Bishampton, and Thomas Molinton, rector of Alvechurch.

Two servants from Bordesley Abbey were in trouble in 1278 when they were caught shooting the king's deer by a forester on horseback. The forester marched them towards the abbey to hand them over to the abbot. When they reached the piggery and the sheep-shearing house, two monks saw the little procession and ran out. The forester was very poor so the monks were able to bribe him to let the two men go with half a mark (about 36p). Then the forester was in trouble for letting the men go. However, the case took a year to reach the courts and, as the forester had no money for a fine, the case was dismissed.

Not only were people fined for hunting the king's game, they were also in trouble for clearing the forest. Despite the penalties, people settled in them, making clearings. William Corbett at Chaddesley paid a fine of one mark for clearing the forest at Chaddesley, and Baldwin de Akeny paid a fine for clearing at Crowle. Many of the offenders were the foresters themselves whose duty it was to guard the forest. They only received a small wage and it was tempting for them to do a bit of poaching or sell some timber. Foresters were imprisoned in 1289 and 1299 and, in the early years of Henry III, John the Forester took enormous amounts of wood from Feckenham Forest. He forced men of the countryside to pile it on their carts and take it to Droitwich to sell.

Sometimes, if the lord of the manor was absent for a long period, parts of his land might be cleared without his permission. In the middle of the thirteenth century, Lord Henry Huband, at Ipsley, was in prison for a time and Hugh de Mortimer held his land. While Hugh de Mortimer was looking after the land, eighteen clearances were made in Huband's woods, ranging from 0.5 acres to 2.5 acres.

As time went by, the forests grew smaller. More than sixty villages began as clearings in Worcestershire forests, among them Bewdley, Ripple, Upton-upon-Severn, Welland, Newland, Northwick, Hartlebury, Kempsey, Fladbury, Inkberrow, Hanbury and Stoke. The trees on the Malvern Hills were eaten away relentlessly by Worcester's iron-working. The Wyre Forest gradually disappeared as charcoal-burners attempted to supply the needs of Bewdley's riverside metal-working bloomeries while the forest of Feckenham fed the salt refineries of Droitwich.

By the sixteenth century, most of the great forests had gone. In 1608, a survey was taken that showed that the Wyre and Feckenham Forests had about 40,000 dead and decaying trees and 603 acres of coppice. By 1895, all the Worcestershire forests were owned chiefly by Lord Dudley of Witley Court, the Earl of Coventry of Croome Court, and Earl Beauchamp in Madresfield.

ESTABLISHING A TOWN

The eleventh century saw some villages outstripping others and developing into towns. This was usually because of one or more important factors. In the days when travel by river was the most convenient, Worcester and Bewdley were on the River Severn, Pershore and Evesham were on the River Avon, and Tenbury Wells was on the River Teme. Kidderminster was on the Stour and was crossed by important trade routes, while Bromsgrove was on the River Salwarpe and on an ancient route from Worcester travelling north. Malvern and Redditch served their monasteries, as did, of course, Worcester, Pershore and Evesham. The only exception was Stourport-on-Severn, which was a new town in the 1760s.

A Medieval town was a most unhealthy place for the thatched houses were huddled together, streets were narrow, and down the centre ran the town's effluent.

A town was usually owned by a king, a lord, or a religious establishment. Market rights were given by the king or a great lord who charged for the privilege. Every town wanted market rights as this brought prosperity. A market one or two days a week would be the centre of trade for that area. No other person would be allowed to buy or sell within a radius of 5 or 6 miles. Most market rights were granted in the 1300s, although Evesham received them from Edward the Confessor as early as 1055.

The granting of a fair was even more desirable than market rights. Although it was probably held only once or twice a year, it would bring in traders and buyers from across the county. A fair was usually held on a saint's day – for example, Roger de Somery obtained grant of a four-day fair for Clent in 1253 at the feast of St Kenelm.

Upper Clent

Stourport-on-Severn received permission to hold a three-day fair annually in about 1768 while the town was still under construction. This was a mixed blessing for the residents. It brought noise and dirt and chaos. In Lion Hill were rows of horses, while York Street and New Street held pens full of pigs and sheep. York Street also had cattle from end to end. The noise was indescribable. When they had gone, the townsfolk had to spend the day scrubbing and swilling to get the streets clean again.

Every town aspired to a form of self-government by means of a charter. Only the larger towns were allowed to have charters which they purchased from the king. Under a charter, a town could get rid of the sheriff so that they could manage their own affairs, regulating trade, setting the level of taxation, collecting rents, introducing rules and regulations, and administering justice through their courts. Worcester purchased a charter from Richard I as soon as he came to the throne in 1189 and Droitwich bought one from King John in the early 1200s. Kidderminster didn't bother until 1632 (granted in 1636), and then only because there was a dispute over market rights.

Clent was granted a charter in 1566 by a curious mistake. The village was in Worcestershire in 1086, but when it applied for a charter it was in Staffordshire. The officials were unable to find the village in the Domesday Book. The only place in Staffordshire with a name that bore any resemblance to Clent was Chenet, near Cannock, which was a large village, so the charter was granted. The inhabitants were exempted from the payment of tolls, from contributing to the expenses of sending knights to Parliament and from serving on juries, except those in their own parish.

Pershore has so many forged charters (perhaps made to replace those lost in a fire) that no one is certain when the first charter was given, but by the end of the 1300s the inhabitants were living in a town with some of the following by-laws:

They could not play tennis, football or the 'dyce'. The bakers could only buy grain from the Tuesday market. All tenants were to be home by nine o'clock. Licensees could only sell their wares at one inn, The King's Borde. Taverners could not keep any man's sons, servants or minstrels during church services or after 8 p.m. All pigs were to be under the charge of the common herd. Streets had to be thoroughly cleaned once a month. Inhabitants were not to have any inmates or subtenants in their houses.

3

MONASTERIES, PRIORIES AND FRIARIES

If you had lived in Worcestershire in the early Middle Ages, your landlord would probably have been the bishop or the local prior or even an abbess. The religious houses were the greatest landowners in Worcestershire. The county was made up of 1,200 hides and the Church held 786 to the laymen's 414. Life in Worcestershire revolved round the monasteries. Many of these church lands had special privileges so that the monks could not be arrested nor taken to court; sometimes they also claimed freedom from taxes, military service and various repairs such as town walls.

Those who farmed church land usually gave one-tenth of all produce to the Church; it became law in 787. The tithes were often kept in special barns; those

Leigh Court tithe barn

at Leigh, Middle Littleton and Bredon still exist and are open to the public. Leigh Court barn is the largest.

It was built in the 1300s and was part of the grange or farm at Leigh which was owned by the monks of Pershore Abbey. Eleven huge carved 'cruck' beams support both the walls and the roof. More than 150 feet long and 34 feet wide, it is now under the guardianship of Leigh Court and English Heritage. Middle Littleton barn dates back to about 1260 and held the tithes of the Abbey of Evesham. Bredon tithe barn is situated to the west of the church, down a narrow lane. It has aisles and two porches; in one of the porches is an upper room with a fireplace. The barn burned down in 1980, but has now been restored. Both tithe barns at Middle Littleton and Bredon are administered by the National Trust.

A tithe could be in money or in kind. If in kind, it was often difficult to assess the exact amount and that frequently led to disagreements. At St James Church in Oddingley, the tithes were under dispute for centuries. The matter came to a head in 1806, when the rector, the Reverend George Parker, demanded extra money from his tenants to build a tithe barn. Five eminent parishioners, led by Captain Evans of Church Farm, decided enough was enough and planned to murder him. They were much too high and mighty to do the deed themselves

Bredon tithe barn

and so they hired a local wheelwright, Thomas Hemming, to carry out the murder. Although Hemming meddled in minor crime, murder was new to him and he was nervous about carrying it out. First he shot the Reverend George Parker, then he bludgeoned him and finally set fire to him, taking so long over it that he was spotted by three men out for a walk. Hemming hid in a barn at Netherwood Farm, rented by Thomas Clewes, one of the five parishioners. A few days later, when darkness fell, Captain Evans, Thomas Clewes, another parishioner, and an elderly farmhand by the name of James Taylor, went to the barn to find Hemming. When he emerged, Taylor killed him with blows from a hardwood stick. He was buried under the floor of the barn.

By a strange coincidence, twenty-four years later, his brother-in-law was hired to develop the barn. When he dug up the floor, there was the body of his long-lost relative. By that time most of those involved had passed away, and the judge said that, as those who had actually committed the crime were dead, no one could be charged, therefore the accessories to the crime could not be charged. Thomas Clewes became licensee of The Fir Tree Inn at Dunhampstead near Oddingley, where old newspaper cuttings and other publications giving details of the murder can be found on the walls.

RICHES AND THE WOOL INDUSTRY

The bishop and large religious houses grew rich from tithes, bequests, donations, granting licences and consecrating churches. They also sold indulgences (forgiveness of sins) and blessings. If they possessed the bones of a saint, these were riches indeed, especially those that performed a miracle or two, as pilgrims paid to touch the venerated bones. The monks had sworn a vow of poverty, but found themselves endowed with large tracts of land. They became wealthy landowners and had to become businessmen, running large agricultural enterprises.

Originally, the brethren were pious, holy men, but by the end of the thirteenth century 'the efforts of the abbots seem to be solely directed to the augmentation of their material welfare and privileges' (*Victorian County History*).

In William Langland's *Piers Plowman*, written in the 1300s, he says:

And the more they acquire and control out of capital and goods,
And gain the lordship of lands, the less they give away.

The wool industry was thriving way back in Roman times, and after the arrival of the Norman conquerors in 1066 it expanded so much that by the twelfth

The Walker Hall at Evesham

century it was England's chief export. Worcestershire wool was in great demand; the sheep were fed on the county's lush green grass, producing wool of excellent quality. It has been calculated that there were three sheep to every person.

Monasteries thrived on the proceeds. Bordesley Abbey, in Redditch, kept 1,650 sheep in total and depended upon the income from wool. In about 1275, one of the abbots of Bordesley was deposed and absconded to London, taking with him the great seal of the abbey that served much the same function as a credit card does today. He tricked some Florentine merchants into lending him 300 marks of silver, saying that he would repay them with forty-two sacks of wool. He fled to Feckenham Forest, where he became an outlaw. One day, he gathered together his fellow miscreants and attacked the abbey, but the monks were able to beat them off. The Abbot of Bordesley eventually petitioned Parliament to sort out the matter with the merchants.

During the thirteenth century, the sale and export of wool became carefully regulated. Taxes were paid on all exported wool and, to make sure that none slipped through the net and escaped the taxes, the 'Wool Staple' was introduced. Wool could only be exported from certain markets through certain ports. Worcester, Evesham and Kidderminster formed centres for the manufacture and sale of wool, although none of them were Staple towns – wool had to go to London to be exported. At Evesham the Walker Hall, built alongside the main gateway to its abbey, functioned as a wool-exchange.

———————————

THE BENEDICTINES

Nearly all the monasteries in Worcestershire were Benedictine, following Saint Benedict's rule of poverty, obedience and chastity. In AD 580 there were only some fourteen monasteries throughout Europe, but by 1300 there were 37,000. Those who wished to become monks went through a probationary period of one year. If, at the end of that time, they still wanted to join and had proved satisfactory, they were made full members, but once they had joined, they were expected to remain in that monastery until death. Their motto was, and still is, *laborere est orare*, to work is to pray. The monks had to dedicate their lives totally to God, praying seven times a day, the first service being about two o'clock in the morning. They were required to give away all their property and live in poverty. However, they could employ tenants who would do most of the work so that they could concentrate on their devotions. Although it was an austere life, it was better than that of the average peasant.

The main Benedictine monasteries were at Worcester, Evesham, Malvern and Pershore, with a Cistercian monastery at Redditch (Bordesley) and friaries chiefly at Worcester. The abbot or prior appointed his officers, usually the steward, the novice master, the sacristan (who looked after the music and the books), the hosteller, the almoner (who distributed the poor relief), the infirmarian, the chamberlain, the precentor (leader of the choir), the cellarer, the kitchener and the refectarian.

WORCESTER MONASTERY AND SAINT OSWALD

Edgar's gate at the rear of the cathedral was formerly the entrance to the monastery

In about 680, a church, dedicated to Saint Peter, was built on or near the site of the present cathedral. A bishop was chosen, but he was so old that he died before he could be consecrated. He was followed by Bishop Bosel, who was so infirm he was unable to execute his duties and so he was assisted by the monk Oftfor who became bishop when Bosel resigned. The enormous See was occupied, at that time, by the Hwicce people (see Chapter 1).

Bishop Oswald was appointed in 960. An energetic man, he was the nephew of the Archbishop of Canterbury. Under Bishop Oswald, the cathedral flourished. In about 983, he founded a Benedictine monastery dedicated to Saint Mary which superseded Saint Peter's as the cathedral of Worcester.

The number of Benedictine monks rose from a dozen or so, to fifty. He managed to increase its assets and brought in a system of leasing church land that encouraged small villages to spring up throughout the county. It became a centre of great learning, and many of the monks went on to study at university.

Bishop Oswald also became Archbishop of York but when he died in 992 he was buried in Worcester Cathedral and miracles soon began to be witnessed at his tomb. Unfortunately, after his death his cathedral was burned down and stood in ruins until a new cathedral was built by Saint Wulstan, who completely demolished St Oswald's building.

Within the cathedral, Early English, Transitional, Decorated and Perpendicular styles blend harmoniously together. The walls of the transept are Norman

WORCESTER CATHEDRAL

The building of Wulstan's cathedral, completed in 1089, has already been described. The crypt still exists, of which Nikolaus Pevsner, the architectural historian, said, 'With its about fifty short columns with their block or single scallop or single-trumpet-scallop capitals and with its plain groin-vaults, it represents to perfection the mood of those determined and ruthless years.'

Worcester monastery, adjacent to the cathedral, was closed by Henry VIII in about 1541.

The lands of Worcester Cathedral simply went to the dean and chapter so that they were still in church hands. Wulstan's and Oswald's shrines and tombs were destroyed, their bones were encased in lead, then buried near the high altar.

EVESHAM ABBEY AND MONASTERY

In the centre of Evesham, two Perpendicular churches stand side by side, that of All Saints and that of Saint Lawrence.

Each one served a different parish. All Saints is the older and parts of it are Norman. Behind these two churches are the ruins of a great abbey and monastery.

Evesham Abbey was founded by Saint Egwin. Born in Worcester, he was the nephew of the king of Mercia. He was appointed in 710 as the third Bishop of Worcester and he and his priests went out into the region to preach and baptize. Few churches would have been built at that time – he would have usually preached from well-known landmarks or at preaching crosses.

*Winter aconites bloom before
St Lawrence's Church, Evesham*

Little remains of Evesham Abbey, but this remnant hints at its original splendour

A church was sometimes later built on the site. The old preaching crosses are still standing in the churchyards of Kingston-on-Teme and Suckley. The base of the cross at Suckley was used for sharpening arrows and the marks can still be seen.

Egwin preached especially against working on a Sunday and adultery, which did not make him popular with either the workers or the gentry.

The monks of Evesham Abbey have recorded that, when he was preaching in Alcester (Warwickshire), he was 'tin-panned' out of the town by the hammering of anvils. He appears to have met with the same welcome at Bromsgrove. In each case, Bishop Egwin cursed the town and shook the dust of it from his feet.

He was falsely accused of various misdemeanours and went to see the Pope to vindicate himself. The Chronicle of the Abbey tells the tale that he put fetters on his feet, locked them, and threw away the key into a pool of the Avon before setting out. While he was at Rome, his assistants were cooking a salmon caught in the Tiber when they found the key to the fetters in the fish's stomach. This miracle was naturally regarded by the Pope as a complete vindication, and the bishop was sent home to England in honour.

As to the founding of the abbey, the story goes that Bishop Egwin's swine-

Saint Egwin kneels before King Edgar. From a stained glass window in St Lawrence's Church

Eoves' vision has been commemorated by a statue in the town centre by John McKenna, unveiled in 2008

herd, a man named Eoves, allowed his animals to wander into an overgrown thicket. While he was retrieving them, he saw a wonderful vision of the Virgin Mary with an angel each side, shining brightly and singing psalms.

When he told Egwin about his experience, the bishop went to the spot and lay on the ground in prayer. As he got to his feet, he had a similar vision, but this time the central figure reached out and blessed him by the sign of a cross. The bishop had already vowed that if the Pope allowed him to keep his bishopric after his journey to Rome, he would build a church. This seemed the ideal place. It began in about 701 and received endowments of land in over thirty-five villages across Worcestershire, Warwickshire and Gloucestershire.

Abbot Ethelwig was appointed in 1059, and became the favourite adviser of Edward the Confessor. He designed a new church and, when he died, he left a substantial sum towards the building of it. His successor, Abbot Walter, raised the rest of the money by sending the monks round England with collecting boxes and the shrine of Saint Egwin.

A document from Evesham Abbey dating back to the 1100s records that sixty-seven monks lived there, plus three clerks and

The bell tower at Evesham

three paupers supported by charity. To serve them were sixty-five servants and some of the occupations are listed: five served in the church, two in the infirmary, two in the cellar, five in the kitchen, seven in the bakehouse, four in the brewhouse, four did the mending, two attended the bath, two were shoemakers, two were in the orchard, three worked in the garden, one attended the stranger's gate, four travelled abroad with the monks, four were fishermen, four waited on the abbot, three were in the hall, and two were watchmen. There were also five nuns – their occupation is not stated.

Clement Litchfield was abbot from 1514 to 1539, at a time when Henry VIII was closing the monasteries. He could not believe that the king would appropriate his wonderful abbey and monastery and foolishly continued with a building programme. He built the beautiful bell tower, which still stands on the abbey park, parts of the cloister arch, and partly refurbished the two churches next to the abbey.

The abbot refused to surrender to Henry VIII. However, the cellarer, Philip Hawford, was in league with Thomas Cromwell, the king's vice-regent in church matters. Hawford said that if Cromwell made him abbot instead of Litchfield, he would surrender the monastery. The abbot was forced to resign, Cromwell appointed Philip Hawford as abbot and, piece by piece, he handed the monastery

Evesham almonry is now a well-equipped and interesting small museum

over to Cromwell. For this piece of skullduggery, he received a pension of £240 a year. One of Hawford's first documents is on display in Evesham's museum, housed in the beautiful old almonry at the southern end of the High Street. Built in the 1300s or 1400s, it was once the home of the almoner.

The locals tried to save the old abbey and suggested that it should be turned into a school or an inn, but to no avail, and the building was pulled down in about 1539.

MALVERN PRIORIES

Malvern had two priories, Great Malvern and Little Malvern.

Great Malvern Priory

The Benedictine Priory of Great Malvern began about the same time as Worcester monastery, in 1084 or 1085. Malvern was then a remote region in a great forest.

John Leland, writing in the sixteenth century, says that the site was originally

Malvern Priory was saved from the destruction of Henry VIII by being purchased by the town

occupied by a hermit, St Werstan, a monk who had escaped from Deerhurst (near Tewkesbury) when it was pillaged by the Danes, only to be martyred in Malvern. Two men were somehow implicated, Aldwyn and his friend. Aldwyn decided to make a pilgrimage to Rome to atone for his sin, but Bishop Wulstan persuaded him to stay in Malvern and found a priory. Devotees came to join him one after another, until the number rose to 300. A series of stained glass panels high up in one of the windows of Great Malvern Priory tells the story.

Aldwyn made the priory subject to the abbot of Westminster 'for the time being', although it was in the middle of the diocese of Worcester. A long struggle resulted between the Bishop of Worcester and the Abbot of Westminster as to which one of them held the priory.

This led to one of the most bitter ecclesiastical quarrels in English history. William de Ledbury was elected as prior in 1279 and *The Victoria County History* tells us that he kept over twenty mistresses, 'on whom he lavished whatever he could seize, while the community starved'. The bishop of Worcester, Bishop Giffard, deposed him in September 1282, and he fled. The bishop then put in a new prior, William de Wykewane, who was sent to London with his companions to be blessed by the Abbot of Westminster. However, instead of confirming de Wykewane, the abbot threw the whole party into prison, saying that the bishop did not have the authority to elect a new prior for Malvern. Both the king and the Pope became involved, and letters passed to and fro between them.

The king wrote to Bishop Gifford, saying that the Abbot of Westminster was correct in saying that Great Malvern was subject to Westminster. At this, Gifford seized the abbot's 'temporalities' – presumably the tithes that were due. In retaliation, the king told the sheriff of Worcester to take all the revenues due to Gifford for the king. By June, matters had still not been resolved. All the officials of Malvern Priory had been excommunicated, the monks' pensions, portions and anything belonging to them had been removed, and poor William de Wykewane, the elected prior, was still held in prison in fetters.

The king was determined to put an end to the quarrel and ordered the two parties to appear before him at Acton Burnell near Shrewsbury. There, Gifford was shown letters saying that the abbey of Westminster, with all its cells and priories, *especially that of Great Malvern,* was to be exempt from common law and ordinary jurisdiction. This proved that Great Malvern belonged to Westminster. Bishop Gifford acknowledged defeat and agreed to lift the excommunications. He was given the manor of Knightwick as compensation.

Malvern Priory was closed in about 1539. Bishop Latimer (later to be burned at the stake) wrote to Cromwell pleading for it to be saved. One of his reasons

The gatehouse, Malvern's last remaining monastic building, is now a museum

was that the prior 'feeds many and that daily, for the country is poor and full of penury'.

For many years, the monks had worshipped in a beautiful priory church, much envied by the townsfolk. A place of worship had been provided by the monks for the general public, but this was miserable by comparison and stood where the main Malvern post office is now. The townsfolk decided to buy the priory church which cost £20, and it took them two years to raise the money.

Part of the old priory church has been incorporated into the present abbey church. Of the monastic buildings, nothing but the gatehouse remains but this is a real treasure and, after being damaged by a speeding ice cream van in 1979, it was renovated and turned into the town's museum.

Little Malvern Priory

Great Malvern Priory is in the centre of the town, whereas the priory of Saint Giles at Little Malvern stands isolated in a picturesque setting by the A4104, just below British Camp.

It is thought to have been founded in 1171 by two brothers who were born in Beckford in Gloucestershire, Jocelin and Edred. They, like Aldwyn, probably buried themselves in the Malvern wilderness as hermits, then found themselves

Little Malvern Priory. Of the original church only the chancel, central tower and transept remain

the centre of a little community. It was only a small priory of ten or twelve monks. Unlike Great Malvern, Little Malvern was 'eternally united' with Worcester Cathedral.

The Victoria County History states, 'The spirit of devotion which animated the early founders of the priory does not appear to have largely inspired their successors.' Two centuries after their foundation, in 1323, they were visited by Bishop Cobham, then the Bishop of Worcester, who appears to have been shocked by the state of the priory. Brother Hugh de Pyribrok was charged with immorality. A few years later he became prior!

A best-selling novel by the Victorian writer Sabine Baring Gould (1834–1924) featured Little Malvern Priory. A local vicar, the Revd W.S. Symonds, claims that he found the story among some old papers in a parishioner's attic and turned it into a book that was then adapted by Gould. A monk from Little Malvern Priory disobeyed the strict Benedictine rules by marrying a relative to save her from an unhappy marriage, then became involved in a family feud and committed a murder. For punishment, the prior ordered him to climb up Raggedstone Hill (last hill but one at the southern end of the Malverns) every day on his hands and knees.

After a year, he died, saying, 'My curse be on thee, thou heaven-blasting hill, and on those which laid this burden upon me and all that be like as they

Legend has it that if the shadow of Malvern's Raggedstone Hill falls upon you, you are doomed!

are … May thy shadow and my shadow never cease to fall upon them.' This has been taken to mean that anyone upon whom the shadow of the hill falls is cursed. Among them have been the Prior of Malvern who died soon afterwards, Sir John Oldcastle, priest, who was burned at Smithfield, and Cardinal Wolsey who fell from grace when he failed to persuade the Pope to annul Henry VIII's marriage to Catherine of Aragon.

The precise date of the dissolution of Little Malvern is not known, but was probably about 1534. The chancel, central tower and transept have been preserved and they are now part of the parish church.

PERSHORE ABBEY

Pershore Abbey and monastery were important. The abbot was much respected in ecclesiastical circles. It was a large monastery – in 1346 there were thirty monks, plus lay brothers and servants. The building itself was huge; the nave being 180 feet long and once reaching what is now the entrance gate on the edge of the precinct. All but one of the bays of the nave could be used by the

Pershore Abbey, much reduced after the dissolution but still one of the architectural glories of Worcestershire

townsfolk. The churchyard was used by thirty-four of the surrounding villages; relatives of the deceased paid for the privilege. Those who held no lands – that is, the poor – had to be taken to Little Comberton for burial.

Pershore Abbey was apparently founded twice. First of all, Saint Oswald began a religious house in about 689, then the abbey was refounded by Egelward, Duke of Dorset, in 972 when it received extensive grants. Throughout most of the eight centuries of its existence the brethren seem to have led God-fearing lives and their work with poor travellers was much commended. Unfortunately, their saintliness does not seem to have been rewarded by divine protection. In 1223 the abbey and most of the town were reduced to cinders. In 1288 it burned down again. In 1299 the important registers showing all its holdings were lost in a fire. By 1327 there had been another fire and the church, refectory, dormitory and guest house lay in ruins. By 1327 it had lost two-thirds of its revenue, including thirty of its manors. Not only was it sacked by Danes, but Edward the Confessor took away many of the abbey's possessions and gave them instead to the abbey at Westminster that he had refounded.

Pershore Abbey came into the hands of Duke Alphere (or Delfer or Aelfhere), who led a life of crime and plunder and stripped the abbey of its assets. Retribution came in the form of a lonely death where he was 'eaten by vermin'. According to the *Anglo Saxon Chronicle*, his son, Odda, was 'a good man and pure and very noble' and took a vow of perpetual virginity lest a son of his should be guilty of a similar crime. He became a monk at Deerhurst, and after his death his body was carried back to Pershore. Many years later, after another disastrous fire, the workmen came across a lead coffin containing his bones.

Odda was a generous patron of Pershore Abbey. Edburgha had been the abbess of a convent at Pershore, but was later the abbess of a convent at Winchester, and her body was interred there. Miracles began to occur at her tomb. The Prior of Pershore asked if he could be sent some of Saint Edburgha's bones, to share in the revenue these saintly relics were producing. Odda purchased three bones from Winchester for Pershore. Unfortunately, the miracles stopped occurring at Winchester and began at Pershore, so the Winchester authorities assumed that these were the vital bones and asked for their return. The abbot at Pershore refused. The wrangling continued down the centuries until relics fell out of fashion, then Winchester magnanimously returned to Pershore all Saint Edburgha's bones. It is rumoured that, finding them rather an embarrassment, the Pershore authorities sent them to Yardley, which was having building or rebuilding work done at that time, and they were put under the floor of Yardley chancel. The church is named after Saint Edburgha.

Henry VIII was on the throne when John Stoneywell was elected as Abbot of Pershore Abbey in 1526. One of the monks, Richard Beerley, wrote to Thomas

Cromwell in 1536 that the abbot was preventing the king's commands from being put into effect and accused the monks of drinking and bowling 'after collacyon until ten or twelve of the clock and come to matins as drunck as myss [mice] and some at cards and some at dice and at tables'. Another monk reported that the abbot was overheard remarking to Ralph Sheldon of Beoley (an ardent Catholic) that the diseases and plagues that were rife at that time were divine retribution because of the king's split with Rome.

However, Cromwell does not seem to have taken much account of these letters as it was another three years before the abbey was dissolved and then John Stoneywell received a comfortable pension of £160 per annum together with lodgings, a garden and two orchards with pools.

Only a fraction of this once-great abbey and monastery now remains. The nave and the lady chapel at the east end were pulled down, the north transept collapsed, and the domestic buildings have completely disappeared. Even so, it remains one of the best examples of Norman and Medieval architecture in Worcestershire.

_____

THE CISTERCIANS AND BORDESLEY ABBEY

Bordesley Abbey was the only Cistercian abbey in Worcestershire. The Cistercian order was founded in France in 1098, with one of its leaders being an Englishman, Stephen Harding. They were known as 'the white monks' as their robes were white.

It was a movement famous for its austerity, for the severity of its rule and its plain architecture. By this time, manual labour had been abandoned by the Benedictine monks, but the Cistercians were adamant that this should be an integral part of monastic life. The Cistercians were brilliant civil engineers and often chose waterlogged, isolated places to build their abbeys. The Redditch site was originally nothing but a marshy waste and no doubt the benefactors were glad to get rid of it and gain a few heavenly points in the process.

The abbey was founded during the turbulent civil war between King Stephen and Empress Matilda, the effect of this being that there are two foundation and endowment charters. The first came from Empress Matilda in 1136 in which she says that she and Henry her son founded and endowed the abbey. Earl Waleran (who was responsible for the burning of Worcester city) was a witness. A second charter was made two years later. This time it was given by Earl Waleran and there was no mention of Empress Matilda. Historians are still trying to unravel this mystery.

People think that, because there is nothing left of the abbey, it was inconsequential. In fact, it was the fifth richest monastery in England, its wealth coming from the sale of wool. It even played a part in national events.

Guy of Warwick sought sanctuary from Edward II here in 1312. He had offended the king by chopping off the head of the king's favourite, Piers Gaveston. Piers had been a thorn in the side of the barons for many years. He had originally been brought in as a friend for the young prince before he became king, but it soon became apparent that he was a bad influence and, furthermore, it was reported by the local bishop that their relationship 'was not natural'. Piers was insolent, greedy and rude. He gave each baron a nickname – Guy of Warwick he called 'The Black Dog of Arden'. Guy replied that one day he would feel his teeth. Matters nearly resulted in a civil war. Piers was banished abroad, but as soon as Edward II became king he arranged for Piers to return and heaped upon him money, jewels, property and titles, including that of Earl of Cornwall and Regent of England. Piers was captured in Scarborough Castle and seized by the Earl of Warwick who condemned him to death in a rudimentary court. Screaming and kicking, he was taken up Blacklow Hill on the outskirts of Warwick and beheaded. As for Guy of Warwick, 'The Black Dog of Arden', he was poisoned by a friend of Piers in 1315 and buried in Bordesley Abbey. Sometime in the middle of the nineteenth century, James Woodward came to Redditch as tutor to a local family. By this time, Bordesley Abbey had disappeared into meadowland, but James realized the importance of the site and began some minor excavations. He found a stone coffin that he thought belonged to 'The Black Dog of Arden' and various ornamental tiles. He and his friends kept watch over them all night long, taking two hours each. Woodward took the midnight hour and reported:

> It was a dark and cloudy night, and the wind blew in gusts across the Abbey Meadows … St Stephen's clock, striking the hour of midnight, intensified my train of thought, when a louder blast of wind caused me to raise my head – at that instant another head appeared above the heap of soil on the opposite side of the chapel – it was the head of a large black dog. It looked at me for a moment then disappeared. I seized a crowbar and climbed to the top of the mound but my visitor was gone.

Swapping notes the next morning, he discovered that a friend had also seen 'what many might have deemed an embodiment of the spirit of the swarthy Earl of Warwick'. The Black Dog of Arden is Redditch's famous ghost and the story is on the walls of the visitors' centre in the Bordesley meadows.

When Henry VIII was closing the monasteries, the last Abbot of Bordesley,

Part of the red ditch from which Redditch town gets its name

Much of the demolition of the abbey was carried out by the townsfolk
who carted away the building materials to use for their own houses

Courtesy of the Forge Mill Needle Museum

John Day, was reported by the cellarer to be 'aged, impotent, sick, also not of perfect remembrance'. Nevertheless, he seems to have pulled off the best deal of anyone, for all that Henry VIII gained from Bordesley, apart from its holdings, was a derelict abbey and a debt of £200. The abbey was surrendered on 17 July 1538 and, according to the papal letters, by 31 July it had been 'defaced and plucked down, and the substance thereof sold to diverse persons'. As for John Day, he received a comfortable pension and went to live with the Sheldons of Beoley.

THE FRIARS

The Friars came with the gospel of simplicity and poverty and were particularly concerned with the needs of the poor and suffering. The monks tended to shut themselves away in monasteries, whereas the Friars existed by begging and moved among the common people.

The various orders were known by the colour of their garments. The Grey Friars were the first to arrive in about 1224. Also known as 'Franciscans', or 'Minorites', they followed the austere rule of St Francis of Assisi. The Worcester Friary became one of the most important in England. It possessed a considerable theological library, but unfortunately did not produce many learned men.

Monks and parish priests sometimes objected to the presence of the friars, saying that they had no authority to hear confessions, nor to preach. Rivalry between the monks and the friars came to a head in 1289 and 1290 over the body of Henry Poche, a citizen of Worcester. Both monks and friars claimed his body. It went first to the friars, but in March the sacristan and a group of monks from Worcester monastery grabbed the body and buried it in the cathedral cemetery. A fight broke out and some of the friars were slightly injured; others were pushed into dung heaps. The friars appealed to the archbishop, saying that they had been attacked by the monks. The dispute came to the ears of Edward I, with the result that the archbishop wrote to the Bishop of Worcester, Bishop Giffard, explaining the friars' case. Bishop Giffard took no notice. Four months later the archbishop ordered him to have the body exhumed and given back to the friars. The bishop still did nothing.

By December the body had been buried for nine months, and the prior received notice that if the body was not returned, he and the elders would be suspended. At that, the monks agreed that the friars could have the body, providing that they removed it quietly. Instead, the friars took it away with great pomp and ceremony, singing loudly.

The monks came to accept the friars. Bishop Giffard left the friars 100 shillings when he died in 1301 and the next bishop, William of Gainsborough, was himself a Franciscan friar.

Their piety attracted support from all walks of society, including the powerful Beauchamp family. William Beauchamp, Earl of Warwick, made a will in 1296 asking for his body to be buried in the choir of the Grey Friars. Sir John Beauchamp, Baron of Powick, bequeathed his body to the friars and gave them enough money to build a side chapel to house it, together with a priest to pray for his soul. One of the last houses of the Black Friars to be established in England was founded near the centre of Worcester in 1347 by William Beauchamp, Lord of Elmley.

Cromwell's agent arrived in 1538 and reported to Henry VIII that all the friars' houses were in great poverty. He withdrew the common seals, used by the friars to authenticate their documents, so that they could neither buy nor sell. Six weeks later they surrendered to Cromwell. The buildings of the Grey Friars and Black Friars were bought by the municipal corporation and the stones used to repair the walls of the town.

One of the finest timber-framed buildings in the county, Greyfriars, is in Friar Street and open to the public. Sadly, it seems to have been simply a fifteenth-century town house, and its only association with the friars being that it was built on the site of the old friary.

Greyfriars. The architectural historian, Sir Nikolaus Pevsner,
describes Greyfriars as one of the finest timber-framed buildings in the county

OTHER RELIGIOUS HOUSES

Across Worcestershire were many other religious houses. Stones from a monastery at Bredon were used in St Wulstan's cathedral. The remains of a small convent at Cookhill are in a private garden. There was also a convent in Upper Tything, Worcester, on the site of the present grammar school, for Cistercian nuns (white ladies).

We know that a friary once existed at Droitwich because of the name, Friary Street. The Augustinian friars arrived in 1331, and although the site eventually spread over 5 acres, there were probably never more than a dozen friars. It was an enclosed order, removed from the outside world. By the time it was closed by Henry VIII, the friars could not even afford blankets.

A century later, Friary Street was blown up during the Civil War. At the western end of the street was an old church that the Royalists used as an arsenal. In 1646 the Parliamentarians placed a cannon on Dodderhill overlooking the town and fired at the church. A few bits and pieces, such as the windows and a sculptured head, were rescued and incorporated into the front of (what is now) The Old Cock Inn. As for the old friary, the Norbury family built a large house on the site which became a hotel in 1936 and is now apartments, except for a block that has been converted into the Norbury Theatre.

The Old Cock Inn. Opposite was a small friary, closed by Henry VIII

Harvington Hall, where the public are now able to inspect the ingenious hiding places for priests

*This tree trunk is all that is left of an avenue of trees lining the straight drive from the hall
to the village, enabling occupants of the hall to check on approaching visitors*

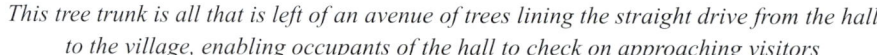

CHURCH PROPERTY SALES

When Henry VIII sold the lands that had belonged to the monasteries, 75 acres of land from Evesham Abbey, situated just across the river at Bengeworth, was bought by Thomas Watson. It included the manor of Bengeworth which had been built on the site of an old Roman camp off Cooper's Lane. In the garden was a ring of six mulberry trees, planted by the monks of Evesham Abbey in an effort to produce silk, but they planted the wrong kind of tree. The descendants of the trees are still there.

One of the purchasers was Henry VIII's favourite lawyer, John Pakington, who bought thirty manors. Among them was Harvington Hall near Chaddesley Corbett, which he bought in 1529 and passed to his nephew, Humphrey Pakington (1555–1631).

Fortunately, Henry VIII never discovered the use to which it was put, for it was used to hide Roman Catholic priests! It is now open to the public and has more 'priest holes' than any other home in England!

4

TWO CIVIL WARS AND THE BLACK DEATH

Henry I came to the throne in 1100, king of both Normandy and England. He was the son of William the Conqueror, and although he was a brusque man who drank heavily, under his rule England became a power to be reckoned with on the European continent.

King Henry managed to father over twenty illegitimate offspring, but only one legitimate son, William, and one daughter, Matilda. She was betrothed to the German emperor when she was only eight and married him when she was twelve and he was thirty-two. Although he died, she kept the title 'Empress Matilda'. Matilda was not a popular character. She was bad-tempered, bellowing at her courtiers with her deep, masculine voice, and was said to be 'puffed up with intolerable pride'.

One dark evening in November 1120, Henry's only legitimate son, William, together with several of the French nobility, embarked on a return journey from England to Normandy. The captain of their vessel, the *White Ship*, was so drunk that a group of monks who were travelling with them chose to return on another boat. Unfortunately, the port side of the *White Ship* struck a submerged rock just off Barfleur on the Normandy coast and the ship quickly capsized. It is said that the only survivor was a French butcher.

Henry I died in 1135. Despite his having sworn loyalty to Matilda, the English throne was seized by Stephen du Blois, one of Henry's illegitimate children. He was the popular 'sporting personality' of his day, a mounted tournament champion, expert swordsman and supposedly a perfect gentleman. His brother, Henry, was Bishop of Winchester. Stephen had reigned for three years when an army invaded on Matilda's behalf and the conflict began.

The lordship of Worcester had been granted by King Stephen in 1138 to one of his great warlords, Waleran de Beaumont, Count of Meulan. In November 1140 news reached the city that Empress Matilda was in Gloucester and planning to attack Worcester. The citizens took sanctuary in the cathedral church, dragging their best furniture with them. A chronicler complains that the cathedral became 'a public inn and a hall of debate', while the chanting of the monks blended with the wailing of the women and crying of children. As the enemy attacked, the monks tolled bells and, dressed in their white vestments, bravely carried the relics of Saint Oswald across the front of the cathedral. However, the enemy was not impressed and rushed through the city gates, burning and looting, with prisoners 'coupled like hounds' for ransom. Afterwards King Stephen himself came to Worcester to see the damage.

Later in the month, Earl Waleran returned to England and when he saw his blackened city, he took his army to Sudeley, which was held by Empress Matilda. A chronicler says, 'What he did is scarce fit to record, he returned evil for evil, seized the people, their property, and beasts for booty and on the morrow returned to Worcester.'

Matters were to go badly for Stephen who, in 1141, was captured at the Battle of Lincoln. Many of his supporters decided it would be wise to change sides, among them Earl Waleran. This was a rather rash act as a little later one of Henry I's illegitimate offspring, Robert Duke of Gloucester, who had declared his support for his half-sister Matilda, was captured. Matilda's only option was to exchange Robert for Stephen so that the king was freed. He decided to mete out retribution to those who had changed sides. This included Count Waleran and once again the city went up in flames. This time the citizens fled to the north of the city to the island of Bevere, situated in the River Severn as it meandered to and fro. From there they managed to fight off the enemy. Bevere still exists, but is a very different place now that the marshes have been drained and the locks built.

The war between Stephen and Matilda lasted for twenty years. It was a time of anarchy. Half-starved armies roamed the countryside, stealing and looting. Peace came in 1153. Stephen's son had been killed in battle, and so it was agreed that Stephen would remain as king for the rest of his life while Matilda's eldest son, Henry of Anjou, would succeed to the throne. Henry had taken over his mother's army, but was running out of financial resources and had to ask Stephen to pay his soldiers their discharge allowance so that he could send them home. This Stephen did in a fit of magnanimity unusual even in the chivalric world.

Henry succeeded to the throne in 1154 as Henry II, the first Plantagenet.

THE PLANTAGENETS, 1154–1399, AND KING JOHN

This is the name commonly given to the family to which the English kings belonged from 1154 to 1399. They are all descended, in one way or another, from Count Geoffrey of Anjou and the nickname came about because the count always wore a sprig of *planta genista* (Latin for broom) in his cap. They were: Henry II, Richard I, John, Henry III, Edward I, Edward II, Edward III and Richard II.

The most important of these kings for Worcester was King John who was a frequent visitor to the county and is buried in Worcester Cathedral. Between 1200 and 1216 a Christmas or Easter rarely passed without seeing the king. One of his favourite saints was Saint Wulstan and he visited his tomb many times.

It would be nice to think that the beautiful cathedral has a man of good character lying at its heart. Unfortunately, King John has been described by various historians as unpredictable, oppressive, violent, idle, frivolous, greedy, extravagant, cruel, false and vindictive.

He was born in 1167 and was the youngest son of Henry II. Despite being his father's favourite, he rebelled and fought against his father. When his older brother, Richard the Lionheart, became king, he was involved in various plots against him.

John was thirty-two when he became king in 1199. Henry II had nicknamed him 'Lackland' as he had no lands left to give him, but John eventually owned more estates than anyone else in the family through his inheritances and his two wives. However, he lost most of them. He tried to raise armies to win back his

King John's tomb in Worcester Cathedral. At his head are the two small effigies of Saint Oswald and Saint Wulstan

estates in France, but he failed to win any battles and the high taxes necessary to fund an army made him unpopular in England.

John had two wives, both named Isabella. He was betrothed at the age of nine to a wealthy heiress, Isabella of Gloucester, and married her when he was twenty-one. Unfortunately, he then became infatuated with Isabella of Angoulême, the twelve-year-old daughter of a French count who was already betrothed to Hugh de Lusgnan. He divorced the first Isabella (although keeping her estates) and married the second, thereby making powerful enemies on both sides of the Channel.

He imprisoned his nephew and murdered him, it is said, 'in a drunken rage'. He quarrelled with the barons and was eventually forced to sign the great charter, the Magna Carta, with its sixty-three clauses. The nineteenth clause is one of the most important and reads: 'No man shall be taken or imprisoned, or dispossessed, or outlawed, or exiled, or in any way destroyed nor will we go upon him, nor will we send upon him, unless by the lawful judgment of his peers, or by the law of the land.'

John repeatedly quarrelled with the Pope. Perhaps it was an act of mischievous spite that the king put forward Roger Norreys as Prior of Evesham, as Norreys had previously been convicted of misbehaviour at the monastery of Canterbury. Norreys took up his new powers in 1191 and lived in great luxury, keeping all the tithes for his own use. The monks were starving and had to beg for food. *The Victoria County History* states that they were unable to preach or go into the town because they 'had no breeches'. The *Chronicle of Evesham* reports that when he visited Bretforton, he squandered a year's rents collected by the Sacrist 'in luxury and drunkenness ... what would have sufficed for many members of the church for a whole year'. The monks were not able to depose him until 1213.

Quarrels with the Pope became so bitter that in 1208 England was placed under an Interdict. No new churches were built and no church service was held for six years; there were no marriages, nor Christian burials. King John was excommunicated in 1209 but, faced with the emnity of the barons, he decided it was wise to make his peace with the Pope.

Yet for all his faults, John was a man of great ability and he was, on the whole, well liked. Worcester looked upon him with affection; the visits of a king gave the cathedral great prestige and John usually managed to benefit them in some way, perhaps to arrange the return of confiscated ground. When John visited Worcester in 1202 he ordered the rebuilding of the magnificent gateway to the cathedral priory, now known as Edgar's Gate, which had been damaged by fire. On a visit in 1207 he was persuaded to grant extensive privileges to Cleeve (now Cleeve Prior) and Lindridge (near Eardiston), and gave them so many rights that they were independent of the Hundred Court and the prior could administer his own justice.

One of the reasons why King John loved Worcestershire so much was that it held some of the best hunting grounds in England. All the early kings of England, including King John, used a hunting lodge at Feckenham. The chapel of St Giles at Heightington was reputedly used by King John when he hunted in the Wyre Forest and we know that he also hunted at Kinver. The Malvern Hills were excellent hunting grounds; he built Hanley Castle and frequently stayed there. The lord of the castle was also lord of Malvern Chase. The castle stood to the south of the village in the south-east corner of the parish. It was a large square structure with four towers, surrounded by a moat with the keep in the north-west corner. One tower was still standing in 1795, but the stones were used to repair the bridge at Upton.

Towards the end of his reign, men of the Earl of Hereford plundered Worcester Cathedral and demanded 300 marks from the monks, for which they were compelled to melt down gold from the shrine of St Wulstan. When King John visited the cathedral at Christmas, he reduced the cathedral's taxes so that the brethren could fund the repairs.

The king renewed his war against the barons; they turned to France for support and in May 1216 a French army marched to London. John ravaged eastern England, and attempted to cross the Wash. While John himself got across safely, he was forced to stand and watch while the quicksands swallowed up the baggage train with his horses, money, arms, provisions and the crown jewels. Understandably, he flew into a rage.

He spent that night at the abbey of Swineshead in Lincolnshire. He then fell ill. There's a legend that he was poisoned by a monk because he had taken a fancy to the abbot's sister and the monk wished to save her honour. The incident is so well known that it was mentioned in *King John*, a play attributed to Shakespeare:

> The King, I fear, is poison'd by a monk;
> I left him almost speechless;

Next morning he was able to continue to Sleaford Castle but then had to be carried on a stretcher to Newark. There he realized death was imminent, so he confessed his many sins and made his will. Amazingly, the library in Worcester cathedral holds the original will, a part of which reads, 'I desire that my body be buried in the church of St Mary and St Wulstan of Worcester'. Three days later he died at Newark on 19 October 1216.

It appears from the *Chronicles* that the Abbot of Croxton carried out a postmortem. John had been tremendously fat and his intestines were found to be very much swollen. The abbot decided to keep his intestines at Croxton, so King John was buried without them.

King John asked to be buried between the tombs of Saint Wulstan and Saint Oswald. In Norman times, the high altar was in a semi-circular recess at the east end of the church, with the shrine of St Oswald on the north side and the tomb of St Wulstan on the south; King John was buried one bay westward. He now lies in the chancel between tiny effigies of the two saints. His effigy is of Purbeck marble and described by the architect historian, Nikolaus Pevsner, as 'one of the finest of its time in England. The drapery is as good as that of any French contemporary effigy'.

Sometime in the fifth or sixth centuries, a wizard and prophet by the name of Merlin was said to inhabit the courts of King Vortigern and Arthur. He prophesied that a king would lie between two saints, so this is thought to be a fulfilment of the prophecy.

The tale is told that King John knew that he would not be admitted through the pearly gates and he asked to be buried between these two saints so that he could slip into heaven unnoticed and, to further achieve this, he wore a monk's habit over his robes. The tomb was opened in 1797 and 'Oh! What a treat for the antiquarian', exclaimed the sexton. The skeleton measured 5 feet 6½ in, the average height of a Medieval man. The remains of the king were intact; on one side of him lay a sword, the bones of his left arm lay across his breast, and his teeth were quite perfect. He was wearing a robe of crimson damask undecayed, although by that time it was largely colourless, and over that was a monk's cowl.

A CLOSE SHAVE FOR KING JOHN'S SON

King John's son, Henry III (1216–72), was nearly murdered in Kidderminster while he was staying with John Biset, lord of the manor of Wolverhampton, in a residential hall near Dudley Street and Orchard Street and near to the church. A relative of John Biset's, Margaret, was also staying there. While she was saying her prayers at midnight she heard a muffled creeping noise. She realized that an assassin was on his way to murder the king and raised the alarm. The king's life was saved. Part of the hall, including the kitchens, was later converted into a Brussels carpet factory which still existed in the nineteenth century.

THE KNIGHTS TEMPLAR

These were exciting times. In 1076, Muslims captured Jerusalem. For the next 200 years, a series of military campaigns, the Crusades, took place to try to recapture the holy city. Knights and nobles went off to fight, among them Richard I, who joined them in 1191 but on the way home was imprisoned by the German emperor. He was ransomed for 150,000 marks, a huge sum that almost bankrupted England. A large proportion was paid by Worcester Monastery. Richard was released in February 1194, came to England and then went to Normandy, never to return.

Dramatic images of the Knights Templar appear in many history books in the chapters referring to the Crusades. We see them galloping on horseback, their white mantle emblazoned with a large red cross fluttering in the wind. They were both monks and knights. To the vows of chastity, poverty and obedience they added a fourth vow, that they would protect pilgrims and fight the infidels. By the end of the thirteenth century there were about 15,000 members while their property included 9,000 castles and manors. Through the research of contemporary historian Elizabeth Atkins, we now know that the order was in Worcestershire. Where Blaze Lane joins the Feckenham Road near Feckenham is a farm known as 'Chapel Farm' and in the adjacent field are depressions in the ground. The site was known as Temple Arly or Ardley and started as a clearing in the Forest of Feckenham occupied by the Knights Templar. In 1312, the order was accused of heresy, immorality and other offences by both the French

The un-named effigy of a Medieval knight lies in Wolverley church

king and the Pope, and was suppressed. Members were subjected to torture and burned to death while their property was confiscated.

The Attwood family were lords of the manor of Wolverley from 1331 to 1391, and there is a tradition that Sir John Attwood went off on a Crusade and remained away for so long that his wife was about to marry again. A milkmaid, however, looking for a lost cow, found a man, emaciated and fettered, asleep in the grass. Only the faithful dog recognized the stranger as Sir John, but fortunately he was able to prove his identity by producing half a ring that he and his wife had broken on parting. Sir John insisted that he had been brought back by a swan, and a swan crest was used by all the families named Attwood. In Wolverley church is the alabaster effigy of a knight in armour. The historian Thomas Habington was unable to positively identify the alabaster knight as Sir John, but he writes that there was (the spelling has been updated) 'one Sir John Atwode who, being imprisoned by the Infidels was miraculously carried from that far remote dungeon of captivity to Trimpley, losed of his gyves [fetters] and restored to liberty, the same is so public, the chapel builded in remembrance thereof so notable, the gyves themselves reserved as a trophy of this glorious redemption so clear a testimony as none but wilful obstinate can deny it'.

Iron fetters said to have been worn by the knight were shown for many years afterwards and there was at one time a rent charge on 'The Knights Meadow' where the knight was said to have been found. The rent was paid 'to someone who should keep the irons polished and show them to all who would like to see them'.

Fighting is an expensive business and the various Crusades meant that many of the Plantagenet kings were short of money. In 1187, Henry II levied a tax of 10 per cent on every man's possessions, down to his last chair. Edward III changed the tax in 1334 to one-fifteenth in counties and one-tenth in towns. It was reckoned that this would come to £39,000 and it was arranged that if it were insufficient he could ask Parliament to increase it. This gave Parliament the power to interfere in the king's financial matters.

SIMON DE MONTFORT AND THE BATTLE OF EVESHAM

The agreement of 1215 between King John and the barons known as the Magna Carta was an early step on the long road to Parliamentary democracy, but friction continued between the monarchy and barons. The acrimony came to a head in 1258, led by Simon de Montfort, Earl of Leicester, against Henry III, the final act being ferociously fought on 4 August 1265 at the Battle of Evesham.

Simon de Montfort and his knights kneel before Saint Egwin.
From the windows of St Lawrence's Church

Simon de Montfort was something of a popular hero, being a dashing and ebullient figure who contrasted with the rather impersonal and aloof Henry III. De Montfort has long been credited with the foundation of the English Parliament, but it must be said that his idea of a governing body did not involve the lower orders but was rather an assembly of 'wise men'. However, he did consult the peasants about their grievances, many of which concerned their loss of the use of forests appropriated by the king for hunting.

Before the battle, everything appeared to be in de Montfort's favour. Henry III had been captured and was imprisoned at the bishop's palace at Kempsey, as a guest of de Montfort. They are said to have celebrated Mass together in Kempsey church prior to the battle.

Simon was expecting large reinforcements from his son at Kenilworth Castle. What he did not know was that his son's army had been defeated. The castle was not large and most of the army had been camped in the grounds outside. During the night, the king's army, led by his son, Lord Edward, had crept into the camp and slaughtered many of the sleeping soldiers. De Montfort's son was lucky to escape with his life by swimming across the moat in his nightshirt.

Flags and banners were taken from the wrecked camp at Kenilworth and displayed by the Royalists so that when the lookout on the priory tower first saw the army approaching he thought that it was de Montfort's son. When de Montfort realized that he was trapped in the loop of the river, he gave a cry of anguish, 'May God have mercy on our souls for our bodies are theirs!' De Montfort was heavily outnumbered; some accounts reckon that he had only 5,000 to the Royalists' 10,000 men. De Montfort decided that his best option was to battle his way up Green Hill, between the flanks of Prince Edward and the Earl of Gloucester. At eight o'clock in the morning he led his army out of the town and up the hill and, as he did so, a shattering thunderstorm erupted. The situation was hopeless. The well-equipped and powerful contingents of Welsh Marcher barons such as Gilbert de Clare Earl of Gloucester and Roger Mortimer Earl of March mounted rearguard actions to cut off any possible escape routes.

Leicester tower, near the Abbey Manor House. On its base is a plaque reading, 'This tower is erected in the year 1842 to the memory of Simon de Montfort, Earl of Leicester, the father and founder of the British House of Commons, who was slain in the Battle of Evesham 1265'

De Montfort kept the captive Henry III with him during the battle. Henry was very nearly massacred with de Montfort's troops. He pulled back his visor and it was only with some difficulty that he persuaded Edward's troops that he was indeed their king.

The Royalists fought with unremitting savagery. It was customary not to kill the enemy's nobility but to take hostages who could, after the battle, be exchanged for a great deal of money, but the king's men went on a killing spree.

De Montfort himself was killed, together with his younger son, Henry. Many of the battered troops sought sanctuary in Evesham Abbey where, despite the protesting appeals of its monks, they were butchered. Others attempted to escape across Merstowe Green, crossing the Avon from Boat Lane, but the river was in flood after the heavy rain and most were drowned – though perhaps a small handful may have succeeded in reaching the opposite bank. Perhaps as many as 4,000 of De Montfort's men-at-arms and 200 of the nobility lost their lives. A Welsh axe, lost in the river by an escaping soldier, was found recently and is now on display in Evesham's Almonry Museum.

De Montfort was savagely mutilated. His head and other parts of his body were cut off and sent to various lords around the country. His head was displayed on London Bridge until it rotted. Monks were later to retrieve his mutilated remains for burial beneath the high altar of Evesham Abbey. A monument to Simon de Montfort was erected in the Abbey Park, Evesham, in 1965. It reads:

> Here were buried the remains of Simon de Montfort, Earl of Leicester, pioneer of representative government who was killed in the Battle of Evesham on August 4th 1265. This stone brought from his birthplace the castle of Montfort-Lamaury in France was erected to commemorate the seven hundredth anniversary of his death. Unveiled by the speaker of the House of Commons and dedicated by his grace the Archbishop of Canterbury on the 18th day of July 1965.

Although never canonized, Simon de Montfort came to be venerated as a popular saint. The enormous number of pilgrims to his abbey shrine was the reason for a rapid enlargement of Saint Lawrence's Church.

———————————

THE BLACK DEATH

The fourteenth century was a period of lawlessness and strife, and its history abounds with instances of brawls and quarrels, robbery and bloodshed.

The crime rate was so high that in 1302 the prior of Worcester took the unprecedented step of excommunicating the bailiffs of the city, calling them 'men of blood and craft'.

In 1315 and 1316 there was a long drought and harvests failed, then a cattle disease broke out. Many starved, but worse was to come. The Black Death first appeared along the English south coast in 1348. Spreading with alarming rapidity, it was raging throughout Worcestershire less than a year later. It was probably bubonic plague, an infection by the *yersinia pestis* bacillus and characterized by large black blisters that could grow to the size of an orange. Thought to be spread by rat fleas, it could also affect the lungs and be spread in an airborne form. Within ten days, half of those infected would have died.

There was not one epidemic but several, recurring time and time again during the next six centuries. The first outbreak of the plague affected the general population, not so much the nobility and the clergy. However, a second epidemic ten years later, perhaps a mutation of the original bacillus, was to strike rich and poor alike and produced a high mortality rate among young children who would not have developed any immunity from the earlier outbreak.

Ombersley plague trough. It was placed on the outskirts of the village during the plague to receive food and other essentials

At least one-third and perhaps half of the population perished. The death rates of the Bishop of Worcester's estates in Worcestershire ranged from 19 per cent of manorial tenants in Hartlebury and Hanbury to 80 per cent at Aston. Rarely can an English society have been flung into such long-lasting and fundamental chaos by a natural event. A chronicler records that corn lay rotting on the ground for want of reapers while cattle and sheep roamed over the country for want of herdsmen: 'Everywhere was desolation, towns were empty, fields unworked, estates deserted.'

Some villages, including Clent, Kenelmstowe and Gannow, were completely depopulated. Abbeys and monasteries were not immune; at Bordesley Abbey in Redditch between 1348 and 1349 four abbots died of the plague in rapid succession.

A bishop's palace had been built in Alvechurch in the thirteenth century and one of the bishops, Reginald Brian, died there of the plague in 1361. Local tradition has it that victims of the plague are buried on the outskirts of the town in Pestilence Lane, the end of which is near the M42. During the building of the motorway, local historians casually mentioned to the contractors that there was supposed to be a plague pit nearby. Work was held up while the soil was thoroughly tested for contagious diseases. Nothing was found and the Hopwood Services was built on the site in 1998.

The deserted village of Elmley Lovett

This terrible catastrophe changed the whole English economy. The manorial system was overturned and peasants now had the upper hand. With far fewer mouths to be fed, food prices generally fell, and in Worcestershire agricultural land lost a third of its pre-plague value. Labour was in short supply. Wages rose by 50 per cent for men and 100 per cent for women. The Abbey of Westminster owned many large Pershore estates and within ten years of the first outbreak their wages bill had doubled. The poor priests, who relied on tithes, were so impoverished that a historian of that time, Thomas Arnold, stated, 'many priests were forced to steal'. Some priests simply left their parishes and went to live in the towns, usually London.

Many landowners found themselves in financial difficulties, so, to increase their revenue, they offered to sell to peasants their freedom. The plague years brought about the concept of the free man. In addition, the freeholder was able to buy land from the lord of the manor and become a country squire of some importance. Most of the peasants became copy holders who could hold anything from 3 acres to 100 acres. The slaves were now free as it was more economical for the lord to pay a slave and leave him to fend for himself, but he had few, if any, legal rights to the land on which he lived. He could be turned out of his house at the landlord's whim.

The peasant now enjoyed unprecedented freedom and power. Any unpleasantness and he could simply move and work for another lord. Many peasants who could not afford to pay for their freedom simply left the manorial holdings for more attractive prospects in the towns where wages were higher as prices of manufactured goods were soaring. If a peasant lived in a town for a year and a day, then he would be free. Sometimes, men still lived on the lord's estates, but the women went into town each day to become weavers, brewers, dyers and innkeepers.

There was a general disregard for authority. A series of laws were passed, such as Edward III's Statute of Labours which tried to prevent the drift into towns, but they were largely ignored. At the same time, prices were rising, partly because of the costs of the opening campaigns of the Hundred Years War.

The shortage of labour after the Black Death caused landowners to shift from agriculture to sheep-rearing. Huge areas were enclosed and given over to the sheep that fed on the lush Worcestershire grass, providing high-quality wool. Open fields, common land, heath and moorland were all affected by enclosures, changing the face of the Worcestershire countryside and bringing about a revolution in lifestyle and work practices.

HUNDRED YEARS WAR AND EDWARD I, II AND III

So great was the impact of the Black Death across the region that it made all other events of the period, including Edward I's wars against the Welsh princes, and the internal turmoils during the reign of his son (Edward II), pale into insignificance by comparison. Edward III unwisely became involved in the Hundred Years War on the Continent in 1337 and was at war with France. Every man who had property worth £5 was called up, but could buy a substitute. Taxes rose so that Edward could maintain an overseas army, and prices rose as imports had to reach England via the Mediterranean. A great international scandal erupted as Edward borrowed money from Lombard merchants and was unable to pay it back, bankrupting the whole city of Florence.

EVESHAM AND THE LOLLARDS

During the fourteenth and fifteenth centuries the Church was losing much of its power. The Black Death had reduced its revenues, and also people began to question its dogmas. John Wycliffe was the leader of the Lollard movement, which was partly named after him as he had a slight speech defect with a rolling tongue. He was a Yorkshireman, born in 1324, educated at Oxford, and he became a popular scholar and preacher. In 1378 he began producing 'Wycliffe's Bible', translating the scriptures from Latin into everyday language so that the man-in-the-street would be able to read them. He was, however, not popular with the clergy. Among his twelve articles were his views that the Church was eaten up by worldly pride, and that the veneration of relics (by which the Church gained a healthy income) caused idolatry. He also preached that, at communion, the bread and the wine did not turn into the flesh and blood of Christ as the priests maintained, and he sent out missionaries to spread the word that transubstantiation did not exist.

The movement was met with enthusiasm in parts of Worcestershire. Although the majority of followers were ordinary folk, some powerful lords saw it as a means of striking against the power of the church dignitaries. Even priests were caught up in the movement. Nicholas Hereford, John Ashton, John Perney, John Parker and Robert Swynderby were all Worcestershire priests, said to have 'honied words in their mouths, but venom under their lips' and were banned from preaching.

In 1401 a law was passed whereby secular authorities could hand all heretics, including Lollards, over to the Church who could then inflict death by burning. Between 1401 and 1532 forty-seven Lollards were burned to death, among them Thomas Badby, a tailor from Evesham who supported Wycliff's belief that transubstantiation did not take place. He said, 'If every host, being consecrated at the altar, were the Lord's body, then there be 20,000 Gods in England.' He was dragged before the Bishop of Worcester who handed him over to the Archbishop of Canterbury and the Bishop of London who condemned him to be burned to death in London before the Prince of Wales. A huge bonfire was built on Smithfield public recreation ground, never before used for burning heretics. Badby was put in a barrel and placed on the bonfire. When he cried out in pain, Prince Henry ordered him to be removed and promised him a yearly allowance from the royal treasury if he would recant. Badby refused and, in 1410, was burned to death.

THE PLANTAGENET PEASANT
AND GEOFFREY CHAUCER

It was customary, for those who could afford it, to go on a pilgrimage. During excavations in Worcester Cathedral in 1986, archaeologists were surprised to come across a fully clothed fifteenth-century skeleton, complete with pilgrim's staff and a cockle shell pierced so that it could be worn as a badge. The shell showed that he had returned from a pilgrimage to the shrine of St James in Santiago de Compostela in north-west Spain.

In Geoffrey Chaucer's *The Canterbury Tales* we have thirty or so London folk on horseback off to the tomb of Thomas à Becket in Canterbury. Chaucer was not a Worcestershire man but as he was a close relative to the mistress, then wife, of the powerful John of Gaunt (the father of Henry IV) who owned Kenilworth Castle, he probably spent some time in the Midlands including Worcestershire. Chaucer lived from about 1343 to 1400 and by the time he was writing his *Canterbury Tales*, the Black Death had petered out, and the country was enjoying a period of relative peace. English towns were becoming prosperous. Few were unemployed, the sick and the poor were cared for, while monasteries and social guilds looked after the old and infirm.

There is no other book that gives us such a wonderful insight into the lives of the ordinary folk at that time. Through Chaucer, we eavesdrop on their everyday conversation. Almost all classes of society are represented, either in person or through the narrative, from the knight who claimed to have fought in fifteen mortal battles around the Mediterranean, to the story of the elderly widow who lived in a two-bedroomed cottage, grimed with soot, and subsisted on milk and dark bread. She owned three pigs, three cows, a sheep and a cockerel (by which she knew the time), and struggled to support herself and three daughters.

Among the travellers are the knight's son, a yeoman, a miller, a rich widow, and a merchant, who says of his wife, 'even if the devil were coupled with her, she would master him'. There was also a wealthy landowner, a haberdasher, a carpenter, a dyer, a tapestry-maker, a doctor of medicines, a sergeant and a reeve, together with a well-bred prioress accompanied by a nun and three priests. We even learn how they were dressed. The yeoman was probably a forester. He was well-tanned, and his hair was close-cropped; he was dressed in a coat and hood of green and a silver Saint Christopher medal shone on his breast. Chaucer says that a sheaf of arrows were beneath his belt, he carried a bow, and on his one side was a sword and shield and, by the other, a dagger. The rich widow was ostentatiously clad in a hat as broad as a shield, she wore scarlet hose laced tightly, a foot mantle was about her ample hips, and on her feet a pair of sharp spurs. Unfortunately, she was 'gap-toothed'.

Through their tales we learn how they lived, their attitudes and what was important to them, all told with an earthy humour. We have a picture of Medieval society, with its hopes, fears, tragedies, triumphs, difficulties, domestic conflicts and desires, much like our own.

THE LANCASTRIANS

Richard II was the last Plantagenet king. When his right-hand man, John of Gaunt, died in 1399, John's son, Henry Bolinbroke, returned from exile in France to take the throne as the first Lancastrian king, winning support from both nobles and the populace. Richard II abdicated and was imprisoned in Pontefract where he died a few months later in mysterious circumstances.

Violence was the dominant theme of Henry's reign. In the north, he quarrelled with Henry Percy, immortalized by William Shakespeare as 'Hotspur'. In the south the French were launching raids, while to the west Owain Glyn Dwr (anglicized as Owen Glendower) was leading the battle for Welsh independence.

Glendower was born in 1355 of aristocratic parentage so he proclaimed himself 'The Welsh Prince'. He was educated in England and fought for Richard II. However, a long-running land dispute over some property escalated into a rebellion. His supporters attacked towns on the Welsh border so that Henry IV was forced to take action and invade Wales.

Woodbury Hill. Owen Glendower and his army camped here in 1404

The English army camped on Abberley Hill. This photo has been taken from its summit

Glendower joined forces with the French. In 1404 a French expeditionary force landed at Milford Haven and joined with the Welsh to march towards Worcester, capturing several important castles as they went. According to local tradition, this combined Welsh and French force was encamped to the south of Great Witley on an old Iron Age fort at the top of Woodbury Hill.

For eight days, the two armies watched each other. There was some light jousting, some skirmishing, and the capture of some English supply wagons. The English army made preparations for a great battle but when they woke in the morning, prepared to fight, the enemy had melted away. Glendower was never captured and no one knows when and where he died.

A local legend says that a French captain, Jean de Hangest, was captured by the English and imprisoned at nearby Wichenford Court, then home of Lord Washbourne. The lord was called away, and Lady Washbourne fell madly in love with the Frenchman. He spurned her advances, and so one night she gave him a sleeping draught and stabbed him to death. Filled with remorse, she wandered the corridors of Wichenford Court, cup in one hand, dagger in the other, and she roams there still.

Wichenford Court

THE YORKISTS, 1461–85, AND THE WARS OF THE ROSES

The Wars of the Roses culminated in the 1450s under the Lancastrian king, Henry VI, and continued through the Yorkist reigns of Edward IV, Edward V and Richard III. Both sides chose the rose as their symbol; the Lancastrians had a red rose and the Yorkists a white.

While the nobility of England were engaged in killing one another, the day-to-day life of the Worcestershire peasant continued as normal. No battles took place in Worcestershire and although the war dragged on for thirty years, the amount of time spent in actual battle, when put together, amounted to one year only.

Worcestershire folk were usually only involved where tenants were called upon to support their lord. The riverport town of Bewdley had, in 1425, become the property of Richard, Duke of York, and the town prospered under his control. The Duke of York was killed at the Battle of Wakefield in 1460, but the town still

The riverside town of Bewdley

held his nineteen-year-old son, Edward, in their affections. The following year, Edward was fighting the Lancastrian lords at the battle of Mortimer's Cross. Bewdley supported him with enthusiasm, he won the battle against all odds, and became the first Yorkist king, Edward IV. Honours were heaped upon the town; it became a borough in 1472 and in 1478 was appointed as the seat of Edward IV's Council for Wales and the Marches. It was also given the privilege of becoming a sanctuary town, although this was not wholly desirable as the town was invaded by thieves, robbers and murderers, all seeking sanctuary.

The respectable folk lived near the river and the miscreants on the edge of the town, too far away from the bridge to be dragged back across. Until 1544 it was not certain whether Bewdley was in Worcestershire or Shropshire, a great advantage to those fleeing justice.

Some of the Worcestershire peasants found themselves serving a different lord. The good folk of Martley lost their lord of the manor at the Battle of Wakefield in 1459. The alabaster effigy of Sir Hugh Mortimer lies beneath the perpendicular tower that he built in about 1450.

The Staffords were a particularly unlucky family. In 1450 the manor of Grafton, near Bromsgrove, was owned by Sir Humphrey Stafford, Henry VI's right-hand man. The yeomen and smaller landowners, chiefly in Kent and

Courtesy of Grafton Manor

Grafton Manor. The lords of the manor were involved in the Wars of the Roses with disastrous results!

Sussex, were so exasperated by high taxes and government corruption that they gathered under the leadership of Jack Cade and marched to London. The king's troops, including Sir Humphrey, met them at Sevenoaks but were defeated, and Sir Humphrey was killed. Jack Cade was later arrested and hung, drawn and quartered.

Another member of the Stafford family, the Duke of Buckingham, was one of the most powerful men in the realm. In 1483, he had been prepared to fight against Richard III and had raised an army in Wales. In its ranks were the bishops of Ely, Salisbury and Exeter. The army marched to Upton-upon-Severn, but the river was in flood and they were unable to cross. They marched on to Worcester but were still unable to cross. The Earl of Devon was in hot pursuit and, in their hurry to get away, they lost their baggage train. Like Owen Glendower, the soldiery had camped on Woodbury Hill near Great Witley, but the weather was appalling and their provisions had been lost. Hunger and cold were soon to see much of Buckingham's army begin to defect. Eventually desertion was so great that Buckingham himself fled, later to be captured in Shropshire and executed in London.

The manor of Grafton was inherited by Sir Humphrey Stafford's nephew, of the same name. In 1485, he fought for Richard III at the Battle of Bosworth. The king was killed, Sir Humphrey's estates were confiscated, and he was executed at Tyburn. Opposing Sir Humphrey on the battlefield was Sir Gilbert Talbot who now became the new owner of Grafton Manor. The reign of the Yorkists came to an end and the memorable years of the Tudors began.

5

THE TUDORS

In 1485, Henry Tudor, of Welsh origin, invaded from France, killing King Richard at the Battle of Bosworth, to reign as Henry VII. The long reign of the Tudors had begun.

This is one of the most fascinating periods in English history. They were the years of Henry VII, Henry VIII and his son Edward VI, followed by the Roman Catholic Mary and ending with the death of the Protestant Queen Elizabeth in 1603.

The Tudor period was a time of change. It saw the ending of the Medieval period, changes to the religious structure of the Middle Ages and advances in science and technology. Two great pillars of the Middle Ages, the manorial system and the Roman Catholic Church, were to lose their positions of ascendancy, and there were changes to the economic system that laid the foundations for modern developments. It was also a time of great learning when schools and colleges were founded. Across the Channel, the Renaissance was blossoming. Arts and crafts flourished and the Tudor court played a prominent part in the cultural Renaissance with such luminaries as Edmund Spenser, Hans Holbein, Thomas More and Cardinal Wolsey.

Books flourished with the advent of the printing press. William Caxton set up the first printing press in England in 1476 and, three years later, the Bishop of Worcester, John Carpenter, endowed a library to Worcester Cathedral. In Hartlebury Castle is the unique Hurd Library, founded in 1783 by Richard Hurd who was Bishop of Worcester from 1781 to 1808. Not only does it contain the bishop's own books, but he had been given the libraries of Alexander Pope, William Warburton (writer and Bishop of Gloucester), Ralph Allen (postmaster and Mayor of Bath) and part of the library of George III. It contains the first book to be printed in France dated 1476 and a wealth of books from Elizabethan times, such as Fox's *Book of Martyrs* (1596), Bishop Latimer's sermons (1578) and Holinshed's *Chronicles* (1587).

HENRY VII – WORCESTERSHIRE PROSPERS

The Wars of the Roses had dragged on for thirty years, but Henry VII succeeded in bringing them to an end. As a Lancastrian, he married the niece of the leader of the Yorkists. Elizabeth of York was the eldest daughter of Edward IV and the sister of the two murdered princes in the tower. A white rose and a red rose were combined to give a symbol of unity, the Tudor Rose. He also managed to avoid wars with Spain and France. Campaigns in Ireland brought that country under English rule and Wales no longer fought for independence. However, for Worcester, peace was a mixed blessing. The town was no longer important as the gateway to Wales. Although it still held its position as the leading town of the West Midlands, it was not a great military base and instead became a trading centre.

As soon as Henry VII was crowned, he began a mopping-up operation to remove possible further rivals. Those lords who had supported the Yorkists were convicted of high treason. Their estates were taken from them and they were

Henry VII revived the wool trade

either hung, drawn and quartered or beheaded. One of the most important was the powerful Earl of Warwick. He had inherited the vast south Worcestershire estates belonging to the Beauchamps. Consequently, a set of inexperienced, minor nobles took the place of the great landowners. Many of them were anxious to wring every last penny from the land and continued a change from agriculture to the more profitable sheep-rearing. Unemployment rose dramatically. The ploughman, the blacksmith, the labourer and other workers on the land were no longer needed. Hundreds of soldiers were discharged from the French wars and the Wars of the Roses, adding to an unemployment problem. To make matters worse, the population grew and probably doubled.

By the time Henry VII came to the throne, the English wool trade had declined. Across Worcestershire, about 8,000 people were employed in the wool trade, including half the population of Worcester who worked in the clothing industry, but they were having difficulty finding markets. The king took a number of measures to revive the trade. He encouraged commerce and negotiated various export deals. Flemish weavers and clothiers were having political and religious difficulties in their own country so Henry, like Edward III before him, invited them to settle in England to improve the local expertise. He increased the tax on exported raw wool to 70 per cent and decreased the tax on manufactured cloth to less than 9 per cent to provide work for the clothiers.

Over the next few centuries there were repeated attempts to revive the wool trade. In 1533 Henry VIII decreed that, in Worcestershire, only such persons inhabiting the towns of Worcester, Evesham, Droitwich, Kidderminster and Bromsgrove 'shall make any manner of woollen cloths to be sold upon pain of forfeiture for each cloth XIs' [presumably 11 shillings or 52.5p]. From 1678 to 1814, all bodies were to be buried in wool only, unless they had died of the plague! The penalty for not doing so was £5.

―――――――――

THE BISHOP OF WORCESTER AND HIS MURDERED RIVAL

Henry VII was one of the few kings able to pay his way. One of his money-saving schemes involved the Worcester bishopric. He needed well-paid diplomatic agents to work in Rome, so he decided to appoint one of the Pope's ecclesiastics and, in addition, give him the role of Bishop of Worcester. This would enhance the salary of the ecclesiastic at no cost to the crown. The practice was continued by Henry VIII; consequently, from 1476 to 1534 the See of Worcester was used as a means of paying state officials who rarely set foot in Worcestershire.

In 1497 the See of Worcester became vacant. There was, living in London, an Italian papal agent, John de Gigliis, and it was decided that he should be Bishop of Worcester, thus receiving a handsome salary at no cost to the king. Unfortunately, he died only seven months after his appointment. His thirty-three-year-old nephew, Silvester de Gigliis, who had assisted him in his work, was selected as his successor. In 1504 Silvester came from Rome to England, but does not appear to have condescended to visit Worcester or do anything for the diocese beyond drawing a salary.

However, when Henry VIII came to the throne in 1509, it soon became obvious that he preferred another agent, an Englishman, Cardinal Christopher Bainbridge, who was Archbishop of York. Cardinal Bainbridge was entrusted with the greater part of English political work. In 1512, Silvester was sent to Rome as one of the English representatives but found that he was overshadowed by the cardinal. Silvester deliberately adopted a policy opposed to Bainbridge. In May 1514 the cardinal wrote to Henry VIII accusing Silvester of plotting with the French ambassador in betraying England's secrets. In July of that year Bainbridge died. He had been poisoned by a priest, Raynald de Modena, who had been a servant of Silvester's household. Raynald was imprisoned and confessed to his crime, stating that he had administered the poison at the instigation of Silvester who gave him fifteen gold coins, saying, 'If we do not get rid of this cardinal we will never live quietly in Rome.' Before his death, Raynald withdrew the charge but it was all very suspicious.

Two Italians appointed as English bishops in 1543 were dismissed by Parliament and the first Protestant bishop, Hugh Latimer, was appointed. We shall hear more about him later.

THE GREAT TRAGEDY

The life of Henry VII, and of the whole of England, was overshadowed by a great tragedy.

Henry VII's son and heir was born in 1487 and christened 'Arthur', partly to emphasize his Welsh descent and partly in the hope that he would emulate the hero of the Arthurian legends. Four years later, a second son was born and named 'Henry' after his father. Tradition says that Henry VII and his two sons, the Princes Arthur and Henry, visited Malvern Priory. Henry VII slept in the rooms over the priory gateway and he found his stay so pleasant he ordered the north window in the northern transept of the priory church to be made as a 'thank you'.

When he was about twelve, Prince Arthur was betrothed to Catherine of Aragon, at a ceremony in Tickenhill Palace, Bewdley. She was the daughter of Ferdinand and Isabella of Spain and nine months older than Arthur. This was a good match, as not only did it come with a generous bounty, but it increased Henry's prestige among the European monarchs. Prince Arthur was well satisfied with his bride. She was intelligent, amenable and even at that early age showed signs that she was to become a great beauty, with a mass of golden auburn hair.

At the age of fourteen, Prince Arthur became Justice of the Council of Marches, responsible for a limited government of Wales. Tickenhill Palace had been enlarged to take the Prince of Wales and his retinue, including a large hall a hundred feet long. He divided his time between Bewdley and Ludlow. The young prince and his bride won the hearts of all who dealt with them.

When Arthur was fifteen and Catherine nearly sixteen, they were married in Saint Paul's, London, on 14 November 1501, and set up court in Ludlow Castle. Less than five months later, Arthur was dead. Apparently, they both caught a serious 'sweating sickness' sweeping through Ludlow at that time. Catherine recovered, but for Arthur it proved fatal.

Prince Arthur's Chantry

On a cold March morning, in driving rain and on deeply rutted roads, the funeral cortège set out from Ludlow, first for Bewdley, then across the Severn ford on the outskirts of Stourport-on-Severn, and on to Worcester. Contemporary reports state that the whole route was lined with weeping people.

The body of the prince was met at the city gate by the 'bailiffs and the honest men of the cittie on foot', and at Worcester Cathedral churchyard by the Prior of Worcester and the Abbots of Gloucester, Evesham, Chester, Shrewsbury, Tewkesbury, Hales and Bordesley. The Earl of Surrey led a full contingent of mourning nobility. Arthur's parents were too distraught to attend. Both his young wife and his boisterous younger brother, Henry, then only ten, were advised to keep away from the funeral service.

There were nine lessons; the first was read by the Abbot of Tewkesbury and the sixth by the Prior of Worcester. The prince's embroidered coat of arms, the sword, shield and crested helmet were conveyed between the choir stalls with the son of the Earl of Kildare who wore the armour of the dead prince and was mounted on his charger. The Abbot of Tewkesbury received the offer of the horse. No offerings were allowed to be made by Worcester folk because of the sickness and pestilence raging in the city.

Henry VII had a particular fondness for Worcester Cathedral so that we now have Prince Arthur's lovely chantry chapel, one of the most arresting memorials to be found in the whole of England. It was designed by Sir Reginald Bray who was both an architect and Henry VII's chief financial adviser. He had probably been a pupil of the cathedral's Almonry School. The chapel's delicate beauty is a poignant reminder of the mortality of the most regal of ambitions.

HENRY VIII AND LORD WINDSOR

What was to be done with poor Catherine of Aragon? The suggestion was made that she should marry Arthur's younger brother, Henry, the future Henry VIII, who was five years her junior. Henry VIII has gone down in history as the king with a succession of wives and it is often forgotten that his first marriage lasted for about twenty-four years, during which time Catherine bore him five or six children, including three sons. All died except for one daughter, Mary, born in 1516 and nicknamed 'Bloody Mary' in later years.

Of his six wives, Henry's marriage to Catherine of Aragon was annulled, Anne Boleyn was executed after charges of treasonable infidelity, Jane Seymour died on giving birth to the future Edward VI, Anne of Cleves was divorced, Catherine Howard suffered the same fate as Anne Boleyn, but the sixth wife, Catherine Parr, survived her husband. None of his brides came from Worcestershire although Lady Jane Seymour was related to the Seymours of Ragley Hall, just over the border in Warwickshire.

The story is well known of how and why Henry quarrelled with the Pope. Cardinal Wolsey failed to obtain papal dispensation for a royal divorce so Henry secretly married Anne in 1533, then passed a series of Acts culminating in the Act of Supremacy where he declared himself 'Supreme Head of the Church in England'. Monasteries were closed and destroyed. The smaller houses were

The tomb of Robert George Windsor-Clive (1857-1923) at Tardebigge. Between 1869 and 1905
he was known as Lord Windsor, then he was made 1st Earl of Plymouth of the third creation

dissolved in 1536 and the larger ones in 1539. The closure of the monasteries has already been described in Chapter 3.

It was through the greed of Henry VIII that, in 1542, Lord Windsor took up residence in Redditch. The Windsors were one of the most important families in England, and they were already great landowners when William the Conqueror arrived in 1066.

Lord Windsor lived in Stanwell Manor in Middlesex – until Henry VIII paid him a visit and took a fancy to it. Lord Windsor was summoned to the king's presence and told that Stanwell Manor was to be swapped for Bordesley Abbey. He could not believe it, but documents had already been drawn up and it was evident that if he wanted to keep his head he should leave immediately. Stanwell was stocked with provisions for Christmas and many had to be left behind. He and his retinue arrived at Bordesley Abbey, it is said, one cold and wet November afternoon to find the abbey in ruins, except for one small building used for weaving the Sheldon tapestries. It was suggested that he moved into a modest farmhouse which belonged to the abbey, Hewell Grange. The former cellarer of the abbey was living there but he was packed off to Wenlock. To add insult to injury, the Bordesley estates were larger than those of Stanwell so the king claimed £2,197 5s 8d in compensation.

Lord Windsor died the following year. Hewell Grange was soon developed as an appropriate residence for the family and has been rebuilt at least twice since. Thomas Windsor was made Earl of Plymouth in 1682 after fighting in Spain.

Lady Harriet inherited the estates in 1819; her husband was the grandson of Clive of India and so they used the surname Windsor-Clive. They were appalled by the lawlessness of Redditch. Lord Plymouth was president of a large number of local charitable organizations and gave land and money for a network of churches, schools and Sunday schools. Many Redditch roads have been named after them: Plymouth, Clive, Archer, Ivor, Salop, Ludlow, Bromfield, Hewell Grange and Lady Harriet's Lane.

The present imposing house, Hewell Grange, was constructed in the 1880s. The ruins of the old house stood nearby until the Shah of Peria paid a visit to Hewell in 1889 and then was invited to blow up the old ruins for entertainment. Hewell Grange remained in the family's hands until death duties forced its sale in 1946. The stately home is now a remand centre, while two prisons have been built in the grounds.

Henry VIII netted in the region of £500,000 from his seizure of monastic plate and other valuables and a further sum from the sale of monastic lands. Despite this, he had severe financial problems, caused partly by his gambling addiction – during his lifetime he ran up £35,000 in gambling debts. He debased the coinage that went towards improving his financial situation temporarily, but caused prices to soar after his death.

He left three heirs: Edward VI, who was the son of Jane Seymour; Mary, the daughter of his first wife, Catherine of Aragon; and Elizabeth, the daughter of Anne Boleyn.

EDWARD VI AND LADY JANE GREY

Edward was only nine years old when his father died; consequently England was governed by the King's Council. The reforms introduced in Henry's reign were continued. Statues and stained glass were smashed and broken, walls were whitewashed, and clergy were allowed to marry.

It had been customary for the very wealthy to build and endow small chantry chapels, leading off the main body of the church. These usually contained the tomb of the founder, and Masses for the good of his soul were chanted there.

Often, the endowment included payment for a priest to serve in the chapel, and as these clergy had plenty of leisure time, they usually worked as part-time teachers. Chantry endowments were now banned and the chapels demolished, so that many teachers disappeared. For 300 years after his death Edward VI enjoyed an undeserved reputation as the good boy who had founded schools but, as we shall see later, Edward VI grammar schools were simply those old establishments that his counsellors refrained from destroying.

A new *Book of Common Prayer* appeared in 1552 and made a great impact. Many of the services were changed radically. Some of its views were controversial; for example, all Protestant churches, including Anglican ones, denied the Catholic doctrine of transubstantiation – that is, the fact that the communal bread and wine becomes the actual flesh and blood of Christ. The book also stated that the success of communion depended more upon the receptive heart of the Christian participant than the actual bread and wine used.

Six months later, in 1553, King Edward died, aged fifteen, perhaps from tuberculosis. The country was Protestant, and the heir to the throne, Lady Mary, the daughter of Henry VIII's first wife, was Roman Catholic. Furthermore, both she and her half-sister, Elizabeth, had been declared illegitimate. John Dudley (Duke of Northumberland) had been more or less ruling the country as Lord Protector. He realized that Lady Jane Grey, the daughter of the Duke and Duchess of Suffolk, had a weak right to the throne, as she was the great-niece of Henry VIII and the grand-daughter of Henry VIII's sister. She was also a Protestant. Just before the king died, Lord Dudley hastily married her to his son, Guildford, then persuaded King Edward to declare her as heir to the throne. On 10 July 1553, Lady Jane was proclaimed queen. Mary took refuge in Framlingham Castle in Suffolk; John Dudley followed her there and, in his absence, the ruling Council declared their support not for Lady Jane, but for Mary to be queen.

Lady Jane only ruled for nine days before she was arrested, tried, convicted and executed at the tender age of seventeen. The hosts of The Whittington Inn at Kinver (just over the Worcestershire border in Staffordshire) claim that Lady Jane spent some of her childhood there, as the lord of the manor in the 1400s was Humphrey de la Lowe whose daughter married into the Grey family.

JOHN DE FECKENHAM

The priest responsible for comforting Lady Jane Grey before her death came from Feckenham in Worcestershire. John de Feckenham's real name was John

Feckenham village, birthplace of John de Feckenham

Howman, but he took his ecclesiastical name from his home village. He had chosen a career in the Church, the one occupation where it was possible to move across the social classes. A boy from a relatively poor family was more likely to become a parish priest than a bishop, but it was not impossible for him to rise through the ranks. John was the only male in a yeoman's family of seven children and was obviously a bright boy, so his father arranged for him to be educated at Evesham Abbey. After attending Oxford, he returned to Evesham until the monastery was closed in 1536, then he became chaplain to the Bishop of London. When the Roman Catholic Queen Mary came to the throne, John was taken to the Tower of London, but the queen was so impressed by his eloquence and knowledge that he was made Abbot of Westminster, the last person to hold the title. It became his task to persuade those who were due to be burned at the stake to turn to Roman Catholicism; in this way, he saved many lives.

When Queen Elizabeth came to the throne, she offered him the archbishopric of Canterbury, but he said he could not conform to the new faith. He was sent to the tower in 1560 and remained there for the rest of his life, but it is said that he enjoyed intervals of freedom because of his expertise with medicinal plants and herbs. The monasteries had provided herbs and medicines for the sick and this aspect of their work was very much missed. Wise women or herbalists were under suspicion as witches and, as witchcraft was a crime, they were forced underground. In 1585 John published a collection of his remedies 'chiefly for the poor, which hath not at all times the learned physicians at hand'.

Feckenham seems to have been a centre of herbalism. The Culpepers lived at Shurnock Court, and although no direct link has been discovered between the Feckenham Culpepers and the writer of the well-known Elizabethan book on herbs, there may well have been a connection. One fact is that until recently, many unusual plants and herbs were to be found in the fields around the court.

QUEEN MARY

Next in line to the throne was the thirty-seven-year-old Mary, the daughter of Catherine of Aragon. She was the first female to inherit a throne in her own right and not through marriage. Crowned in 1553, she became possibly the most unpopular queen in English history.

Mary had moved to Tickenhill Manor in Bewdley when she was nine years old, about the time that her father became infatuated with the two Boleyn girls. Workmen were employed there for eighteen weeks in 1525 to get the house ready. After her parents' divorce, the household was reduced. Letters from her Council to the king asked if sixty-nine of the poorest of those discharged might be bestowed among various religious houses in the neighbouring counties. These were only part of her household and only the poorest!

Mary hated the Reformation. She had seen her mother cast aside, and she herself had been declared illegitimate. She was determined to return the country to Roman Catholicism. The Pope was once more Supreme Head of the Church. Roman Catholic bishops returned. Those who had bought church land were asked to return it, not a popular request. There were several Worcestershire priests who refused to convert and five priests had to leave the ministry because they had married.

Unfortunately, Mary insisted that the best way to deal with heresy was to burn as many heretics as possible. She revived the old laws where heresy was regarded as a religious and civil offence amounting to treason. She banned Edward VI's *Book of Common Prayer* and condemned Archbishop Cranmer, who was chiefly responsible for its production, to be burned to death.

JOHN HOOPER, BISHOP OF GLOUCESTER AND WORCESTER

Mary condemned nearly three hundred people to be killed, of whom two had been Bishops of Worcester, John Hooper and Hugh Latimer.

John Hooper preached against the hierarchy and superstitions of the Roman Catholic Church and his views were so unpopular that he had to escape abroad, disguised as a sailor. After Henry VIII's death he was recalled to England and became chaplain to the king's uncle, the Duke of Somerset.

He was invited to be Bishop of Gloucester, but refused as he had preached against the appointment of bishops! Consequently he was thrown into prison, where he decided, in 1550, that being Bishop of Gloucester was a better fate than lying in prison. He accepted the lordship of several manors including Abbots Morton and Offenham, but refused to live in Hartlebury Castle and gave it to the king.

Bishop Hooper tackled his new role with enthusiasm. Most of his Gloucestershire clergy spent their time hunting and gambling. When he questioned them, he discovered that 168 could not repeat the Ten Commandments, 41 did not know where the Lord's prayer was situated in the Bible, and 31 did not know that Jesus had taught the Lord's prayer! He made sure that they studied more and instructed them to preach twice on Sundays.

He ordered all painted images, screens, rood lofts and tabernacles to be removed, and we have Bishop Hooper to blame for the damage to Worcester Cathedral in 1551. His men, known as 'King's Commissioners', pulled down the choir, damaged the organ, defaced the altars and chapels, and smashed the stained glass windows. The early Medieval stone carving in the college hall was plastered over and even sculptures in Prince Arthur's Chantry were defaced.

The following year the current Bishop of Worcester was thrown out by the Council of Edward VI because he refused to use the new prayer book. Bishop Hooper was appointed in his place. He was now Bishop of both Gloucester and Worcester, and the two Sees were united.

However, Hooper's satisfaction was to be short-lived. The next year, in 1553, King Edward died and the Catholic Mary was on the throne. Hooper was eventually thrown into prison accused of heresy and was one of the first bishops to be condemned to death by Mary. It so happened that his chaplain was also John de Feckenham, who tried to convert him to Roman Catholicism but failed.

Bishop Hooper suffered a painful and gruesome death at Gloucester on 9 February 1555. The fire refused to burn properly and had to be relit three times.

Hooper's death was followed by the famous burning of the three harmless intellectuals known as the Oxford Martyrs. Hugh Latimer and Nicholas Ridley were burned together in October 1955, Thomas Cranmer in the following March.

———————————

HUGH LATIMER, BISHOP OF WORCESTER

Hugh Latimer was born in Leicester in 1485, the same year that Henry VII came to the throne. His life spanned four monarchs: Henry VII, Henry VIII, Edward VI and Queen Mary.

Hugh Latimer believed that people were saved by faith alone: each individual could have direct contact with God, so that the Church, including the priests and bishops, were unnecessary. He was also critical of the rich, saying that they exploited the poor. In 1531 he was appointed Rector of West Kington in Wiltshire. He was, of course, very unpopular with the Roman Catholic Church, but he was a powerful preacher and people came from miles around to hear him.

His views came to the ears of Henry VIII who was looking for support of his break with the Pope, hence Latimer was appointed chaplain to Anne Boleyn in 1535.

Hartlebury Castle

One of his tasks was to work with Archbishop Cranmer and Bishop Ridley on a Protestant version of *The Homilies,* to be read in a church 'on any Sunday or Holy Day when there is no sermon'. However, King Henry and Latimer repeatedly disagreed. Latimer had been Bishop of Worcester for about four years when he resigned in 1539, but he lived on in Hartlebury Castle in grinding poverty.

He had to sell his clothes and his precious books in order to stay alive. Henry VIII wanted to have him executed, but Thomas Cromwell managed to dissuade him. 'Consider', he wrote to the king, 'What a splendid man he is, and cast not that away in one hour which nature and art hath been so many years in breeding and perfecting'. A tragic irony is that Latimer escaped the quick death of execution to suffer an agonizing one later. Queen Mary condemned him to be burned at the stake. He met his end in Oxford on 16 October 1555, together with his friend and colleague, Nicholas Ridley, the Bishop of London. Watching the final moments of their sufferings was their other colleague, Thomas Cranmer, who was later burned to death on the same spot.

Ridley walked to the pyre dressed as a bishop in his splendid robes which he took off one by one and threw to the crowd. Latimer was by now seventy and he walked to the pyre in a simple white shift which he removed. An eye-witness wrote, 'And though in his clothes he appeared a withered, crooked old man, he now stood bolt upright.' His last words to Ridley have been quoted many times, 'Be of good comfort, Master Ridley, and play the man; we shall this day light such a candle, by God's grace, in England, as I trust shall never be put out.'

A DISASTROUS REIGN

Mary married Philip, King of Spain, who was eleven years her junior. The marriage was unpopular in England and the alliance with Spain dragged England into war with France. Mary hoped to produce an heir, but she was past child-bearing age and her husband eventually returned to Spain to live. However, we may have the King of Spain to thank for the existence of Mary's successor, Queen Elizabeth. Mary imprisoned Elizabeth in 1554 and was probably toying with the idea of cutting off her head but, at Philip's request, she reluctantly released her and eventually accepted Elizabeth as the next heir to the throne.

Mary only reigned for five years, but she lost all the territory in France that had been won by the English and she turned the religious situation into chaos. Dogged by ill health, Mary died on 17 November 1558, possibly from cancer, leaving the crown to her hated half-sister Elizabeth.

Good Queen Bess

By strange quirks of history, the daughter of the dependable, reliable wife of Henry VIII nearly brought about the downfall of England when she became queen, while the daughter of the wife who caused such trouble and strife in England, and was in many ways responsible for the break with Rome, brought peace to the land. Elizabeth's mother, Anne Boleyn, had been beheaded; Elizabeth herself had been imprisoned in the Tower and feared for her life – and now, in 1558, she was queen!

For the forty-five years of her reign, England prospered. Shakespeare said of this Elizabethan age, 'Oh brave new world!' A host of adventurers, such as Sir Walter Raleigh and Sir Francis Drake, established a great seafaring tradition as England became one of the leading European powers. The powerful Tudor monarchs enforced peace on the land so that aristocrats changed from warlords to cultivated courtiers. Elizabethan architecture flourished as houses no longer had to be built as fortresses.

Built the year that Queen Elizabeth I came to the throne, this beautiful Merchant's house at Avoncroft Museum of Historic Buildings has an open fire on the ground floor with smoke escaping through a hole in the roof

Landowners became prosperous; Jon Pakington was extending Harvington Hall, and the Wintours were building Huddington Court. Both families were later to be caught up in the Gunpowder Plot.

The monasteries had provided shelter and food for travellers and this had largely disappeared. Travellers now tended to be more wealthy – merchants and a range of traders were needing overnight accommodation, and consequently inns were made more comfortable and hospitable. Most of our oldest inns are not aware of the date of their foundation; however, we know that The White Lion in Upton-upon-Severn had an excellent reputation by the time of the Battle of Worcester in 1651 and Oliver Cromwell watered his troops at The Ketch in Broomhall, just outside Worcester. The Lygon Arms in Broadway dates back to the sixteenth century, and The Angel Hotel in Pershore has an inlaid overmantel and a painted female figure dated 1575.

Born in 1533, Elizabeth was charming, witty and glamorous. Examples of her wit have survived the centuries; there was, for example, the incident of the courtier who was unfortunate enough to pass wind as he bowed to the queen and was so mortified that he went abroad for seven years. On his return to court, the queen's first words to him were, 'My Lord, we have forgot the fart.'

The Lygon Arms

Queen Elizabeth I public house at Elmley Castle

She had the knack of enchanting and captivating her subjects, and one way in which she did this was by touring the country. Her visit to Worcester in the summer of 1575 is well recorded.

She rode side-saddle upon a white horse in her velvet riding habit, and behind her streamed the ladies and gentlemen of her court. They stopped at White Ladies for a rest and refreshments, where the queen removed her plumed riding hat and changed her habit for a richly embroidered dress. Jewels sparkled in her red hair, round her neck and on her fingers. Her face was framed by a high, gauzy ruff. The bishop's retinue greeted her at The Mitre Oak at Crossway Green, about 1½ miles south of Hartlebury, and she stayed at the castle overnight. She is also reputed to have slept at the inn bearing her name at Elmley Castle.

The story goes that the citizens wanted to make her approach to the city attractive, so they uprooted a black pear tree covered with ripe pears from White Ladies and replanted it at the gate of the city. In the late summer and autumn this becomes a pretty tree with colourful fruit and leaves. The large fruit has a dull green skin with a reddish brown flush, sometimes with a purple sheen that gives it a black appearance.

Queen Elizabeth stopped to admire the tree and tradition has it that she suggested that the black pear be used in the town's coat of arms. The coat of arms of Worcestershire is now emblazoned with three black pears. It's a pity to spoil a good story, but the fact is that a drawing of 1415 shows that the Worcestershire flag with its emblem of black pears led the English knights into battle at Agincourt as they cried, 'for Harry, England and Saint George'. The tree dates back to Roman times and is now very rare, with only a few examples existing. The pear can be cooked but not eaten raw.

On another visit to Worcestershire the bishop either forgot Queen Elizabeth was coming or mistook the dates. She reached Hartlebury, but there was no one to greet her. According to the historian Francis Bacon (1561–1626), the queen was furious, she stopped at the village inn, sent for the bishop, 'rated him soundly', and went back to London, very angry.

Under Elizabeth, the country became Protestant again. Priests became tutors or vanished abroad, chapels were converted into drawing rooms or libraries, statues were removed or hidden, wall paintings whitewashed. The Recusancy Laws were introduced in

Hamid Habibi of Keepers Nursery, Kent

The famous black pear

1559 where non-attendance at church was punishable by fine or imprisonment. Churches were also obliged to use Edward VI's *Book of Common Prayer* that had been banned by Queen Mary.

THE SPANISH ARMADA

Not everything was peace and tranquillity though, and England became very close to being invaded by the Spanish at this time. Queen Mary may have passed away, but her husband, Philip of Spain, had become one of the most powerful men in Europe. He considered it to be his mission in life to restore England to Catholicism by putting his daughter, Isabella, on the English throne. His naval fleet was the greatest of the age, with 130 ships and 30,500 men. In 1588 it was ready to invade England. Panic spread through Worcestershire. Many of the county's uplands were hastily put in readiness as signal-stations, to be lit with cartloads of kindling and barrels of pitch. Bonfires were sited on the Malverns' Worcestershire Beacon, the Lickeys' Beacon Hill and other prominent high points. The story goes that the Spanish Armada was sighted off Plymouth Hoe but Frances Drake calmly insisted on finishing his game of bowls before he set sail. In defeating the Armada, he was the hero of the hour, but in actual fact he was helped by the bad weather. We may complain about the English weather, but it saved us from a Spanish invasion.

THE HOMELESS

The reforms of her father created many problems for Elizabeth. Brethren and servants from the closed monasteries and friaries added to the unemployment problem. Bands of sturdy beggars roamed the countryside, alarming society. Worcestershire suffered more than most because the great forests of Worcestershire – Feckenham, Wyre and Arden – made ideal hideouts for outlaws. The old nursery rhyme describes them:

> *Hark, hark, the dogs do bark*
> *The beggars are coming to town.*
> *Some in rags and some in tags*
> *And one in a velvet gown.*

Elizabeth was determined to wipe out the 'ruffians'. In the time of Edward VI it became a legal requirement to keep a list of the poor in your parish. Five years into Elizabeth's reign, in 1563, justices of the peace were given the power to raise funds (these later became taxes) to feed and/or clothe the deserving poor – that is, the very young, the old, and the sick. The undeserving poor, those who refused to work, were to be whipped. Overseers of the Poor were appointed in 1597. Records show that, by 1633, throughout Worcestershire, 80 unemployed had been found apprenticeships and 134 rogues and vagabonds had been identified, whipped and sent away.

THOMAS HABINGTON AND THE BABBINGTON PLOT

Perhaps the worst of Queen Elizabeth's problems was the constant threat of assassination.

England had been Roman Catholic since the Synod of Whitby in 664, then, as we have seen, it became Protestant under Henry VIII and Edward VI; Roman Catholic again under Queen Mary; and now it was Protestant under Queen Elizabeth. Many of the leading families in Worcestershire refused to convert from

Roman Catholicism to Church of England. The Bishop of Worcester wrote to Lord Cecil in 1596 that Worcestershire was as dangerous a place as any he knew. 'Nine score recusants [i.e. Catholics] of note besides retainers, wanderers and secret lurkers' were indispersed in 'forty several parishes and six score and ten households'. Of these, about forty were 'families of gentlemen who whether themselves or their wives absent themselves from the church ... Many of them are not only of good wealth but great alliance, as the Windsors, Talbots, Thogmortons [sic], Abindons, Talbots, Middlemores, Blounts, Pakingtons, Foliots, Lygons and Woolmers.' The recusants were not only the wealthy; they came from all walks of life, and among them were labourers, fishermen, watermen, husbandmen, and yeomen, with more women than men.

One of the recusants, Edward Habington of Hindlip Hall (now the headquarters of the West Mercia Constabulary), was involved in the Babbington plot of 1586. This was the most important of four plots to assassinate Queen Elizabeth. The plan was to kill Queen Elizabeth and put on the throne Mary Queen of Scots, who was the daughter of James V of Scotland and also a French princess, and who was languishing under a twenty-four-hour watch in Chartley Hall in Staffordshire. Letters between Mary and Anthony Babbington, a young aristocrat from Derbyshire, were smuggled in and out in beer barrel stoppers, but the letters were intercepted.

Two groups of conspirators were sentenced to be hung, drawn and quartered. The killing of the first group of six was so horrendous that Queen Elizabeth ordered the second group of seven to be hanged and pronounced dead before they were cut open and their internal organs produced for the crowd. Edward Habington was included in the second group. His younger brother, Thomas, was also implicated, but escaped conviction, partly because Elizabeth was his godmother. He was later involved in the Gunpowder Plot.

Queen Elizabeth had been warned for many years that while Mary was alive, her throne was in danger and this last conspiracy forced her hand to sign a warrant for Mary's execution. In 1587 Mary was beheaded, but she left behind a twenty-year-old son, James, who was not only king of Scotland but heir to the English throne.

Queen Elizabeth was nearly seventy when she passed away peacefully in 1603. A messenger galloped northwards to tell James that the English throne was now his.

So ended the eventful reigns of the Tudors.

6

CIVIL WAR AND THE GUNPOWDER PLOT

James seemed to be an ideal successor to Elizabeth. He had ruled Scotland well and, in addition, although his mother was a Roman Catholic, he was raised in a country that had become fiercely Protestant, so he was in an ideal position to negotiate between the Catholics and the Protestants. His father, Lord Darnley, had been murdered before James reached the age of one, and his mother, Mary Queen of Scots, had been forced to abdicate in 1567; consequently, James had been crowned king of Scotland when he was only thirteen months old.

When Elizabeth died, James was thirty-six and not an attractive man. He had thin brown hair, a straggly beard and, although he was tall, his legs were thin and spindly. His tongue was too large for his mouth, leading to a speech impediment, and he dribbled as he drank. He was untrustworthy, deceitful, tactless, thriftless, slovenly and swore freely. To make matters worse, he believed in the divine right of kings. When a bishop stated that the king spoke through the spirit of God, a cynic remarked that the spirit was rather foul-mouthed. His sexual inclinations made Henry VIII look positively saintly; however, he adored his wife, Anne, daughter of Frederick II, King of Denmark. Their three children were Henry, who died in 1612, Elizabeth, and Charles I, from whom the present royal family are descended.

On the other hand, James was not lacking in intelligence, coupled with a sensitivity for all the arts. By the age of ten he was able to read a chapter of the Bible in Latin and translate it fluently into French, then English. He recognized the genius of the Italian Renaissance architect, Andrea Palladio (1508–80), who revolutionized English architecture in a classical style, with columns, cupulas, dormers and balustrades based on Greek and Roman remains. Nearly all the stately homes in Worcestershire were built to that design for the next few centuries. Hagley Hall (about 1747) and Witley Court (1683, extended in 1860) are two magnificent examples.

James set up a commission that produced the much-loved and admired King James I Bible, which had a lasting influence on the English language and is still used and quoted today. Churches throughout the country, including

Worcestershire, would have changed over to this version.

At first all went well. He maintained a liberal attitude towards the Catholics and the new Bible was acceptable to most sects. In 1604 he brought to an end the long war with Spain, but then found himself dragged into the Thirty Years War.

THE PURITANS AND EDWARD WINSLOW

One of his first quarrels was with the Puritans. He had only been on the throne a few months when he told them that unless they converted to the Church of England, he would 'harry them out of the land'. A small group of pilgrims sailed to Holland to find freedom, but twelve years later they decided to return and, in 1620, sailed for America on the *Mayflower*. One of those sailing in the *Mayflower* was Edward Winslow, from Droitwich.

A storm blew the boat too far north so he was at sea for sixty-six days before he landed in New Plymouth. There he founded a British colony and was elected governor three times. Winslow returned to England to promote his colony in 1623 and when he travelled back to New Plymouth he took some heifers and a bull – 'the first beginning of any cattle of this kinde in ye land'. He returned to England a second time in 1635 where he was clapped into prison for various offences such as religious intolerance and performing marriages when he was only a layman. He impressed everyone with his defence, so much so that he became a favourite of Oliver Cromwell. When a naval force was despatched to the West Indies in 1655, Winslow

Edward Winslow's statue in Droitwich shopping centre shows him taking his first unsteady steps on land

went with them as a civil commissioner. Unfortunately, it was his last voyage as he died of yellow fever. A memorial tablet was erected in his memory in St Peter's Church, Droitwich Spa, and in January 2009 a statue by the sculptress Sara Ingleby-McKenzie was unveiled in the shopping centre, showing Edward Winslow taking his first unsteady steps on dry land.

1605 – THE GUNPOWDER PLOT

In 1604 King James brought back the fines for recusancy. No doubt this was the catalyst that sparked the horrific Roman Catholic plot. The plan was to blow up the Houses of Parliament, kidnap the five-year-old Prince Charles, and govern the country in his name. Its supporters were wealthy, well-educated young men, the flower of Worcestershire; some of them were happily married, prepared to risk all for their religion. Most of them were related in some way.

Robert Catesby, a northerner, was thought to have hatched the plot; his uncle was Thomas Throckmorton of Coughton Court, just over the border in Warwickshire.

Coughton Court is just over the border in Warwickshire and is famous for its association with the Gunpowder Plot

The plot was probably planned in Huddington Court near Droitwich, home of Robert and Tom Wintour. The Court is now a private house. Robert Wintour was the elder of the two, and had inherited Huddington Court and a considerable fortune. He was steady, reliable, respected by his workers and a staunch Roman Catholic. His father-in-law had spent twenty years in prison for his faith. Tom was intelligent and lively; he was trained as a lawyer, but went to Spain to fight on behalf of the Protestant rebels, then changed sides. Many of the other Catholic gentry who were involved were from Worcestershire.

As everyone knows, Guy Fawkes, a mercenary explosives expert, helped assemble the gunpowder below the Houses of Parliament. But the plot was exposed when Lord Monteagle, a Catholic, received a letter warning him not to go to Parliament that day. No one has ever discovered who sent it.

At Coughton Court on the evening of 4 November 1605, three female relatives and three priests waited for news. At Huddington Court, the mother of Robert and Tom Wintour watched from her window.

The messenger was to come in through the gate with his hat on if the plot had succeeded, and with the hat off if it had failed. On an upstairs window is 'erk hope, erk care' (without hope, without care), said to be scratched by Lady Wintour when she heard that the plot had failed. The tale is told that she

Huddington Hall is now a private house

committed suicide before the window and her ghost now roams the balcony, wringing its hands.

Guy Fawkes was discovered and tortured, and eventually began to reveal the plot on 7 November. Meanwhile, the conspirators headed homewards. Some reached Warwick Castle and stole four war horses. Thirty-six of the conspirators arrived at Huddington Court on the afternoon of 6 November and stayed overnight. They raced on to Hewell Grange, now a remand home, but then the home of Lord Windsor. The then Lord was only fourteen so he had been sent away. They took gunpowder and arms from the armoury and a large sum of money. In the pouring rain, a group of them rode on to the home of Stephen Littleton, Holbeach House, just inside the Staffordshire border.

Stephen Littleton and Tom Wintour returned to Grafton Manor, home of John Talbot, a relative of the Wintours. There they were misinformed that all were dead. Tom Wintour returned to Holbeach to die with his friends. Littleton met up with Robert Wintour and fled to a relative at Hagley Hall.

About fourteen conspirators arrived at Holbeach, but four of them managed to slip away. The gunpowder had been in an open carriage and was wet from the rain and from fording the River Stour, so they spread it before the fire to dry. It exploded. Three of the men were burned and one of them, John Grant, was blinded.

The home of the High Sheriff of Worcester at Shelsey Walsh

Holt Castle

The following morning, 8 November, Sir Richard Walsh, the High Sheriff of Worcester, who lived at Shelsley Walsh, surrounded the house with 200 of his men.

Four of the plotters were shot dead, two of them were killed by one shot from John Streete, who was rewarded with a pension for life. Tom Wintour was shot in the shoulder. They were all rounded up ready for the Tower of London except for four injured men, presumably Tom and John Grant among them, who were taken to Holt Castle, home of Sir Henry Bromley, Lord High Chancellor, to recover until they were well enough to stand trial.

By December, only Robert Wintour and Stephen Littleton were still at liberty. They were hiding in the outbuildings of Hagley Hall, tended by Perks, a tenant farmer, and Barford, his servant.

Unfortunately, in January, the cook noticed the large amount of food disappearing into the outbuilding and informed the authorities. Stephen was hung, drawn and quartered at Stafford, and Robert Wintour at St Paul's in London. This was a death usually reserved for those found guilty of high treason. Perks and Barford were merely hanged at Worcester.

The conspirators had now all been rounded up, but the search was on for any priests who had been involved. Grafton Manor and Huddington Court were

Hagley Hall

turned over by the high sheriff and his men, and furniture, property, papers and arms were removed. Hindlip House or Hall, now the headquarters of the West Mercia Constabulary, was the home of Thomas Habington who had refused to have anything to do with the fugitives, but he was a known recusant. On 20 January Sir Henry Bromley, Sheriff of Worcester, was ordered to search the house. A rich bounty was promised for each priest caught and so the sheriff's men began with great enthusiasm. Thomas Habington denied all knowledge of priests and offered to die at the gate if a priest were found. Eleven hiding places for priests were discovered. He feigned horror and surprise. They searched for four days and had given up hope when two men sauntered through the gallery, 'Owen' and Ralph Ashley, a lay brother. 'Owen' may have been Nicholas Owen and an important catch. Known as Little John, he was a very small cripple who constructed hidden refuges for priests and therefore knew all the hiding places across several counties. The two had only eaten one apple between them over the past four days and were starving.

Six days later, on 26 January, Humphrey Littleton of Hagley Hall tried to save his own neck by revealing that at least one priest was definitely in Hindlip House. The search was renewed. On Monday, 27 January, Father Garnet and Father Oldcorne emerged, so thin and grey that at first their pursuers took them to be ghosts and ran away. Although they had been fed liquids through a tube, they had been sitting in a hiding place not large enough for them to stretch their legs and with no toilet facilities.

All the main conspirators were hung, drawn and quartered. As for Thomas Habington, he was released on condition that he never moved out of Worcestershire, so he spent his time compiling a history of the county, on which many further histories have been based, among them *The Victoria County History* of 1900. The story goes that when he came to write the history of Tardebigge church, he could only inspect one-half of it because the other half was in Warwickshire.

A series of anti-Catholic laws came into effect. Catholics had already been ordered to marry in the Anglican Church, take their children there for baptism, and bury their dead in Anglican ground. But now they could neither practise law, nor serve in the army or navy. No recusant could vote in local elections, act as executor of a will, act as guardian to a minor, nor even possess a weapon.

THE LAST OF JAMES I

As James believed in the divine right of kings, there were the inevitable quarrels with Parliament, usually over money, which he needed to equip his armed forces. His legislation constantly upset the gentry; for example, in 1617 he decreed that anyone who owned land outside London and did not have any property in London had to leave the city and return to their estate to manage it properly.

His treasured elder son died in 1612 and his beloved wife in 1619. James died, grief-stricken, vulgar, a little senile and prematurely aged, in 1625. His reign in Scotland and England had amounted to fifty-eight of his fifty-nine years. Opinion is divided as to the success of his reign. Some historians believe that he was one of the best and ablest kings England has ever seen, while others state that he set the country on a downward spiral that brought England to the worst civil war in English history.

CHARLES I

Charles was totally unlike his father. He was one of the nicest kings in English history, courteous, sober, dignified, conscientious and a little shy. He is one of the few kings with no known mistresses or lovers. A small man, with a long, sensitive face, his wife, Henrietta Maria, the sister of Louis XIII, burst into tears when she first saw him but eventually they became a devoted couple and had five children. A cultured man, he continued to sponsor Palladian architecture, together with the painters Van Dyck and Rubens. Yet his reign was one of the worst in history, culminating in the English civil wars. It has been said of Charles, 'so good a man, so bad a king'.

Like Henry VIII, Charles did not expect to become king, but when he was twelve years old, his eighteen-year-old brother Henry died, perhaps from typhoid.

———————————

THE PLAGUES IN WORCESTER

Virulent diseases frequently rampaged throughout the known world, terrifying the population. The open market at the end of Angel Street is probably built over an old plague pit.

Worcester was visited by the plague nearly every summer. Some of the most serious outbreaks came in 1583, in Queen Elizabeth's time, when thirty-eight died from the St Johns area alone, and again in 1610 when James I was on the throne.

Worcester's open market

The population of St Johns only amounted to 130 families and 83 of them died, including the vicar, Thomas Leonard, and seven of his children. The worst outbreak came in the days of Charles I, in 1637. The city lost one-fifth of its population. The death toll amounted to 1,551, of which 236 were from St Andrews Parish. People tried to escape from the city but no one wanted them in their area in case they bought the plague with them; consequently, many took refuge on Bevere Island. Everything in the city stopped except for the grave diggers.

A new cemetery at Angel Lane filled up rapidly; another was dug near the cathedral then, when that was full, the site that is now the market place was chosen. It was originally a little orchard belonging to the Dominican friary, but had been purchased by the Corporation thirteen years previously. The historian Bill Gwilliam, writing in 1977, says that he remembers seeing a mass of bones being removed when the foundations of the market were laid.

Starvation threatened. The townsfolk and those at Bevere were kept alive by a few kind folk outside the infected area who left food at designated collection points outside the town. It was customary, where a town or village was a victim of the plague, to have these dropping points from where the villagers could collect food. What appears to be a large horse trough on a little green in the centre of Ombersley village (see page 85) is, in fact, a Plague Stone for the reception of food, moved here from the outskirts of the village as a reminder of those tragic times.

CIVIL WAR IS DECLARED

Charles's great undoing was that, like his father, he believed in the divine right of kings. This set him on a collision course with Parliament. He dissolved Parliament in 1629 and ruled without one for eleven years. However, it was from Parliament that his finances should have come to equip his army and navy. He raised money by selling monopolies and imposing a tax known as 'ship money', levied to rebuild the fleet. All this made him very unpopular.

The Archbishop of Canterbury tried to impose the English Prayer Book on Scotland in 1637 which led to war with the Scots; also, trouble was brewing in Ireland. Charles was forced to recall Parliament in 1640. A series of Acts were passed that deprived him of his powers. Matters came to a head when Charles decided to arrest five leading MPs, but when he arrived with his soldiers 'the birds had flown'. In fear for his safety, Charles fled north with his queen. By August, he had secured enough supporters to strike. At Nottingham, on 22

August 1642, he raised the standard, making the symbolic and ancient summons to all his subjects to come to his aid. Both sides took steps to raise men. Even in the same family and the same village, men fought on different sides. In Salwarpe, the lord of the manor tried to levy a force for the king while the MP, Sergeant Wylde, either tried to prevent men from enlisting or persuaded them to fight for the Parliamentarians.

KIDDERMINSTER AND THE
REVEREND RICHARD BAXTER

Those who were Church of England tended to be Royalists and those who were Protestant (sometimes known as Roundheads) generally fought for Parliament, but this was not always the case. One of the Kidderminster's well-known char-

The statue of the Reverend Richard Baxter

acters is the Reverend Richard Baxter, whose statue overlooks the Kidderminster ring road.

The saying 'There, but for the grace of God go I' is attributed to Baxter when he saw a young man being led away to prison. Although he was vicar of St Mary's, which was Church of England, for twenty-five years with just a few breaks, he had Protestant leanings that brought him into conflict with both authorities and townsfolk. One of his beliefs was that there should be no pictures or statues to distract the congregation. He destroyed the old statues and effigies in St Mary's, but when he tried to smash the carved crucifixion on the processional cross, he was attacked by an angry mob shouting 'Down with the round-head', so much so that he had to leave to live in Coventry.

When Cromwell was made Lord Protector, Baxter was reappointed in 1647. He should have lived in the handsome vicarage but he refused to turn out the incumbent, George Dance, and inhabited a humble room in a nearby attic instead. He was eloquent and caring; he visited the sick and as there was no doctor in the town he became skilled in medicine. It was said that he converted the inhabitants of Kidderminster from a lawless and amoral community into 'as godly a people as any in the kingdom'.

When Charles II came to the throne, Baxter was offered the bishopric of Hereford but he refused as he believed that all ministers were equal. Charged with preaching against the Church of England, he came before the 'Bloody' Judge Jeffreys who sentenced him to eighteen months in prison. He died in Christchurch in 1692.

Baxter is not only well known for his work in Kidderminster, he was also a writer on spiritual matters, and his book, *The Saints Everlasting Rest,* is still in use today. The Baxter Congregational Church has been built in his memory. A site in Ring Street was purchased in 1694, but a larger church with a steeple was built in front of the old one in 1884.

THE ENGLISH CIVIL WAR

The historian J. W. Willis Bund wrote, 'Worcestershire is one of the smaller English counties … yet … more fighting went on during the great Civil War than in most other Counties … In every year of the war there was more or less fighting within it.' Worcestershire was on a direct route between Wales, Oxford (where King Charles had his headquarters) and London and great armies tramped across the county. There was often fighting all along the line of the Severn. A large part of Worcestershire belonged to the Crown and was a valuable recruiting ground.

Nearly every village in Worcester suffered in some way. Husbands and sons were sent off to fight. Ill-disciplined and starving troops plundered and pillaged. Ironworks were converted to make weapons and cannonballs. Bakers were made to provide bread for nearby troops; sometimes they were paid, sometimes not. Bridges were wrecked. Pershore Bridge was blown up in such a hurry by the Royalists that some troops were still on the bridge. Two or three officers, their major and twenty-six privates were drowned as well as some eighty countrymen. Their hats floated off down the river.

By a strange quirk of fate, both the first battle and part of the last battle of the Civil War took place at Powick, about 2 miles outside Worcester.

*Evidence of the 1651 Battle of Worcester. These holes in the wall of
St Peter's Church, Powick, were created by musket shot*

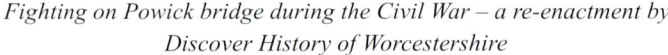

*Fighting on Powick bridge during the Civil War – a re-enactment by
Discover History of Worcestershire*

Powick Bridge has been preserved but is no longer used

The first was only a skirmish. One hot day in the summer of 1642 a contingent of mounted Parliamentarians trotted over Powick Bridge straight into a detachment of Royalists, who were resting and enjoying the sunshine. The Parliamentarians were new to war, but Princes Rupert and Maurice of the Royalists had already been involved in battle. The princes jumped on their horses and charged. The Parliamentarians tried to turn and flee, but the lane was too narrow. Some were trampled by horses, others fell into the river. As many as fifty Parliamentarians were killed, wounded or drowned. The Royalists escaped with nothing more than sword wounds.

OLIVER CROMWELL

At this point, Oliver Cromwell began to develop his New Model Army.

Oliver Cromwell was born in Huntingdon in 1599. With his halting speech and dishevelled appearance, people thought he was just a country bumpkin but in actual fact his family was quite prestigious. His great-grandfather had married the sister of Thomas Cromwell, Henry VIII's right-hand man, who had helped in the closure of the monasteries. Cromwell went to Cambridge for a year, but returned home on the death of his father when he inherited the Huntingdon estate; later he studied law for a short time in London. In 1628 he was elected MP for Huntingdon and then for Cambridge. When war broke out he organized his own district for military purposes and at the Battle of Edgehill he had the command of a company of horses that he had trained. It was so successful that he was entrusted with the task of raising and training forces in the eastern counties.

The Parliamentarians began to dominate the conflict. In the Battle of Marston Moor, between York and Knaresborough, in 1644, about 3,000 Royalists were slain. That same year the king was nearly caught at Oxford, but escaped, going through Broadway, Evesham (where he stayed for a few days), Pershore, Worcester and Bewdley.

HEROES AND VILLAINS

There were many heroes of the war. In 1644 the Parliamentarian Colonel Thomas Fox, known as Tinker Fox, had been routed in a minor battle on Stourbridge Heath and was looking for a way to redeem himself. He learned that the Royalists had gone from Shrewsbury to Oxford, passing Bewdley, and there were likely to be stragglers. Bewdley was a royal garrison of some 120 troops with Thomas Lyttleton as governor. On Bewdley Bridge was a gatehouse, and from there the one and only road led from the bridge through the town and along to Tickenhill Palace, where Lyttleton lodged. Fox reached Bewdley after dark and selected about sixty of his troopers to go with him. He ordered the guard to open the gate, saying that he was a Royalist detachment. The guard let him through without question. A chain across the road signified the main guard in the town. Again Fox demanded admission and again it was granted. Then Fox sent some of his men on to Tickenhill while others went to each house where soldiers were billeted, demanding surrender. Five or six sentinels had to be killed to prevent them raising the alarm. Leaving a guard over his prisoners, Fox marched on to Tickenhill and surprised everyone in their beds including the governor. Taking the most important prisoners with him, he rode off with forty-four horses and a great store of provisions. Knowing that the alarm would soon be raised and the Royalists would be in hot pursuit, Fox went in another direction to Coventry.

Lyttleton was sent to the Tower but his bail was paid. He was rearrested then again set free. He died soon afterwards and is buried in Worcester Cathedral.

There were heroes on the Royalist side, too, one of them being Colonel Legge who commanded what he described as 'a scanty force' who had entrenched themselves in a garrison on the north-eastern side of Evesham with large forti-fications, palisades and a ditch. Evesham was in an important strategic position. It so happened that the commander of the Parliamentarians, Colonel Massey, had just been defeated at Ledbury and, like Tinker Fox, was anxious to prove himself, so he decided to capture the town. His reinforcements had arrived so a considerable force gathered outside the garrison. Colonel Massey sent a message to Colonel Legge inviting him to surrender, but he replied: 'You are hereby answered, in the name of His Majesty, that this garrison, which I am entrusted to keep, I will defend so long as I can, with the men, arms and ammu-nition therein being nothing terrified of your summons.'

Massey ordered his men to throw bundles of twigs into the ditch in order to reach the fortifications. It was dangerous work as the Royalists were firing down on them and casualties were heavy. The soldiers retreated, but Colonel Massey could not risk losing face again and ordered them back into the firing line. Finally, the Parliamentary cavalry managed to break through the defences. Colonel Legge was forced to surrender, and 70 officers and 480 soldiers were taken prisoner.

Charles marched through Inkberrow, Droitwich and Bromsgrove to Naseby, where, in 1645, his army was defeated. About 1,000 were killed and 5,000 taken prisoner. The conflict dragged on, but the Royalists began to realize that their cause was hopeless.

Towards the end of the war supplies for the Royalists were not getting through and troops were often ill-disciplined and hungry. In 1645 a Royalist contingent visited Kidderminster and were described by a Parliamentary writer as 'the most rude, ill-governed and ravenous horse that I believe ever trod upon the earth'. In Hartlebury, Thomas Brooke complained that his house had been plundered three times. There was so much plundering and stealing of goods and cattle that armed bands of farmers and labourers formed them-selves into gangs that they called 'Clubmen' to protect their property. On the summit of Woodbury Hill in the Abberley Hills is an information display giving an account of the Woodbury Hill Clubmen on 5 March 1645. One thousand clubmen, humble villagers from north-west Worcestershire, met to protest at the ravages of the Civil War. Their crops and livestock had been seized by both sides in the conflict, their houses set on fire, and their wives and daughters raped. The Clubmen drew up a charter to be presented to the high sheriff of the county, listing their grievances and affirming their support 'for king and country and the maintenance of the true Reformed Protestant Religion ... against all Popery and Popish superstitions and all other heresies and schisms whatsoever'.

Even the bishop's residence was involved in the war. Hartlebury Castle had been given to the bishops of Worcester by the king of the Mercians in about the year 800, and in the sixteenth or seventeenth century it became the principal residence of the bishops. It was important geographically, because close by, at Areley Kings, was one of the few fords across the River Severn and a main route to Wales. At the beginning of the war, the castle was garrisoned for the king by Colonel William Sandys with 120 foot soldiers and 20 horse and was of great importance as it had been chosen to house the royal mint. It was never captured, but when it was obvious that the Royalist cause was lost, Colonel Sandys surrendered on 9 May 1646. The Parliamentarians then used the castle as a gaol to keep their prisoners.

The remaining Royalist garrisons were at Madresfield, Strensham and Worcester. Strensham surrendered about the same time as Hartlebury. The terms of surrender for Madresfield were that the occupiers were to walk out and leave behind their arms and provisions, but in return the owner of the house would receive £200, his troops were to have 30 shillings each and his foot soldiers 10 shillings each. Who could refuse these generous terms?

THE SIEGE OF WORCESTER

Worcester was the last place to surrender. The walls had been repaired, earthworks had been thrown up in front of and behind each wall to strengthen them, and the Medieval city outside the walls had been flattened so that Parliamentary forces could not creep up unnoticed.

It will be remembered that Worcester was a walled city, and people could only go through its gates with a pass. A contemporary survey estimated its citizens at about 7,000. Those residents that were 'of no use' were allowed to depart. Statistics vary, but it was reckoned that about 1,500 were left in the city compared to an army of 5,000 outside.

The Parliamentarians arrived on 21 May 1646 under Colonel Whalley and built huts on the outskirts of the city. These huts accidentally burned down, but were hastily rebuilt. The action mostly consisted of minor forays and pot shots with cannons. An early attack by the Royalists killed forty. A later incursion by the Parliamentarians cost the lives of 100 men. One cannon shot from the Parliamentarians killed a couple in bed in the Trinity; another hit the mayor's house and yet another landed on the bishop's pantry. Edgar tower was damaged by another shot. Worse damage was done to the Royalists by their own cannon placed in the centre of the city which exploded. A number of people were injured and a large section of it fell on The Rose and Crown, near St Helen's Church.

Captain Hodgkins, or 'wicked Will', got very drunk, sallied over the bridge to St Johns, killed one of the Parliamentary guards and returned in safety. He was so drunk that he fell off his horse twice.

The cows had to be turned out to eat the grass under the city walls. The Parliamentarians devised various ways to capture the cows. They tried tethering a cow to a stake and surrounding it with fires. They hoped that, by its bellowing, the Royalist herds would move across to join it, but the plot failed.

On 23 June, news came that Oxford had fallen. The officers refused to believe it, until a high-ranking secretary arrived with a pass and confirmed it. A Council of War was held in the bishop's palace and negotiations were begun for the raising of the siege. On 23 July, the last Church of England service was held in the cathedral for fourteen years. Among the besieged were over thirty wealthy landowners, such as William Habingdon of Hindlip, and Henry Bromley of Holt. They were allowed out of the city (in fact they were *told* to get out within ten days), but had to promise never to bear arms against Parliamentarians again, and were fined 25 per cent of the value of their estates.

THE SECOND CIVIL WAR

Charles had already, in April 1646, given himself up to the Scots who handed him over to the English. Over the next two years, while he was prisoner, there were so many Royalist plots and so much guerrilla warfare that the period is sometimes known as the 'second civil war'. The illegitimate son of Lord Dudley, Dud Dudley, lived in Worcestershire but was discovered training a guerrilla army in Boscobel Woods in Staffordshire. Dud owned some ironworks and is famous for inventing the process of smelting iron by coal instead of wood. He was taken to Hartlebury Castle where he was stripped naked, subjected to many insults, and made to ride almost naked through the streets. Dud managed to escape, was recaptured, and taken to London. He was condemned to be shot, but managed to escape again. He was wounded in the leg and could only move with crutches. Miraculously, he reached his home in Worcester but his wife and children had gone, his house was sold and his ironworks destroyed. Dud was told that his family were at Bristol and he managed to reach them safely. He lived there until he died but his body was returned to Worcester for burial and there is a magnificent memorial to his wife, erected by him in St Helen's Church, Worcester.

CHARLES I IS EXECUTED

Oliver Cromwell then played a leading role, negotiating between Parliament and the king. Parliament finally lost patience with the many plots to reinstate Charles, and in 1648 he was brought to trial in Westminster Hall before 135 judges and the decision to execute him was carried by sixty-eight votes to sixty-seven. Cromwell's name is fourth on the list of those agreeing to the execution.

Charles's beloved wife, Henrietta Maria, had fled to France; of his family, only his thirteen-year-old daughter Elizabeth, and his ten-year-old son, Henry Duke of Gloucester, were with him to say their farewells. He asked Elizabeth to tell her mother that his thoughts had never strayed from her, and that his love should be the same to the last. He was beheaded on 30 January 1649 at Whitehall.

Henrietta lived on until 1669, long enough to see her son restored to the throne as King Charles II.

THE SCOT INVASION

Meanwhile, the son of Charles I – that is, Charles Stuart – had been in exile on the Continent. He was proclaimed King of Scotland and, in 1651, crowned on the Stone of Scone. That same year, he decided to raise an army in Scotland and march down to England to regain the throne, hoping to recruit on the way.

Cromwell was a man to be feared. No mercy was shown by his troops to anyone who was in arms. He crushed an uprising in Wales in 1648, then in Ireland in 1649 where he massacred the entire population of Drogheda, amounting to 2,500, followed by the slaughter of 2,000 at Wexford, and he had routed the Scottish army at Dunbar in 1650.

Cromwell's tactic was to let Charles march well into England then trap him between two armies, one from the north and one from the south. After a few skirmishes in the north, Charles marched to Worcester. Both Wales and Worcester were chiefly Royalist and he knew that he could rely on their support for supplies, ammunition and, hopefully, recruits.

Worcester was reached on 22 August 1651. Charles was given a royal welcome and his troops, who had marched 300 miles in three weeks, were supplied with new shoes and stockings. Orders went out to surrounding parishes to send in men to work on the fortifications of the city. Salwarpe, for example, was told to send thirty men with spades, shovels and pickaxes.

The front line ran from Powick, about 2 miles south-west of the city, to Pitch-croft, where the racecourse is now. Powick Bridge was blown up, together with bridges at Bewdley, Upton and Bransford. In the city itself, earthworks were thrown against the walls, gates were blocked, and at Sidbury Gate a star-shaped fort was built, Fort Royal, so huge that part of it still exists.

Before the battle Charles stayed with the vicar of Inkberrow and we have proof of this because he left his maps behind. Succeeding vicars kept them for centuries, but they have now been passed to the Worcestershire County archives.

Local folklore says that Cromwell spent the night in nearby Nunnery Wood where he sold his soul to the devil for victory and seven years' good fortune. The battle took place on 3 September 1651 and he died on 3 September 1658, which is exactly seven years. In actual fact, he probably stayed at the house of Mr Justice Berkeley at Spetchley, 3 miles from Worcester.

Cromwell planned to push all the Royalist forces into Worcester, where they would be trapped. He began making two makeshift bridges across the Severn and the Teme by lashing boats together and, to distract the Royalists, he put one cannon on Red Hill and another on Perry Wood.

These cannons were a great nuisance and the Royalists decided to try to capture them. On the night of 31 August, two groups of soldiers left the town and made their way towards the cannons. Unfortunately, a Worcester tailor, Guise, who was in the city, let himself down the city walls on a rope and informed the Parliamentarians of the plot. The Royalist soldiers had decided to wear white shirts for easy identification, which meant that they were easily picked off by the opposing side. Eleven bodies were found on the road the following morning. The tailor was arrested and hanged, but during the following years his widow received compensation totalling about £1,700, a large fortune.

THE BATTLE OF UPTON BRIDGE

The River Severn runs from north to south through Worcestershire so it was necessary to cross the river to get from one side of the county to the other. At Upton-upon-Severn there was a sturdy bridge. By 28 August, five days before the actual battle, the Royalists were holding the town; one arch of the bridge had been blown up and replaced by a single plank. A number of soldiers had been left to guard the bridge, but for some reason they had left their posts. The White Lion nearby claims they had sneaked off to enjoy its hospitality. The Royalists had no idea that the Parliamentarians under General Lambert were nearby, nor that he had been ordered by Cromwell to capture Upton-upon-Severn at any cost.

The White Lion at Upton-on-Severn

Eighteen of Cromwell's men were chosen to negotiate the plank. As soon as dawn broke, they gingerly began their journey across the deep river, knowing that they could be fired on at any moment. They were spotted as soon as they reached the other side, but managed to reach the safety of Upton-upon-Severn church where they fired at the Royalists through the windows.

General Lambert managed to find a section of the river that, with difficulty, could be forded. His dragoons floundered across and attacked the Royalists from the rear. There were losses on both sides, but eventually Upton-upon-Severn was taken by the Parliamentarians. Lambert was hailed as a hero and Cromwell himself came to thank his men for their bravery.

The next day, the bridge had been repaired and a Parliamentary force of 12,000 had crossed the river and were camped on the west bank of the Severn. It cut off the Scots from Wales and from the west, so that no further supplies, munitions or recruits could come from there.

The White Lion still exists, the Georgian front is only a façade, and the interior is thought to go back as far as the 1500s. As for the church, the main body was rebuilt after the Civil War but pulled down in 1937. Only the old tower, dating back to the 1300s, has been left standing. A cupola was placed on top in about 1769, so that the tower ever since has been popularly known as 'The Pepperpot'.

Upton-on-Severn

THE BATTLE OF WORCESTER

The battle began on the mid-morning of 3 September 1651. With their battle cry 'Lord of Hosts', the Parliamentarians attacked, beginning at Powick Bridge, then spreading to Lower Wick and towards the city. Charles watched the battle from the top of the cathedral tower. He realized that Cromwell was trying to drive his troops into Worcester city where they would be trapped, so he rode to Powick and St Johns, emphasizing that they must stand firm. Then he returned to the city.

Reinforcements were at Pitchcroft, with a Scottish general, Leslie, who had the whole of the Scots cavalry with him. Several times he could have saved the day for Charles, but he refused to join in the fighting.

Charles decided to attack the Parliamentary strongholds at Red Hill and Perry Wood. He led an assault on Red Hill, while the Duke of Hamilton took his battery to Perry Wood. They succeeded in capturing the guns, but the duke was shot in the leg. He was carried to the Commandery in the city centre. The duke and several Scot lords were lodging there, and it had probably become a temporary field hospital. When Cromwell heard that the duke had been shot, he sent his own surgeon to see to him. Charles Stuart's surgeon was already at the Commandery and the two surgeons argued whether or not the duke's leg should be amputated. After four days, the duke died of gangrene. According to the historian Willis Bund, 'His blood was in recent years shewn on a board in a room in the ground floor.' His family wanted him buried near his home, Hamilton Palace, but the Parliamentarians refused permission. Instead, he was buried in Worcester Cathedral, wrapped in lead. In 1862, during renovations, a workman accidentally put a pickaxe through his head.

The Scots fought bravely but finally they had to retreat into the city itself, leaving behind their dead and wounded. Fort Royal was stormed. The troops rushed down the hill to Sidbury gate, but it was so narrow that only a few could pass at a time. There they were jammed in tightly and the Parliamentarians mowed them down without mercy.

Afterwards, bodies were piled high at the gates. Charles was inside Sidbury gate and his escape was nothing short of miraculous. Years later, a certain William Bagnall claimed that one of Cromwell's troopers had recognized Charles and ridden his horse at him, but Bagnall had dragged a team of oxen across his path and enabled Charles to escape. It seems unlikely that a slow-moving team of oxen could be dragged in front of a fast-moving horse, but William stuck to his story and was rewarded for it.

Charles managed to reach his headquarters in New Street (now the King Charles II Restaurant) and slipped out of the back door as the Parliamentarians entered the front. Lord Wilmot was holding a horse for him; they galloped along a lane to Barbourne Bridge and away.

The victorious Parliamentarians rampaged through the town with their battle cry 'Lord of Hosts!', killing and looting. A letter from Worcester on 6 September reads:

King Charles II Restaurant

On the wall of the bridge next to the Commandery is this commemorative sculpture

'Things at Worcester are in great confusion. Lords, knights and gentlemen were there plucked out of holes by the soldiers. The common prisoners they were driving into the cathedral, and what with the dead bodies of the men and dead horses of the enemy filling the streets there was such nastiness that a man could hardly abide in the town.'

The number of Royalist prisoners was so great that the Parliamentarians did not know what to do with them. They were kept in the cathedral where they did more damage than the rampaging enemy! Tombs and effigies were smashed and pews were used as lavatories. The cathedral was afterwards disinfected 'with pitch and rosen'. A thousand prisoners were taken to Bristol to be transported. The slave market came to a standstill!

It was the end of Worcester as a great city. Cromwell ordered that the town walls should be demolished. There are now only a few remnants left, chiefly in the aptly named City Walls Road. Around Sidbury, the Commandery was the only building left standing in a sea of destruction (three centuries later it even survived the destruction of town planners and is now a tourist attraction).

Furthermore, the city authorities and its occupants had to face heavy fines for backing the wrong side, so that no one could afford any rebuilding. It took 100 years for Worcester to get back on its feet.

THE FLIGHT OF CHARLES II

So began Charles's famous six weeks on the run with a price of £1,000 on his head. Together with about 200 other Royalists, he headed north, stopping after 5 miles at an inn in Ombersley (probably the present Kings Arms), then on towards Hartlebury. All bridges and fords were heavily guarded and it was impossible to cross the River Severn. When they reached the Kidderminster

Road, Charles Stuart, Lord Wilmot and a small group decided to take the road to Kinver while the others went on to Kidderminster. This was fortunate for the king, because when the Royalists reached Kidderminster they were confronted by the local Parliamentarians and many were killed.

Charles Stuart rode on safely, probably through Chaddesley Corbett, Hagley, Pedmore and Stourbridge to Boscobel House, 8 miles north-west of Wolverhampton. Here we have the famous story of Charles hiding in the oak tree while soldiers searched the ground beneath him. At some point, it was decided that he should aim for Bristol. He stopped in Moseley Old Hall (near Wolverhampton) where you can still see the bed where he slept, then continued to Bentley Hall, home of the Catholic Jane Lane.

In 1651 it was illegal for Catholics to travel more than 5 miles away from their homes without a pass from the sheriff of the county. Before the Battle of Worcester, Mistress Lane had obtained two passes, one for herself and one for a manservant, to travel to Bristol to visit a friend who was having a baby. Lord Wilmot heard about the pass and intended to disguise himself as the manservant and travel with Mistress Lane; however, when he heard of Charles Stuart's plight he gave the pass to him. Charles's long hair was cut and he was clad in the dress of a serving man. No shoes could be found to fit Charles's large feet so a pair were cut down the sides.

In later years, this was one of Charles's favourite anecdotes:

> We took our journey towards Bristol … We had not gone two hours on our way before the mare I rode cast a shoe, so we were forced to ride to get another shoe at a scattering village, whose name began with something like 'Long-' and as I was holding my horse's foot, I asked the smith the news. He told there was no news that he knew of, since the good news of the beatings of the rogues, the Scots. I asked him whether there were none of the English taken that joined with the Scots. He answered that he did not hear that rogue, Charles Stuart, was taken, but some of the others, he said, were taken, but not Charles Stuart. I told him if that rogue were taken he deserved to be hanged more than all the rest for bringing in the Scots, upon which he said I spoke like an honest man, and we parted.

Many historians believe that the village was Bromsgrove. Near the centre of the town on the Worcester Road is Ye Olde Black Cross.

In 1651 it was not a public house, but a smithy, so that Charles could have had his horse shod here. In the pub floor is a small glass panel where visitors should be able to look down into the cellar to see the rungs where Charles tied his horse, but the glass is now very scratched.

Ye Old Black Cross in Bromsgrove

After six weeks of hair-raising adventures, Charles managed to find a ship that took him to France and safety.

The Battle of Worcester was one of the most important conflicts in English history. It was the last great battle to be fought on English soil. It brought to an end the fighting between the Parliamentarians and the Royalists, and increased the power of the army under Oliver Cromwell.

Some historians have calculated that, in proportion to its population at the time, the number of fatalities exceeded England's losses in action in the First and Second World Wars combined. The effect upon Scotland was catastrophic. Eleven thousand Scots never returned home. Children went hungry as the bread-winner had disappeared. Mills lay idle and fields were left to grow wild as there were no men to work them.

ENGLAND UNDER THE PURITANS

The Puritans wanted to create a God-fearing society. They dreamed of an England where the whole of society was on a spiritual plane, where everyone was honest, reliable and trustworthy. Unfortunately, the laws to bring this about were draconian.

Courtesy of Sealed Knot.

Two re-enactors from the Sealed Knot condemn local housewives to perpetual washing up!

Theatres were closed, public houses were not allowed to open on Sundays, and many were closed. The Sabbath was to be spent in spiritual contemplation: in prayer, Bible-reading and going to church. Dancing was banned. Swearing, gambling and drunkenness came in for heavy fines. Adultery received the death penalty. It was even suggested by Parliament that the traditional festivities at Christmas and Easter be replaced by a weekly fast on Wednesdays. Clothes were to be plain and hair short or tied back. Money was given to strolling players to prevent them playing in Worcester. At Cropthorne, some of the parishioners were sent to trial at sessions by their vicar, for playing the banned game of football.

Anything that could be a distraction from prayer and contemplation in a church was destroyed. Statues in churches were smashed and paintings white-washed over. In recent years several ancient churches across Worcestershire have discovered traces of Medieval paintings under the whitewash. Three levels of wall paintings were uncovered on the north wall of the nave in St Nicholas's Church at Warndon. Pinvin Church has wall paintings going back to the late 1200s showing the adoration of the Magi and the crucifixion, which were discovered in 1855.

Under Cromwell, more than thirty Worcestershire ministers lost their living. This often meant that they and their families were thrown out of their homes without any means of support. George Durant at Blockley was one of these. He

*During Cromwell's time, the number of sects began to increase enormously,
but few new sects could afford a place of worship. This problem was alleviated by the
Victorians with 'tin tebarnacles' supplied in kit form. This 'mission church', now at
Avoncroft Museum, was erected in 1891 in Yardly by the Methodists*

had ten children, some of them very young, and a party of horsemen dragged
them out of the house. The neighbours, feeling sorry for them, let them move
into a poor cottage nearby.

Cromwell's vision for England included civil liberty, where Christians could
worship without persecution. Consequently, a whole series of various sects and
cults evolved.

The Fifth Monarchy Men were influential from about 1649 to 1661. They
hoped to reform Parliament and the government for the imminent coming of
Christ's kingdom on earth. At least two Worcestershire vicars were involved,
Thomas Wilmot of Wolverley and Robert Brown from White Ladies in
Worcester.

The Unitarian Church was another early sect. By about 1708 they had fled from
Birmingham to escape persecution to Dark Lane, in Hollywood on the Birm-
ingham/Worcestershire border. The chapel had only been standing for seven years
when it was damaged by riots. One of the arsonists was hanged at Worcester.
In 1791 the chapel was burned down completely and so the congregation erected
a new building nearby in Packhorse Lane, Wythall, which is still there.

The Baptist church at Bewdley, dates back to 1649 and is one of the earliest in the Midlands

The Kidderminster vicar, Richard Baxter, was involved in a terrific fight in the old church in the centre of Bewdley (St Annes) against the curate, John Toombes, who had Anabaptist sympathies. Baxter went over to Bewdley early one morning in 1646 for a debate, but it became a battle, starting at 9 a.m. and not finishing until 5 p.m. Contemporary reports say that the two sides 'became like two armies' and 'the civil magistrate had much to do to quieten them'. The costs of the repair to the church furniture were considerable. Afterwards, John Toombes founded the Anabaptists in the town, but kept his position as curate so that he ran both communities.

Evesham had a tradition of hostility against the established religion, going right back to the burning of Thomas Badby in 1410 (see Chapter 4).

In the time of Oliver Cromwell, it was, to some extent, left to the magistrate in each town to deal with the dissenters as he thought fit. In Evesham, the Society of Friends, sometimes known as Quakers, was founded in about 1650. The Church of England vicar George Hopkins preached such a tirade against them in 1655 that an angry mob marched to Bengeworth where the Quakers were holding their services, and surrounded the house. The Quakers remained quiet and the crowd eventually dispersed.

From then on, the Friends were arrested, fined heavily, whipped and beaten. All their valuable books were burned in the market place and their possessions were confiscated. They were treated so badly that it reached the ears of Oliver Cromwell who ordered that their property should be returned.

Some Quakers were imprisoned in a dungeon without daylight and without toilet facilities for as long as fourteen weeks. The underground room is thought to have been below a building at the junction of Bridge Street and the High

The Evesham Quaker meeting house in Oat Street

Street, on the High Street side, usually occupied by a shoe shop. The room was about 12 feet square and had one hole nearly 4 inches square through which food was passed. Visitors were locked in with them and had to pay the goaler a fee to be released. Two women asked if they could visit, and merely for asking they were put overnight in the stocks. The weather was freezing and one of them died soon afterwards. When those who had been persecuted returned to normal life, their trades had died out because of their long absence and they suffered from poor health for the rest of their lives. They never recovered.

After the Restoration, Parliament decided to tighten up on dissenters. In 1662, soldiers arrived, rounded up the Quakers and ordered them to appear at Worcester the next day. They were all released except for popular, respectable 60-year-old Richard Walker. The soldiers drove him on foot before the horses, and when he collapsed they dragged him by force. The major beat him and threatened to shoot him. He was taken to Worcester gaol and died soon afterwards.

The Quaker movement survived and played an important part in the development of Worcestershire; for example, they helped to finance the early days of the Worcester Porcelain, and they also paid for some of the Worcestershire railways to be built. The Sheward brothers, who helped to develop the needle industry, were also Quakers.

OLIVER CROMWELL – THE LORD PROTECTOR

This is the only period in English history when England has been a dictatorship.

It was Cromwell's dream that England should be ruled by Parliament, but his dream proved to be impossible to carry out. Members had dwindled to about sixty and, with so many different ideas and sects, agreement on almost any topic was impossible. In 1653, after four years of Parliamentary lethargy, Cromwell's patience ran out when they failed to come up with a working constitution. He jumped up from the back benches, described the assembly as corrupt, fraudulent, unjust and self-seeking, and brought in thirty of his musketeers – who were waiting outside – to clear the chamber. He had no ambition to be king and so he ruled as Lord Protector. Having destroyed the monarchy, Cromwell could find nothing to put in its place.

When Cromwell died in 1658 he was one of the most hated men in English history. His army had put down risings in Scotland, Wales, Ireland and across England with great brutality. His body was buried in Westminster Abbey, but when Charles II came to the throne it was dug up and hung on the gallows at Tyburn. The head was placed on a pole at Westminster Hall. Worcester's hatred of Cromwell persisted for centuries, and when the new Guildhall and was built in the eighteenth century, a strange effigy was placed over the doorway, said to be Cromwell nailed by his ears.

Cromwell's two eldest sons had died from smallpox when teenagers. A third son, Richard, succeeded his father but was unsuited to the post. Heavily in debt, he changed his name to John Clarke and retired first to the Continent and then to Cheshunt in Hertfordshire, where he died.

The authorities decided that they had no alternative but to invite Charles to return to England as king, if he agreed to an amended constitution. He was crowned in 1660.

What a complete and utter waste the years of fighting from 1642 to 1651 had been. The nation had undergone tremendous suffering in a bid to get rid of the monarchy and now it was back again, admittedly with constitutional amendments. They had fought to introduce the policies of the Parliamentarians and these were a disaster. As for the Scots invasion and the Battle of Worcester of 1651, if Charles had simply bided his time in exile he would still have been offered the crown and it would have saved more than 11,000 lives.

The image over the door of the Guildhall, a poor likeness of Oliver Cromwell

The Guildhall, Worcester, is one of the most splendid town halls in England.
It was built between 1721 and 1723, probably by Thomas White

7

POLITICAL HIGHLIGHTS

After Charles II was crowned, a nasty shock awaited him.

One of the reasons that the son of Charles I was offered the throne was the publication of a book known as *The Eikon Basilika*. It was printed a few days after Charles I was executed and widely circulated; there is a copy in the Hurd library at Hartlebury and another in the cathedral library.

The title page reads *The Pourtracture of His Sacred Majestie in his Solitudes and Sufferings*. It was said to be written by Charles I and gives his thoughts during the period leading up to his death. He appears to be a dedicated, conscientious, thoughtful and sensitive character. People in general were horrified by the execution of Charles I and the book created a great deal of sympathy for the

The Hurd library in Hartlebury Castle

Royalist cause, especially as people were suffering under the strict regime of Oliver Cromwell.

However, who should turn up asking to see Charles II but John Gauden, saying that *he* had written the book, not Charles I. Gauden was an educated cleric holding several high posts in the Church and had visited the king while he was in prison. To keep Gauden quiet he was promptly made king's chaplain. The posts of bishop had disappeared under Cromwell, but Charles was able to bring them back again and Gauden was appointed Bishop of Exeter. Gauden did not believe this to be sufficient reward as the living was a poor one, so the king made him Bishop of Worcester. Fortunately for Charles II, Gauden was only in the office for a few months before he died, leaving his widow to pick up the bill for his expenses. Nevertheless, she found the money to pay for a monument in Worcester Cathedral. It graces the wall near the door to the cathedral library.

Once again, Church of England was the official religion. An Act of Uniformity in 1662 insisted that all religious services throughout the land used the latest version of the *Book of Common Prayer* with its revised service. All vicars were to make a declaration that they would use the book, and over 1,000 across England refused. Despite fierce persecution, the number of nonconformists grew until, in 1672, Charles had to admit that the policy of oppression had failed. He issued a Declaration of Indulgence, which not only suspended all penal laws against Protestants and nonconformists, but allowed their buildings to be licensed. At last, they were to exist separately from the Church of England. Licensed in Worcestershire were fifteen Presbyterians, six Congregationalists (that is, Independents), one Baptist and two other nonconformists. Catholics were still penalized, for Parliament insisted that they were to be excluded not only from public office but from all professions.

The worst of the religious controversies had blown over when, in 1678, a fraudulent priest, Titus Oates, arrived in England from Spain. He was born in Rutland in 1649, had been expelled from school, expelled from Cambridge, and imprisoned for perjury. When he was about twenty-eight, he decided to become a Catholic but was expelled from the Jesuit College in Spain. Back in England, he managed to convince those in high places that he had discovered a Roman Catholic plot to kill the king, invade Ireland, and massacre the Protestants. Panic spread throughout the land. All Catholics were to leave London and no Catholic anywhere could travel more than 5 miles without being stopped and questioned. Huge bonfires were made of their books and relics and Catholic priests were hunted down. One such priest was Father Wall who came to Worcestershire, and went to visit a friend. It so happened that the magistrate came to the house to take another man for debt. Father Wall was taken by mistake. The magistrate was suspicious, thought he might be a priest, and asked him to swear the oaths of supremacy and allegiance. He refused and was identified, imprisoned at Worcester, tried and put to death.

For several years Titus was the hero of the nation. He then made the mistake of describing Charles's brother, James, as a traitor and so when James came to the throne he was able to get his own back. Titus was tried, given a heavy fine, whipped through the streets of London and imprisoned for life, although he was released when William and Mary came to the throne. He died poverty-stricken and forgotten in 1705.

The year 1664 was a bad one for Charles. Plague swept through London, followed by the Great Fire. There was war with Holland, which lasted ten years.

Curiously, Charles II converted to Catholicism shortly before he died in 1685. For how long had he nursed Catholic sympathies? He was given the last rites by Father Huddleston, who had hidden him at Boscobel after the Battle of Worcester.

JAMES II AND WILLIAM AND MARY

Charles's brother, James, inherited the throne. He was a Catholic but quite ambivalent; for example, he kept two Protestant mistresses. He visited Worcester in 1687 and upset the mayor and corporation by going to hear Mass at the Roman Catholic chapel. They refused to accompany him further than the door. Catholics began to be appointed to high places.

The reign of James II was not a success and after three years he retired to France, leaving the throne open to Mary, his elder daughter. She had married William of Orange, who had inherited the title from birth as he had been born eight days after his father's death, and from 1672 he had governed the Netherlands as Stadtholder (head of state). It was not a joyous marriage. William was twelve years older than Mary, taciturn, asthmatic and in feeble health. Mary was devoted to religion. There was no heir.

They were both Protestants, but they introduced an Act that they later amended to make the Oath of Allegiance more acceptable to dissenters. However, not only did the Quakers refuse to swear – several churchmen also refused, saying that they were already under oath to James II. One of them was Thomas Morris, a minor canon at the cathedral. As a result, he was never promoted.

He asked to be buried after his death in the cathedral at the foot of the steps that are now just outside the gift shop, saying, 'I have been walked over in life, I will be walked over in death.' He asked for the covering of his coffin to be carried by six girls in white, all with a white rose, and for his gravestone to have only one word on it, 'Miserrimus', meaning 'O miserable one'. The stone slab is still there and is so famous that in 1828 it inspired Wordsworth to write a sonnet that contains the following lines:

> *He marked also for his own*
> *Close to these cloistral steps a burial-place,*
> *That every foot might fall with heavier tread,*
> *Trampling upon his vileness.*

The locals say that under no cicumstances must you step on this stone because you will invoke the ghost of Thomas Morris. One local retired policeman states, 'I joined the police force in Worcester in 1962 and worked that area for two years. If you were new you were put on a quiet beat which included Worcester Cathedral. Some of the old hands had worked the area for twenty-odd years and they made sure that you knew the story of the Miserrimus ghost before you set out on your beat. Then sometimes they would hang a cassock over the door so that as you opened the door this black thing would come floating down on you.' Among those who have seen the Miserrimus ghost was the late Albert Price, who unfortunately passed away in 1995. He was a verger for over fifty years and his relatives say that his favourite party piece was the tale of the night he saw the ghost of Thomas Morris. Then in 1934 a young courting couple were lying under the walls of the cathedral when a monk appeared at a ruined window with such an expression of disapproval that the couple moved on. It was only the next day that the young man discovered that the window was inaccessible.

The Miserrimus door

JOHN WESLEY

In the 1700s a new denomination arrived in Worcestershire. Methodist Wesleyism was founded by John and Charles Wesley who had no desire to start a new sect and always considered themselves to be part of the Church of England. Methodist Wesleyism was only separated from the Church of England four years after John's death in 1791.

John was born in Epworth Rectory in 1703, the fifteenth child, although nine had died in childhood. When he was six years old the rectory burned to the ground and he loved to tell the tale of his dramatic rescue. He went to Charterhouse School, then Christchurch, Oxford, and Lincoln College where he was a fun-loving, lively and not particularly religious student. He became more serious in his early twenties and took holy orders when he was twenty-two. Charles also went to Christchurch where the two brothers established a religious club nicknamed 'the Methodists'. In 1735 both John and Charles went to Georgia (near Atlanta in the Southern States) for three years where they were inspired by the calm faith of the Moravians, an old Lutheran-type sect.

Both John and Charles began preaching in the open air in 1739, first at Bristol, then in London, Yorkshire, and Newcastle-upon-Tyne. They attracted other preachers, and Methodism spread rapidly round the country. John travelled about 5,000 miles a year. When he visited Worcestershire, he was nearly drowned in a flash flood. The Redditch diarist William Avery, writing in 1800, reported, 'On his way from Wednesbury to Evesham, accompanied by Messrs Walsh and Bruce in August 1756, they came to a place which was flooded and Mr Bruce, seeing a footbridge, walked over leading his horse by a long rein through the water. In an instant the horse disappeared. However it soon emerged and gained the bank. Mr Wesley gaining experience from this, found a safer place further down.'

York Street in Stourport-on-Severn is famous as the place to which John Wesley wrote his last letter just before he died. It was addressed to Aaron York, after whom the street is named. John Wesley himself came to Stourport in 1787 when he was attacked by a rough crowd and had to be rescued by Aaron and two of his friends. He preached in a makeshift meeting place at the back of a house in New Street. A year later John Wesley visited Stourport-on-Severn again, this time to open the tiny Methodist chapel in Parkes Passage. The Methodist chapel still has its galleries and contains a wealth of alabaster carvings by Joseph Ward.

The town was chosen to be the head of the Worcestershire Methodist circuit,

Stourport Methodist Church

a great honour. A team of ministers lived in a house in Litchfield Street and every Sunday, no matter what the weather, each minister would walk miles to preach at one of the churches within the circuit. One minister nearly lost his life in snowdrifts up to his neck on the Clee Hills, while another, John Saunders, fell into the canal one dark night. The Reverend John Mantle walked 11 miles through snow to preach at Frith, and when he got there the church members, thinking he could not have made it, had gone home. The church was locked and he had to turn round and walk the 11 miles back.

Methodism made even faster progress after John's death. There's a story about the way in which the Methodists came to be accepted in Redditch. In 1800 a traveller in wire was so appalled by the godlessness of the town that he left a guinea in Birmingham for a preacher to go to Redditch. Services were held in a private house, where, during each service, a mob stood outside, shouting, jeering and banging saucepans and kettles. One Sunday evening, the lady of the house, Mrs Turner, was so determined to bring the interruptions to an end that she grabbed her carving knife, marched into the middle of the crowd, and plunged it into the drum. After that, they were left in peace.

THE BREAD RIOTS

Between 1688, when William and Mary arrived, and 1815, England was involved
in seven great wars. France was Britain's chief opponent. Battles were chiefly
naval, with the French and the English blockading each other's ports. Until the
late eighteenth century, England was able to provide enough grain for the population, but then harvests were poor and with the French cutting off foreign
supplies, the price of bread soared. In 1800 there was a national uprising about the
price of bread. In Redditch and its outlying districts an army of women marched
to the home of the lord of the manor at Hewell Grange near Bromsgrove to
protest, banging anything that would make a noise – kettles with wooden spoons,
saucepans with ladles, and so on. Lord Windsor hastily summoned all the
respectable citizens, swore them in as police constables, and sent them off to quell
the riot. However, when the volunteers saw the army of angry women
approaching, they turned tail and fled, locking themselves in The Fox and Goose,
a public house halfway between Redditch and Bromsgrove. The local poet, Crane,
was one of the volunteers and wrote:

> *A line of stout women, with ladles three deep,*
> *Determined to drive us or send us to sleep.*
> *The leader well-armed with a stout wooden crutch*
> *Ten women to one Bromsgrove man is too much.*

The ringleaders were arrested but discharged after promising to be on good
behaviour in future.

England declared war on France in 1803 and the situation was serious,
Napoleon was marching across Europe and extending the French empire. Both
the 29th and 36th Worcestershire Regiments, later the 1st and 2nd Battalions,
saw a great deal of the fighting. Those who were called up but did not want to
join in the conflict were usually able to pay some young blood to take their place
for a cost ranging between £20 to £40. The Napoleonic Wars ended in 1815 at the
Battle of Waterloo. There were celebrations throughout England, none greater
than in Redditch. William Avery, the diarist, wrote that never before or since was
there such jollity. It was decided to present a 'Miracle Play' entitled 'Napoleon
imprisoned at Elba'. He describes it as follows:

> A young apprentice of the town (who afterwards became one of our most
> respectable manufacturers) having had his face blackened, was dressed as

Napoleon. He was then seated on a cask and escorted by two mounted Cossacks with huge lances in their hands. They were accompanied by the multitude to the coal-hold prison ... For this brilliant exploit the Cossacks had so inflamed their courage with beer that they began, regardless of nationality or other just cause, to use their weapons on the crowds, who were forced to set on and disarm them, and secure them in safe keeping until they had slept off their exuberant patriotism.

THE FRANCHISE

By the early 1800s, the old voting system was in a muddle and so a Reform Act of 1832 made sweeping changes. Those towns that had grown in size, usually because of the Industrial Revolution, were awarded more seats in Parliament while those towns that had grown smaller (known as Rotten Boroughs) had seats taken from them. Voting had previously been the preserve of the wealthy, but now any man owning a household worth £10 or more could vote, adding 217,000 middle-class voters to an electorate of 435,000. About one man in six or seven now had the right to vote.

The population was wildly enthusiastic. There were two main parties – Liberal, known as Whig, and Conservative, known as Tory. Election day was an excuse for a punch-up. Stourport-on-Severn was passionately Whig while Bewdley, although in the same Division, was the home of the Tories; consequently, whenever the results of an election were to be announced, Stourport men would march to Bewdley to hear the election results armed with sticks and bludgeons. The two sides would fight for hours until they were exhausted.

Voting was usually done by raising a hand; therefore it was not in secret and everyone knew who was supporting whom. This led to bribery and corruption. In 1847 the Bewdley Tories paid twelve guineas to screaming women to drown the political speeches of the Whigs, and some Bewdley supporters who would probably have voted Liberal were spirited away by the Tories to Stanford Bridge, entertained with fishing, eating and drinking and kept under surveillance until voting had closed.

In another Act of 1867, the right to vote was extended to include some working-class men, adding a million voters. Bribery and corruption were outlawed, but continued.

In 1869 Sir Richard Glass, the Tory candidate, stayed at Stourport-on-Severn for a few days, during which time he visited a total of thirty-three pubs and supplied everyone with free beer. As many as 100 people were often crammed into these little pubs. Alfred Baldwin (father of Stanley Baldwin, three times Prime Minister) reported Sir Richard Glass for bribery and corruption. It made the national press. The editor of *Berrows Worcester Journal* wrote, 'The *Telegraph* revelled in the subject, the *Birmingham Post* could not conceal its joy and the *Chronicle*, while rejoicing in the result … described Bewdley as a peasant borough where corruption is ingrained.'

It turned out that the Liberal Party was not squeaky clean either. There had been a rally at The Anchor at which over 150 were present and several 10-gallon casks of beer had been brought in and distributed. The election result was annulled.

In Kidderminster, Robert Lowe had been the local MP for some years but, in 1857, was opposed by William Boycott, a local solicitor, who was popular with the carpet weavers.

A wooden platform, the 'hustings', was always built specially for the elections, from which candidates were nominated, election speeches made, polling declared open, and the results announced. Unfortunately, the mayor had decided that the hustings should be built in an open area near to the church, and this was where the broken stones were held for road building. Two polling booths had also been erected.

St Mary's Church, Kidderminster

At 2 p.m. the factories closed and 8,000 carpet weavers poured into the streets. At first they gathered round the polling booths. Voters only managed to get to the booths with police assistance. As soon as the state of the polls began to be revealed, anyone who voted for Lowe was grabbed, spat on, punched and kicked. The mayor had declared the poll open and a procession to support Mr Lowe was just about to set off when the stones began to fly. Some women were holding up the edges of their pinafores to make a basket and filling them with stones.

When Boycott's defeat was announced, the crowd was furious. There were shouts of 'Come out and let us kill the ...' Facing the crowd estimated at 8,000 were thirteen police officers including the special constables. They formed a line in front of the hustings.

The mob continued to throw stones. One of the Conservatives was hit on the head and the blood poured. Robert Lowe himself was hit and his grey hair was red with blood. Lowe and six of his supporters ran along a wall at the back of the church, found an unlocked door, and bolted themselves in. At half-past four the police managed to whisk Mr Lowe and the mayor away.

Police constable Jukes was carried into a house unconscious. He had been cut all over his body. His nasal bone was fractured and his skull lacerated. At 5 p.m. the mayor telegraphed Birmingham for assistance. A troop of the 10th Hussars arrived on horseback at 11.50 p.m., formed up in the yard of the Lion Hotel, and the mayor read the Riot Act. The hussars policed the streets until 4 a.m.

The surgeon announced that Jukes was in an unsatisfactory condition. A local antiquarian, Ebenezer Guest, says that he died a few days later. Among the ringleaders were John Hayes, John Cook, James Tranter and James Slater who were fined 30 shillings each. It was proposed that the reserve force of eight officers at Worcester should be increased.

Women were not granted voting rights until the end of the First World War, and then it was only awarded to women over the age of thirty. Even after the Reform Acts of 1832 and 1867, most of the working classes were not able to vote because they could not afford the required property. This was one of the factors leading to the Chartist Movement.

THE CHARTISTS

On the northern tip of Bromsgrove, the M42 joins the M5. To the west of this junction is Dodford village, now a conservation area, and originally a settlement of thirty-nine red-brick bungalows and two houses set in spacious gardens.

This is a Chartist village, of which there are only about six in the whole of

Chartist cottage at Dodford, near Bromsgrove. Of the 39 cottages,
this is the only one that has not been developed

the British Isles. Behind the movement lies a sad and dramatic story of how one man's struggle to better the life of the poor came to a bitter end.

Disgusted by the feeble electoral reforms of the 1832 Act and the way in which the ordinary working man was still not able to vote, the London Men's Working Association produced 'The People's Charter', with six basic demands. These were abolition of the property qualification for MPs, payment for MPs, vote by ballot (that is, a secret vote instead of a public one), the right to vote for all men, equal electoral districts and annual Parliaments. Representatives travelled up and down the country getting signatures. Finally, in 1838, the petitions with their millions of signatures were presented to Parliament with great ceremony. However, they were ignored, but were presented again in 1842. Again they were ignored.

The Association had a radical section, the head of which was the red-headed Feargus O'Connor. He was born in Ireland in 1796, trained as a lawyer, and became editor of the *Northern Star* newspaper through which he made his views known. He was appalled by the plight of the workers who toiled for long hours in terrible circumstances for a pittance, such as the nailers of Bromsgrove. He came up with an idea to improve the life of the working man. He proposed, in 1845, to found a company with a capital of £5,000 raised by 2,000 workers buying shares. This would enable the company to buy 120 acres of land on which to build. Further income could be realized in various ways. The working man would be independent and own a property of sufficient value to enable him to vote. Not all the houses could be built at once, though, so names for the next available house would be pulled out of a hat.

The scheme caught the public imagination. The first thirty-five settlers moved into their cottages in 1847. O'Connor was elected MP for Nottingham.

People rushed to buy shares and money poured in. Some 60,000 workers held 180,000 shares. Three more villages were built, then the one at Dodford.

Money was raised from a nationwide raffle. Thousands of tickets were sold and the prize was a tea-tray. This was won by someone in Scotland. Perhaps there's an ancient cottage in Scotland where an old tea-tray sits under the aspidistra and no one is aware of its historical value!

But there were innumerable problems. The company's legal status was uncertain, and consequently that of the tenant as well. Tenants who had never seen a cow were taken from an industrial background to manage a small-holding. When they did manage to produce a crop, they couldn't find the markets. Some of the tenants at Dodford were quite enterprising – they grew strawberries and made jam for markets at Bromsgrove and Birmingham, while wives and daughters started making bonnets. Even so, some of the Dodford families decided that life as a nailer was preferable to life on the land and left to return to nailing.

Money melted away. Assets were £7,000, but there were debts to the Land Bank of £6,800 and O'Connor personally was owed £3,000. Total subscriptions amounted to £91,000. Some £35,000 had been spent on buying land, £50,000 on forming and building estates, and £4,000 on management expenses. O'Connor was accused of stealing the money, so a Parliamentary Barrister arrived to check Dodford's accounts. He announced that not only could O'Connor account for every penny, he had put a lot of his own money into the scheme.

The plan was said to be unworkable. The number of subscribers was 70,000 and the cost per allotment £300; therefore £21 million was needed to provide everyone with a house and an allotment. A committee told the House of Commons that the company was illegal and should be wound up.

Everyone seemed to turn against O'Connor. MPs pointed out that the scheme was never authorized by them, and subscribers were terrified of losing their precious savings. Rival newspapers were only too happy to attack him. Even his staff were anxious to separate themselves from him, and the London Working Men's Association said that he was a bad example.

Despite everything, building continued at Dodford. Then in 1851 the whole scheme was wound up and closed down.

O'Connor had begun drinking heavily for some time. His behaviour became increasingly irrational, possibly as a result of syphilis. In 1852, he was declared insane and sent to an asylum in Chiswick. In 1854 he began to have epileptic fits. The following year his sister took him to her home to nurse him for the last few months of his life. He died on 30 August 1855.

He was buried in Kensal Green, a couple of miles south of Willesden in London. Large crowds followed his coffin to its final resting place. On his tombstone is engraved:

Reader, pause,
thou treadest on
the grave of a patriot.
While philanthropy
is a virtue, and
patriotism not a crime,
will the name of
O'CONNOR
be admired
and this
monument respected.

8

ENTERPRISE AND INDUSTRY

❧ *Worcestershire's rural produce* ❧

Worcestershire is predominantly a rural county. During the civil wars of 1642–51, a soldier wrote home to his family telling them about the wonderful county of Worcestershire, where you could pick apples and pears freely from the trees. Four and a half centuries later, south Worcestershire is still well known for its fruit. Within a radius of 10 miles of Pershore are 15,000 acres dedicated to fruit growing. The plums have 9,000 acres, the apples 3,000, and the strawberries

A busy farmer's market in Pershore

Large-scale crop production at Offenham in the Evesham valley

2,000. Other fruit and vegetables from the Evesham plain include peas, asparagus, cabbage, tomatoes and lettuce.

Pershore is so proud of its plums that in August each year it holds a month-long Plum Festival. Especially famous is a yellow jam-making plum, the Pershore Yellow Egg Plum, which was saved from extinction in 1871 when George Crooks, licensee of The Butcher's Arms in Church Street, discovered a seedling in nearby Tiddesley Wood and, out of curiosity, took it home.

HOPS AND HOP-PICKING

For hundreds of years, Worcestershire was famous for its hops. Round about the mid-1500s, hops began to be used in beer-making for flavouring and as a preservative. The distinctive conical chimneys of the oast houses, where the hops were dried, were a common sight. West Worcestershire and Herefordshire were especially suitable for the growing of hops, with their rich soil.

The hop-picking season ran from about the middle of August until the end of September. The hops needed to be picked by hand, and thousands – perhaps

*Walsgrave Mill, one of the few remaining oast houses in the Teme valley.
Most of them have been converted into dwellings*

Hops growing in the Teme valley. This was once a common sight but is now much reduced

millions – of mainly women and children travelled from Birmingham and the Black Country to the areas around Pershore, Worcester and the Herefordshire borders for a free holiday in the country, lots of camaraderie and some pocket money. Farmers sent wagons into the towns to pick up hop-pickers, or chartered a special Sunday train service that could bring in 2,000 pickers in one day.

The industry began to decline in about 1934, when hop-picking machines began to be introduced, together with other factors such as cheap imports. Most of the great hop fields have now been ploughed into the ground, although the Teme Valley still has some hopyards.

THE MISTLETOE MARKET

Mistletoe mainly grows in four counties: Worcestershire, Herefordshire, Gloucestershire and Somerset. This is a parasitic plant, growing on old trees, particularly apple trees, and the old orchards in the extreme west of the county provide a plentiful supply of hosts. Because it remains green in winter, it has been associated with fertility rites. The Druids apparently worshipped it and

Tenbury Wells

thought it had healing and magical powers. The custom of kissing under the mistletoe is thought to go back to Norse myths. For every kiss, a berry should be plucked, then when all the berries have gone the kissing stops.

For over 100 years, in late November and early December, farmers have brought their mistletoe to the cattle market in Tenbury Wells, to be auctioned. The town is said to be the mistletoe capital of the world.

In 2003–4 the old cattle market was closed, but auctions still go ahead at a venue outside the town. In order to continue the old tradition, the town now stages a Mistletoe Festival within the town itself. National Mistletoe Day was endorsed by Parliament in 2005 and takes place on 1 December (or the nearest Saturday) every year.

BEWDLEY AND THE WOOL TRADE

Worcestershire wool was of exceptionally good quality (see Chapters 3 and 5) and was developed in some towns to provide a specialized product.

From the time of Queen Elizabeth to the end of the reign of Charles II, cap-making was Bewdley's most important trade and is said to have given employment to 1,000 people. The caps had seamless stocking stitch throughout, with flat double brim and were knitted in coarse, thick, two-ply wool. The cap industry was heavily regulated. An Act of Parliament fixed the price in 1488 and heavy fines were imposed on anyone wearing a cap from overseas. Later, in Queen Elizabeth's reign, an Act of Parliament decreed that Bewdley caps had to be worn and those not wearing one were fined 3s 4d!

By 1667, the trade had declined and by the mid-1800s it had disappeared altogether.

KIDDERMINSTER AND THE WOOL TRADE

Kidderminster's woollen industry developed into the manufacture of carpets. The waters of the River Stour are said to contain Fuller's earth and iron, which produces long-lasting and particularly bright dyes. The manufacture of cloth in Kidderminster was first mentioned in 1235 when the townsfolk were making a variety of cloths, but particularly a coarse cloth known as Kersey. In 1533, during the reign of Henry VIII, an Act was passed limiting the making of cloth to certain towns and Kidderminster was one of those chosen.

Preserved in Avoncroft Museum of Historic Buildings is the 1853 Counting House from Bromsgove cattle market where money was handled for the buying and selling of sheep and cattle

The most popular colours were blue from woad, yellow from weld, and red from the root of the madder plant. Dyeing was best done outdoors – stale urine was used to fix the dye. The dyers balanced on tiny platforms over the River Stour and swirled the fabric round with a long stick.

The manufacture of cloth was originally a cottage industry. A weaver needed to have four looms on the go at once to make a living. The whole family were involved – wives and daughters wound the bobbins, and children from the age of eight were employed to draw the bobbin across or for various menial tasks. The masters bought the raw wool and collected the finished product from the weavers; consequently the masters became rich while the weavers worked long hours for a pittance, creating a great deal of unrest.

In 1677 there were 150 master cloth weavers controlling 400 looms. Eight years later, the cloth trade in England had a stroke of luck. Louis XIV encouraged the persecution of the Huguenots who were skilful weavers and many fled to England. As a result, the quality and variety of cloths improved.

In 1817, England was hit by a great tragedy. Princess Charlotte, the only child of George IV and Caroline of Brunswick, died in childbirth, together with her baby. Two clothing companies knew immediately that there was going to be a great demand for the black cloth known as bombazine, and so that night buyers from two London companies rushed to Kidderminster in the hope of acquiring all the stocks before George Talbot Senior, a bombazine cloth manufacturer in Mill Street, heard the news. Although the two tradesmen hammered on his door, George refused to get out of bed until the morning. By that time, he realized that there was some special reason why the two men wanted so much bombazine and refused to sell until they had told him the news. Old George made a small fortune that day.

As far back as the sixteenth century, Kidderminster was famous for a coarse, wool-based cloth, known simply as 'Kidderminster Stuff', used where a heavy cloth was an advantage, such as for wall hangings, blankets and shawls. The looms to weave this type of cloth were heavy and expensive, so they were often brought together in a loom shop or a carpet hall. One of these halls was managed by John Pearsall and John Broome and in 1735 they adapted the 'Stuff' so that the pattern appeared on both sides. The Kidderminster carpet was born. Over the next few years other carpet manufacturers learned how to make Kidderminster carpets and so John Broome needed to find a new development.

He was by then middle-aged, but he had heard about a new type of looped-pile carpet being made at Brussels, so he decided to go there to learn the secret of its manufacture. He journeyed on to Tournay, where he found a weaver who was willing to accompany him back to Kidderminster. Broome smuggled the Belgian into an upstairs room in the Park Butts area and, in 1749, in great secrecy, they built a new type of loom for Brussels carpets. News of this wonderful new type of carpet spread through the town. The tale is told that Broom and the Belgian worked at night by candlelight, and that a local carpet master paid a workman to climb up to the window at night to see how the carpet was produced. Once the secret was out, the manufacture of Brussels carpet was copied by a number of companies. The trade expanded so much that in 1753, Lord Foley, living in Witley Court, laid out new streets and built 200 new houses. By 1800, there were over 1,000 looms of that type in Kidderminster. The population rose from about 3,000 in 1700 to about 8,000 in 1811 and an enormous 17,000 in 1851!

The carpet halls were terrible places. Windows were small and the only lighting was by candles standing near piles of wool. The stench was overpowering from the dyes and the urine bins. Children worked in this environment from the age of eight. The government had made an attempt to improve the conditions of children in factories. The first Factory Act had been passed in 1802, stating that children were not allowed to work more than twelve hours a day and not later than 9 p.m., and that they were to be taught the three Rs during work time. Unfortunately, there was no official body to enforce the Act and it was not until 1833 that factory inspectors were appointed.

Brintons Carpets no longer use their old factory. It has now been redeveloped

In 1828, the carpet masters of Kidderminster were losing trade to the weavers in the north of England who were on lower pay. On Saturday, 15 March, posters were put up around the town saying that payment for 1 yard of Brussels was reduced from one shilling to ten pence. Two thousand angry weavers marched through the town. On the first Monday one weaver went into work. He was stoned and his home was attacked with stones and manure.

The Reverend Humphrey Price was a vicar at a church near Litchfield, but he had been born in Kidderminster and had a great sympathy for the weavers. He took part in the strike, distributing inflammatory leaflets. One of his poems was about a carpet master who proposed to build a sumptuous house and paint the door vermilion. John Broome, the son of the original John Broome, had a vermilion front door to his house. Broome took him to court for libel.

Two months later, the weavers were still on strike and many of them were starving. Then the masters offered thirty shillings to every married weaver who returned to work and twenty shillings to unmarried weavers. To a starving community, this was an offer they could not turn down. They returned to work on 16 August. Their strike had achieved nothing. As for Humphrey Price, he was arrested and sent to prison for a year.

The carpet manufacturing business in Kidderminster never fully recovered.

Other towns had taken the opportunity of a brief gap in the market to set up their own carpet factories. A carpet mill was built in Bewdley and other mills at Stourport-on-Severn. Some of these developed into huge concerns; for example, the Bond Worth factory employed 1,500 in 1935. Some Kidderminster carpet factories went bankrupt, among them the mill belonging to John Broome with the vermilion door.

Ten years after the strike there were about 2,000 looms in the town, most of which were lent by the manufacturers to outworkers. Three-quarters of these were used for Brussels carpets. The looms were heavy and complicated and had to be operated manually by strong men. The answer was steam power, but it was expensive to install.

William Grosvenor was elected Mayor of Kidderminster in 1851, and his civic duties brought him into contact with the very wealthy Lord Ward (later the Earl of Dudley) who had bought Witley Court. The mayor persuaded Lord Ward to invest £20,000 in building one of the first steam-powered carpet factories in the town, known as the Stour Vale Mill Company. Weavers could rent one of the nine sections of the shed and connect to a common lane shafting powered by a 35 hp steam engine. Some of those renting a unit became large manufacturers – for example, William Green, who built New Road Mill. Other steam mills followed.

Unfortunately, the new machinery gave rise to severe unemployment. One steam-powered loom could do the work of several men and, even worse, as the heavy work was now done by steam power, the machines could be operated by women. Disagreements between the weavers and the carpet masters came to a head when 2,000 angry workers massed outside the factory gates of Long Meadow Mills, throwing stones and other missiles. The Dragoon Guards and the Birmingham police were called out. The vicar of St Mary's and the mayor asked the MP for Kidderminster to sort out a compromise and peace was restored.

Kidderminster carpet companies were at the height of their prosperity in the 1950s and 1960s but they were unable to compete against foreign manufacturers and were forced to close. One of the few to survive is Brintons which was founded in 1783 and is still exporting carpets across the world.

––––––––––––––––––

THE TANNERIES

Hand in hand with the development of the wool trade went expertise in tanning. In Medieval times, every village had its tannery, supplying leather for anything from horse harnesses to bellows for furnaces and belts for water-powered machines. As two essential ingredients in those early days were urine and sometimes dog faeces, the tanneries were usually on the edge of the town.

At Tenbury Wells 'Tannery Court' marks the site of an old tannery. Tanner's Hill and Bark Lane in Bewdley show that the town was once famous for its leather. The Bewdley leather workers were prosperous enough to found a chantry in Bewdley chapel and, in 1591, the tanners gave the land for a school and enough money to maintain it. In Worcester, a huge tannery in Hylton Road overlooked the Severn.

The tannery at Stourport-on-Severn claimed to be the largest outside London. It was built in 1702 and eventually stretched across both sides of Lombard Street, backing on to the canal where the company had a wharf. A huge tannery chimney was built in 1831 by Thomas Ward and remained a local landmark for years. It was 203 feet tall and twenty-five workmen could sit around the top. From the canal side of the building, you would have seen men patiently pushing the hides down into pits with their long poles. Wagons would arrive bringing great loads of bark from Ribbesford woods to be piled into giant ricks. Stripping bark was considered to be a woman's job.

In about 1860, the tannery was completely burned down. No one ever found out how the fire started. At that time it was owned by the Rogers brothers and when Joseph Rogers saw the flames, 'he was speechless'. A splendid new factory was built, but after the rebuilding Mr Rogers seemed to lose interest and the tannery went into liquidation. It was sold at a quarter of its value to Mr Beakbane (a Celtic name meaning worker in bone and leather). He failed to make it profitable and the tannery closed in 1901. Then in 1908 Mr Beakbane's son returned from America, having learned new methods of tanning. The old tannery was modernized and the chimney stack demolished. In the 1920s they began to supply fine sheepskin leather to the Worcester glove trade.

Disaster struck again in the 1960s when there was another terrible fire. The business moved to Kidderminster.

Worcestershire is still known for its fine leather products. Two Worcester companies, Fownes and Dents, are still making top-quality gloves. Fownes' old factory was built in 1884 and is now a hotel on the eastern side of City Walls Road. Dents was founded in 1777 by John Dent, followed by his two sons, John and William, who continued to expand the company with a healthy export trade to Europe, North America, Asia and Australia. The family became rich enough to buy the run-down Sudeley Castle in the Cotswolds where it was chiefly John's wife, Emma, who restored the property.

THE SPA TOWNS

Malvern Spa

Dr John Wall was a brilliant artist and scientist who was responsible for the founding of both Worcester Porcelain and Malvern as a spa town. He was born in Powick, near Worcester, in 1708 and was the son of a former mayor. His wife was a relative of Lord Sandys. He lived at 43 Foregate Street, later occupied by Sir Charles Hastings, the founder of the British Medical Association. Dr Wall went to King's School, then Oxford, where he qualified as a doctor in 1738.

Dr Wall was a great philanthropist and it was his ambition to build a charitable infirmary in Worcester for the benefit of the poor and for medical research. He was joined by Bishop Maddox and, between them, they raised enough money to purchase an old house in Silver Street and convert it into an infirmary. It opened in January 1746, but they were not able to purchase any beds until June, then only five, and they had to wait until the end of the year for the surgeon's instruments!

The infirmary needed to expand and so, in 1765, 2 acres were bought on the Butts site in the centre of the town. The new infirmary was completed five years later. Over the next two centuries, more and more buildings were added until it became the largest hospital in the county.

It has now been replaced by the Worcester Royal Hospital on the eastern edge of the town, which opened in 2002. Most of the old infirmary was pulled down in 2005 and replaced by university buildings, but the original infirmary has been preserved as part of the campus.

Dr Wall was intrigued by the cures attributed to Malvern waters. Since Medieval times, the springs and spouts had been claimed to cure a number of diseases, especially those of the eye. In 1622 Richard Banister had written *Breviary of One Hundred and Thirteen Diseases of the Eyes and Eyelids*, recommending the Malvern waters. Dr Wall analysed the water and found it was exceptional for its purity. The waters are from underground springs and are uncontaminated. In 1756 he wrote *Experiments and Observations on the Malvern Water* in which he described seventy-nine case histories of water cures. The book was reprinted many times. One wit wrote:

Malvern water, says Dr John Wall
Is famous for containing just nothing at all.

St Anne's Well has had a reputation for curing eye diseases since Medieval times

Over 100 springs and wells have now been traced in the Malvern Hills, the best known being Saint Anne's, which was once a holy well, visited by pilgrims and cared for by the monks of Malvern Priory. Its waters were bottled between the 1620s and the 1980s. Dr Wall's workers took them to use at the infirmary.

When Queen Anne 'took the waters' at Bath in 1702, bathing and drinking natural waters had become very fashionable. Dr Wall laid the foundations for Malvern to become a spa town. Before he died in 1776, he had enlarged the Priory's Abbey House and built The Crown Hotel. A guide for visitors was drawn up in 1796 and the Pump Room and Baths were built between 1819 and 1823.

Then, in 1842, the hydropathic (water cure) doctors, Dr James Wilson and Dr James Gully, arrived. There were many hydrotherapy clinics in Malvern, but Wilson and Gully were the two most famous (and wealthy) practitioners. In 1845 they built the exclusive Priessnitz Hotel at a cost of £18,000, named after the Czech who invented hydrotherapy. The following year Gully wrote his famous book, *The Water Cure in Chronic Disease*. Gully was an excellent speaker and became an international figure, travelling to America to set up clinics there. They were bitterly opposed by various medical men, including Sir Charles Hastings.

Wilson and Gully's therapy aimed at stimulating the circulation and driving out toxins from the body. Their patients were woken at 5 a.m., undressed, wrapped in wet sheets, and then blankets. After an hour they were unwrapped and buckets of water were thrown at them. This was followed by a 5-mile walk sustained by bottled water from the wells. Then back home to a breakfast of dry biscuits and more water. For entertainment during the day, the patient could select from a range of baths. Dinner was always boiled mutton and fish, followed by a few hours in bed – but this time in a dry one.

Amazingly, it brought the rich and famous to Malvern. Among their patients were Queen Victoria, Prime Minister William Gladstone, author Charles Dickens, famous nurse Florence Nightingale, Prime Minister Benjamin Disraeli, novelist George Eliot, art critic John Ruskin, and the poet Alfred Lord Tennyson.

Dr Gully was at Edinburgh University at the same time as Charles Darwin, famous for his then radical theory of evolution. Darwin suffered from nervous dyspepsia which improved under Dr Gully. Darwin had a ten-year-old daughter, Annie, who suffered from indigestion. Darwin took Annie to see Gully on 24 March 1851, and left her in his care. However, she died on 23 April. The death certificate reads 'Bilious fever with typhoid character'. She was buried in Malvern Priory.

Twenty years later, when he was sixty-four and married with a family, Dr Gully fell madly in love with one of his young patients, Florence Ricardo, whose husband had died in mysterious circumstances, leaving her a large fortune. In 1873 Dr Gully and Florence travelled together to Germany; Florence became pregnant and Gully performed an abortion. They separated, and Gully returned to London. Two years later Gully received a letter from a friend telling him that Florence had married. He tore the letter to shreds in a rage and went to see her in London. Only about four months into the marriage, in 1876, Florence's husband died from antimony poisoning. The antimony was traced back to Malvern, so that Dr Gully became a suspect but was later cleared. The culprit was never found. Two years later Florence died from alcohol poisoning.

Droitwich Spa

The spires of the palatial Louis XIV-style Chateau Impney are a well-known landmark in Droitwich. Built in 1875, this was the home of John Corbett, known as 'the salt king'. He married an Irish girl whom he met at a French finishing school, and perhaps it was to please his wife that he built the Chateau.

He was born at Brierley Hill in 1817 where his father owned the local boatyard. Corbett could trace his ancestors back to Norman times and the family emblem was a raven, hence The Raven Hotel and its symbols. Corbett joined his father's business, but by the 1850s canalboat owners were finding it difficult to compete with the railways, and so the company was sold. With his share of the

Courtesy of Chateau Impney

Chateau Impney

The sculptures of salt workers in Victoria Square, Droitwich, were cast in bronze by John McKenna and erected in 1998

money, Corbett acquired, in 1851, some bankrupt salt works in Stoke Prior near Droitwich. He used the latest highly efficient means of extracting the salt and the works expanded to an enormous extent. He even bought two locomotives and 400 wagons to help in transporting the salt.

The salt industry was beginning to decline in Droitwich in the mid-1800s, partly because people were now buying their salt from Stoke Prior, which was purer and cheaper. John Corbett turned his entrepreneurial genius on Droitwich by developing it as a spa town.

Immersion in warm salt water had long been recommended by doctors for a variety of ailments, especially for rheumatism and arthritis, and brine baths had been built in Droitwich in

1836. They were sold to Corbett who opened a second baths in about 1891, known as St Andrew's baths, containing a swimming pool and nine private bathrooms, each with their own bath. Their popularity led to the number of private bathrooms being increased to forty-eight. In 1933, two additional storeys were added for X-ray machines, electro-medical equipment and a gymnasium. In addition to the public brine baths and a remedial pool for hydrotherapy, there was an aeration bath (presumably some kind of jacuzzi), and a douche room. Guests could choose from first- or second-class facilities.

Comfortable hotels were needed, so Corbett built The Salter's Hall and a number of hotels including The Raven, The Worcestershire and The Royal Hotel. He also paid for the rebuilding of Droitwich railway station.

Corbett was a philanthropic employer. He created a model village for his employees at Stoke Works including Mission Church schoolrooms and he endowed both Bromsgrove and Stourbridge cottage hospitals. He also funded the Corbett Hospital in Stourbridge and made numerous other gifts far and wide, including the rebuilding of the church at Stoke Prior. He did much to improve the working and living conditions for his employees as testified by a stained glass window in St Michael's Church, Stoke Prior, paid for by local folk.

The Droitwich Spa Heritage and Information Centre now stands on the site of Corbett's Brine Baths, although the present black and white building, known as St Richard's House, only goes back to the 1930s. New brine baths, opened in 1985, were built near the Square, but have now closed.

The Droitwich Spa Heritage and Information Centre

As for the salt industry, by 1912 only one mine was operating and the industry came to an end in about 1922. A salt mine has been preserved in Vines Park, and on view in Gurneys Lane are the base of the chimney and part of the pipework of the last remaining pumping station.

Tenbury Wells and the wells

It was not until 1839 that Tenbury discovered that the town lay on a bed of natural mineral water. The local lord of the manor, Septimus Godson at Tenbury Court, was not happy with his drinking water and decided to bore a deeper well. Imagine his surprise when he discovered that he was drinking delicious-tasting water with an unusual flavour. The local vicar sent the water off for testing and discovered that it contained iodine, and therefore had healing properties. Drinking the water was reputed to cure liver diseases, scurvy and glandular swellings, while bathing in them relieved gout and rheumatism.

A spa specialist was called in, Dr Granville. He had visited spas across England and Germany and written books about them. He recommended that the town be developed into a first-class spa with pump rooms, promenades, hotels and lodging houses. The result was that a small red-brick bathing house was

The fairy-like pumphouse at Tenbury Wells

built by the Court. It had two baths, one for each sex, and consultation rooms where patients could discuss their ailments with a doctor. After bathing or drinking the water, folk could wander round the grounds of the Court, accompanied by the music of a small band. The baths failed to draw the crowds and were closed in 1855.

In 1861 the railway came to Tenbury. The town officials thought that this was the time to restore the baths. The Tenbury Wells Improvement Company decided that the town should attract the working classes, with lodging houses rather than hotels. They found a new site and put out tenders for an architect to design new pump rooms. They chose a local architect, James Cranston, who had already designed the renovations for the church at Shelsley Beauchamp and several buildings in Tenbury.

The new pump rooms were the first prefabricated building in the county. The wrought iron plates and clips were made in Birmingham and erected on site. In spite of the fact that Cranston was inspired by the design of a greenhouse, the final design was attractive and unique. A large boarding house and hotel were built next to it and another hotel and a boarding house nearby were extended to take more visitors. Town officials decided to add 'Wells' to the Tenbury and renamed themselves 'Tenbury Wells'.

Unfortunately, the flood of visitors never came. The working classes didn't have the money for such luxuries. The pump rooms gradually went into decline. By 1986 they were in a very poor state and so Leominster District Council purchased them, and restored the exterior to its original condition. Thirteen years later a thorough renovation began with well-deserved grants from various sources. The pump rooms are still standing and have proved to be a popular background for wedding photos.

❧ *Worcestershire and iron-making* ❦

When looking at the development of industry in Worcestershire, it should be remembered that the north of the county was in the Black Country. Until a series of Acts passed in the early 1900s, Dudley, Halesowen, Stourbridge, Kings Norton, Northfield and Yardley were all in Worcestershire. The glass-making town of Stourbridge was once in this county, so was Herbert Austin when he built his first cars at Longbridge. Dud Dudley, who lived at the foot of Dudley Castle and was the illegitimate son of Lord Dudley, was a Worcestershire man. He was one of the first to discover that coal could be used for smelting iron (see Chapter 6).

People tend to think that early iron-working was only carried out in the north of Worcestershire, but this is not so. Iron forging was also carried out by itinerant charcoal-burning forges working across Malvern Chase and the Feckenham and Wyre Forests. During the second century AD, a major iron-smelting industry developed in Worcester (see Chapter 1).

A tutorial by the blacksmith at Avoncroft Museum of Historic Buildings

Courtesy of Avoncroft Museum of Historic Buildings

ANDREW YARRANTON

We first met the enterprising Andrew Yarranton in Chapter 1 when, during the time of the Civil War, he noticed the large quantity of iron slag left in Worcester city and he obtained a licence to transport it to his iron furnace at Astley. An enormous furnace was discovered near Sharpley Pool close to Glazen in 1924, which is almost certainly Yarranton's furnace. In use between 1653 and 1668, it was a new type of blast furnace with a round hearth and has now been preserved as a Scheduled Ancient Monument.

Yarranton began his career by running away from his apprenticeship with a draper and ended it in 1684 in a London brawl, when he was reported to have been beaten and thrown in a tub of water. According to Gordon Lovett's history of Astley, Andrew Yarranton made enemies easily, tortured his opponents, bribed where necessary, and was involved in many a fight. He fought in the Parliamentary army and rose to the rank of captain.

Nevertheless, his achievements were enormous. He introduced the art of tin plating which he learned in Saxony; he wrote a series of knowledgeable books on a variety of subjects and, most astonishing of all, he claimed to have made the River Stour navigable from Stourbridge to Kidderminster. In Nash's *History of Worcester* there is a quotation from Yarranton who writes: 'I ... made it completely navigable from Stourbridge to Kederminster, and carried down many hundred tuns of coales, and laid out near one thousand pounds, and there it was obstructed for want of money, which by contract was to be paid.' Heavy flooding destroyed the canal in 1670, but the remains of three of his locks can still be seen on Dick Brook.

THE FOLEYS

From the mid-1600s to about 1820, the Foleys were one of the richest and most influential families in Worcestershire.

Their good fortune began with Richard Foley who was born in Dudley in 1580, the son of a humble nail-maker. Not only was Richard expert in nail-making, he was also a first-class violinist and he earned a second income by busking in the local hostelries. In the 1600s, the nailers could not split rods to the size required for nails and were having to forge the nails out of a piece of iron which made the labour heavy and the nails costly. The Swedes had discovered the secret and were therefore able to make nails much more cheaply. An iron-master by the name of Brindley lived at Hyde in Kinver and it is said that he suggested to young Foley that he went to Sweden, ostensibly as a fiddler but secretly to try to find out the secret of rod-splitting. After three years Foley returned and Brindley made a machine to his instructions, but it didn't work – to the amusement of the iron-workers. Foley returned to Sweden, where the Swedish nail-makers were so delighted to see their fiddler back again that they locked him in the machine house at night so that he wouldn't escape. There he was able to sit and draw the machines.

After two years he returned to England. His wife had died so he married Brindley's daughter. The machine was a success; he went into partnership with Brindley and, between them, they revolutionized the trade in England, making a small fortune in the process. Whether or not the story is true, Richard Foley set up one of the first slitting mills in Stourbridge in 1628.

There is always someone who profits from a war, and during the Civil War of 1642–51 Brindley and Foley became even richer by supplying cannons, cannonballs and other armaments. By the time Richard Foley died in 1657, he had furnaces across the whole of Worcestershire. In the Stour valley alone he had nineteen furnaces, together with a large warehouse at Bewdley.

Courtesy of English Heritage

Witley Court. The Foleys built the central core then the Dudley family enlarged the house and converted it into a palace fit for kings

His second son, Thomas, married a rich heiress and bought the Great Witley estate, rebuilding Witley Court. Richard's third son was High Sheriff of Worcestershire, a grandson was Speaker of the House of Commons, while another was Bishop of Ireland. The family was prominent politically, but it was not until 1712 that a descendant was elevated to the peerage to become Baron Foley of Kidderminster.

The seventh Lord Foley was fat, lazy and a compulsive gambler. The press nicknamed him 'Lord Balloon'. He gambled away the entire family fortune so that in 1827 his grandson was forced to sell Witley Court to the wealthy Dudley family.

THE IRONWORKS AND THE PRIME MINISTER

A Shropshire ironmaster, Thomas Baldwin, arrived at Stourport-on-Severn in about 1791 to work at a mill in the centre of the town. At that time there were about thirty water-powered ironworks along the River Stour, slitting (cutting) mills, forges and wire mills. Thomas Baldwin specialized in good-quality cast iron hinges. He purchased the mill in which he worked in about 1814 and expanded so much that his factory filled the site now occupied by the public library, fire station, police station and medical centre. The mills and factory were the main source of employment in Stourport-on-Severn for five generations.

The factory made a huge range of products, from plates and saucepans to hand grenades, during the First World War. In 1879 Baldwin & Son bought patents for enamelled steel hollow-ware, a secret process that had been invented in America; this was only the fourth factory in the world to process it. The factory became known as the Anglo American Tin Stamping Company, later Anglo-Enamelware Ltd.

The Baldwins bought and developed an ancient foundry on a steep embankment at Wilden where the River Stour flowed under the works. In 1879 Thomas's grandson, Alfred Baldwin, after working at Wilden for many years, moved from Bewdley into Wilden House opposite the site, and took over the running of the works. The company employed somewhere between forty and fifty men, and each year produced 75,000 boxes of tin plate and iron sheet. Alfred Baldwin's only son, Stanley, born in 1867, became Conservative Prime Minister three times – in 1923, 1924 and again in 1935. He led Britain between the wars, and one of the crises he was forced to face was that of the marriage of Edward VIII to Mrs Wallis Simpson. In one of his speeches he spoke of his factory:

It was a place where I had known from childhood every man on the ground, where I was able to talk to men, not only about troubles in the work, but troubles at home, where strikes and lock-outs were unknown, and where fathers and grandfathers of the men had worked and their sons automatically went into the business. It was also a place where nobody ever got the sack, and where we had a natural sympathy for those who were less concerned with efficiency than this generation is. There were a large number of old gentlemen who used to spend the day sitting on the handle of a wheelbarrow and smoking their pipes. Oddly enough, it was not an inefficient community. It was the last survivor of that type of works, and ultimately was swallowed up in one of those great combinations to which the industries of the country are tending.

Both factories closed their doors in the 1950s.

THE METAL BOX COMPANY

The Victoria Institute in Foregate Street

In about 1855, an expert in the tin plating business, William Blizard Williamson, decided to leave Wolverhampton and try his luck at founding a new company in Worcester. He arrived with his wife and family and a few craftsmen. His first enterprise was in Lowesmoor where he had a shop with living accommodation. The first part of his factory was built in 1858 in Charles Street, and known as 'Providence Works'. He specialized in 'japanned' products, decorated by hand. The process was complicated and a single coal vase would take about four days to complete and sell for £2. The cleaning, varnishing and polishing were done by women, but highly skilled men carried out the artwork. These early products, especially those made before 1920, are now collectors' items.

In about 1868 the Metal Box Company began making canisters for soups and biscuits. Ten years later Williamson died, but fortunately he was followed by two very able sons, William and George.

William and George were both involved in local politics; William became mayor in 1883 and George in 1894. George was the driving force behind many new developments in Worcester. He promoted the building of the Victoria Institute in Foregate Street, which is still there in all its Victorian magnificence. He was responsible for promoting the building of Diglis Lock, which brought in more river traffic and raised the level of the River Severn by several inches.

He was partly responsible for the building of the hydro-electric power station at Powick on the confluence of the Rivers Severn and the Teme. It was the first hydro-electric power station in Europe and the second in the world. It provided electricity for street lighting, but unfortunately the electricity was most needed in winter when the rivers were often in flood, so that the turbine failed to work. Later, a steam engine was installed, hence the tall chimney at Powick Bridge. Eventually a new power station was built in Hylton Road. The station has now been converted into apartments and the chimney is a listed building.

The remains of the old power station at Powick

William was bought out by George in 1890 and the company was renamed Williamson & Sons Limited. By 1914, their catalogue was showing 2,000 items including tin baths, cash boxes, watering cans, etc. One of the trustees for the debenture holders of this new limited company was Alfred Baldwin, father of the Prime Minister, Stanley Baldwin. Over the years there was a close co-operation between the two companies.

After the First World War, the company was in the hands of George's son, Captain Williamson. The company was failing, so Captain Williamson decided to try out a new venture, that of canning on mass-produced lines, which was already being carried out in America. It was a great success and they soon managed to achieve 300 cans per minute. In May 1931, a new factory was opened in Perry Wood, and by 1937 they were employing 10,000 factory workers and producing two million cans per day. The demand for canned fruit and vegetables fell with the arrival of the freezer, but consumers instead bought canned pet food and beverages. By 1981 Metal Box had 26,000 employees in thirteen factories.

The Perry Wood factory is now one of the factories of the Crown Food Europe Division.

BROMSGROVE AND THE NAILERS

Courtesy of Avoncroft Museum of Historic Buildings

Avoncroft Museum of Historic Buildings has preserved a nail shop from Sidemoor in Bromsgrove

Bromsgrove turned from the making of linen and woollen cloth to become Worcestershire's nail-making centre. No one knows when nail-making first came, but it was thriving by 1584 when there was an attempt to pass an Act regulating the number of apprentices held by the masters in Shropshire, Staffordshire and Worcestershire.

The introduction to the 1842 *Bentley's Directory of Worcestershire* states:

> Nails are manufactured here [Bromsgrove] to a greater extent, and in greater perfection, than in any other place; some idea of the vast amount of labour employed in this business may be inferred from the fact of there being 538 people in this parish alone, entirely engaged in it, who employ from 3 to 15 to 30 hands each.

Until well into the 1800s, nail-making was a cottage industry. The nail-making shop was sometimes in a brick-built hut next to the nail-maker's home, but a family might use one room of a two-roomed house.

Perhaps the best account of nail-making comes from a schoolboy writing in Bartley Green, a small village about 8 miles north of Bromsgrove, in 1907:

> Until the 1880s many of the men, women and children of Bartley Green earned money making nails. Bartley handmade nails were famous. They were made in small forges, one of which could be seen at the back of almost every cottage. The iron rod was heated, a bit cut off and hammered to a point. It was then dropped into a hole in a nail-block. Then the Oliver (a foot-operated hammer) came down and 'bumped' a head on it ... Women could earn ten shillings a week and men more. Every Friday afternoon the nailers took their week's work to the nail-master to be weighed and to get new bundles of iron rods. The nail-master sold the nails at Shaw's nail warehouse, Park Street, Birmingham.
>
> The Bartley Green nail-master used to carry a considerable amount of money on his return journey from Shaw's and it is said he carried under the seat of his cart a large knife to defend himself in the event of an attack.

A nailer was independent; provided he manufactured the required quantity of nails, he could work when he liked. The nails were made in pairs, bent double, so that one firing did for a pair of nails. He had to adjust his blocks for different nails. A nailer had the reputation of working from Thursday to Saturday only, then getting drunk on the other days! He also had the reputation of living hand to mouth, spending as he earned.

Some of the men were farm workers but turned to nail-making in the winter. Sometimes the whole family worked side by side. Babies were hung in cages between the anvils of the father and the mother. Boys and girls began work at seven years old. Women and children were usually given the lighter work of making tacks, but when the nail slipped, the hammer came down on their hands and many children had bent and crushed fingers. It was hot, sweaty work and both men and women sometimes stripped to the waist.

In the 1500s nail-making was a profitable trade, but by the middle of the 1600s nail-makers were becoming poorer. There was still a lot of money to be made, but the profits tended to go into the pockets of the much-hated nail-masters such as the Foleys of Witley Court.

Impending disaster came in 1811 when nails began to be made by machine in Birmingham. Many of the nail-makers were out of work, with no official relief. Some were dying from starvation; consequently, it was decided to establish a Visiting Society. Bromsgrove parish was divided into twenty-five districts and in the first three months of 1842, forty-four ladies made 6,953 visits to 1,264 families, granting 482 relief tickets for food, 112 for fuel and 332 for clothing.

The following month a riot broke out. Several thousand nailers from all the nailing districts marched to Dudley where a conference of nail-masters was to be held. On the way they kidnapped some nail-masters and slashed the bellows of any 'blackleg' nailers. The cavalry were called and the leaders arrested, but they were given light sentences because of their mitigating circumstances. Further strikes followed from time to time.

At Catshill and Marlbrook in the Bromsgrove suburbs, a few nailers continued working at their domestic forges until the outbreak of the Second World War. In the 1920s, a Catshill nailer told the local *Bromsgrove Messenger* newspaper that, 'There are not so many nailers in the village now as there were in March 1914.' At that time there had been fifty-one domestic nail shops on Barley Mow Land but, since the ending of the First World War, only eight were back in business. Fifteen years later, the last nail-maker, William Emus, was still making hobnails for boots in Golden Cross Lane.

REDDITCH, THE SHELDONS
AND THE NEEDLE INDUSTRY

For over 200 years, Redditch was supplying needles, fish-hooks and springs throughout the world. By about 1850 the town was making about 200 million needles a week. Yet no one knows when the needle-making industry came to Redditch. Recent excavations at Bordesley Abbey have discovered a metal-

Forge Mill was built in 1730 and is the world's only remaining scouring mill. It is now a needle museum linked with the Bordesley Abbey visitors' centre

working mill used between the twelfth and fourteenth centuries, so it is clear the monks were experienced in manufacturing items such as tools, nails and swords, but there was scant evidence of needle-making.

Tradition has it that when the abbey was dissolved in 1538, the wealthy Sheldons occupied part of the abbey that was still intact, and used it to weave their famous tapestries. The Sheldon family were lords of the manor of Beoley, near Redditch, from about 1470 until the civil wars of the seventeenth century. William Sheldon was High Sheriff and MP for Worcester and is buried, with other members of his family, in Beoley Church. In 1554 he sent his son, Ralph, accompanied by Richard Hyckes, on the Grand Tour of Europe, where Hyckes learned the art of tapestry-weaving in Flanders. When Hyckes returned to England, William Sheldon established him in a tapestry-weaving business in Barcheston, then at Bordesley Abbey. They specialized in huge tapestry maps to adorn stately homes and castles as well as cushion covers and other small items. They probably produced about twenty tapestries, most of them made to order. A Sheldon tapestry more than 15 feet wide and 6 feet high, woven with silk highlights between 1580 and 1590 and featuring a palace surrounded by a moat, was discovered in the United States and shipped to England in 2007, and went on sale for £1,000,000. The Sheldons have now settled in Warwickshire's Weston Park.

The first evidence of needle-making in the area goes back to 1629, when a London needle-maker, William Lea, settled in Studley, a village about 3 miles from Redditch. He may have been one of the master craftsmen who decided to leave London and settle in the countryside to escape the guilds that were becoming expensive and overbearing. One of the earliest needle mills is that of Studley's Washford Mill, which claims to date back to 1744.

The manufacture of needles requires over thirty operations and was originally a cottage industry. A local resident, Vic Bott, died in the late 1990s just before he reached 100 and, when referring to his younger days, he said, 'One family would buy the wire and cut it into lengths, then they would pass it to a relative or someone a few doors down the road who would straighten it, and so on. William Layton & Company's needles were worked like this. I remember that granny did all the furbishing. Families would put a nice label on them and off they would go, and very often it was only a few people working together.'

As the industry developed, more and more processes were transferred to the factory. One of the largest factories was British Mills on Prospect Hill, part of which still exists.

A needle pointer at work

In the early days, every introduction of new systems or machinery brought trouble with the needle-makers. In 1830 foot-operated stamping presses were introduced to help with the making of the eyes. In protest, a crowd of needle-makers, led by fife and drum, marched towards Studley, smashing the stamping equipment from a local factory on the way. The six ringleaders spent six months to a year in prison. In 1839 Joseph Turner discovered that needles remained straight if they were dipped in oil instead of water. It created a riot, as straightening the needles was the work of the women. A public meeting was held in which it was said that 700 ladies would be out of work if oil was introduced, and they would have to turn to prostitution. Faced with a town of 700 prostitutes, the needle masters gave way, but warned that if it was an improvement, it would have to be used eventually.

The needle pointers were a rough, tough lot. As they worked, they inhaled steel dust that gave them pneumoconiosis, so they were not expected to live beyond the age of thirty. Consequently, they were highly paid and objected strongly to any improvement in their lot. In 1822 Mr Abraham came from Sheffield with a muzzle of magnets to catch the steel dust, but the pointers abused Mr Abraham and smashed the muzzles. In 1844 the pointers went on strike to oppose the introduction of a pointing machine. Two years later they were on strike again for several months with regard to the regulating of prices for pointing.

Needle-making could be well paid. The historian John Noake wrote in 1851, 'What an agricultural labourer might consider the height of superabundance, for instance 10s [50p] or 15s [75p] a week, the needlemakers of Redditch look upon as their extremity of distress.' Consequently, people flocked to Redditch from across England. Experienced needle-makers came from Wales, Scotland, Chester and Long Crendon and were joined by hundreds of ordinary folk hoping to become needle-makers. In 1800, the population of Redditch was about 1,000; by 1901 it was 13,493.

The late historian Margaret Mowbray said that Redditch was worse than an American shanty town. In the centre of Redditch, near to where the Council House now stands, was a large pool into which all manner of rubbish was thrown, including dead animals. The water from this stagnant pool seeping down into the wells may have contributed to the cholera outbreak of 1832, with its terrible succession of deaths.

The outbreak began in Upton-upon-Severn and rapidly spread through the county, but was worse in Redditch than elsewhere. The deaths included over

Cholera began in Upton-upon-Severn in 1832

Victims were buried immediately so that the disease would not spread. The corner of the old Bordesley churchyard in Redditch was used as a cholera pit

thirty children under the age of seven. To prevent the infection spreading, victims were hastily buried in the old churchyard at Bordesley Abbey.

Some could have been buried with undue haste. A young lady from the Ramsay family was pronounced dead, but her father stood over the body with a pitchfork. She recovered and lived to a ripe old age.

In 1838 there was another serious epidemic of smallpox and the government decided to get involved. In 1858 the Health Improvement Act came in and eight commissioners were appointed. They formed a Board of Health which battled to raise the funds to build sewers. A Medical Officer of Health, Dr Edward Page, was appointed in 1874, and his second report a year later gives a description of the town centre. Houses had been hastily erected and were either back to back or built round a courtyard. They were damp, with water in the cellars, and as there was no spouting, water was coming in through the roofs. They were cold, with no fire grates and broken quarried floors. Rooms were small with no windows that could be opened. Some houses were overcrowded and filthy. Pigs and fowl were kept in the courtyards or backyards. There were only seventy-two lavatories for 3,000 people.

All rubbish – including the contents of chamber pots – was tipped on to middens, but these were sometimes next to a house and not covered. Nearly everyone drew their water from wells or pumps.

An earth closet dating back to the early 1700s at Avoncroft Museum of Historic Buildings. The three holes are over a cesspit which could be emptied by means of a trapdoor in the floor

Dr Page stressed the importance of clean water, but by then the cost of an adequate sewage system had increased to nearly £16,000. It was not until 1882 that a local wealthy needle master, Mr Bartleet, was able to use his influence to have a reservoir and water tower built on high ground at Headless Cross, providing the town with clean water. To celebrate, Mr Bartleet presented the town with the pretty fountain in the centre of Redditch on Church Green.

Forge Mill, next to the Bordesley Abbey Visitors' Centre, has been restored as a needle museum and scouring mill.

FISH-HOOKS

The needle industry diversified into several world-famous products. The manufacture of fish-hooks was perhaps introduced into Redditch by a certain Walter Brian in about 1776 (see Chapter 11).

Of particular interest is Partridges of Crescent Works as their factory on the Redditch end of the Evesham Road was turned into residential accommodation in 2002. The last factory owner was Ted Partridge who was interviewed in 1982. He said that his family were one of the earliest fish-hook makers in Redditch and remarked, 'Those were the days when you worked for two weeks then drank for a week!' They employed between fifty and sixty hand-workers and out-workers and specialized in salmon and trout hooks, all hand made and hand finished. Semi-automation arrived in about 1932 when they used English copies of German machines.

Ladies were employed as fly dressers, a skill that took three years to perfect. An experienced fly dresser could work at home. The late Norman Neasom said of the family's maid: 'When she had finished her work, usually in the evenings, she would set up her little industrial vice in the kitchen. There she would sit with her large box of feathers, cottons, twills and silks, tying flies on to the fish hooks. She was as quick as lightning and fascinating to watch.'

The trade declined in the 1960s, partly as a result of foreign competition.

TERRY'S SPRINGS AND THE ANGLEPOISE LAMP

Redditch is still the spring-making centre of England. The largest and earliest spring-making company in Redditch was that of Herbert Terry & Sons Ltd. For more than half a century it occupied the area now known as Trafford Park and stretched across the road to include Millsborough House. By the end of the Second World War, it was employing 1,200 people.

Herbert Terry founded the company in Peakman Street in 1855, but it was his son, Charles, who expanded the company. Their catalogues show an amazing range of springs and clips, including necktie adjusters, pipe bowl cleaners, letter clips, exercisers, tie clips, fittings to hold crinolines in place, cycle clips, etc.

The family was plagued by tragedy. The Dorothy Terry memorial home on the Evesham Road was given to the Red Cross in memory of Dorothy Terry who contracted multiple sclerosis and died. Another family member fell under a train, and Charles Terry lost two of his sons in their early twenties through illness.

Charles Terry built his home about half a mile from the town centre; it is now the Southcrest Hotel. He was a strict teetotaller and his sons say that he would turn in his grave if he could see the hotel's guests sitting in his rooms sipping merrily away.

A Baptist church once stood at the front of the factory, but during the First World War, Terry's needed more storage space and so, to the annoyance of the congregation, the building was requisitioned. The Baptists received enough money to build another church in Easemore Road. In 1932 the church at Terry's factory burned down – the locals said it was divine retribution because a consecrated building was being used for storage.

Throughout the twentieth century many new small spring-making companies appeared in the Redditch area. But Charles Terry always claimed that his company was the granddaddy of them all. He said that many of his employees had learned the craft, saw how easy it was to set up on their own, and off they went.

The Anglepoise lamp is celebrated as an outstanding example of innovative and elegant design, and in 2009 it was featured on a postage stamp. All kinds of distinguished people have used the lamp, from the queen to the late comedian, Ronnie Barker. It was designed by George Carwardine (1887–1948), an automotive engineer who owned a factory in Bath that developed vehicle suspension systems. He invented a variety of products, among them a spring that could easily be moved, but remained in a fixed position when the hand was taken away. An obvious use was as a series of cantilever springs for a lamp so that the light could easily be adjusted. He took his design to the most famous spring-makers in England, Terry's Springs, who agreed to manufacture and sell the lamp.

Over the years the basic design has changed very little. The rights were sold to America, but then bought back again by the Terry family.

ROYAL ENFIELD

In the early 1800s, England was said to be a gin-sodden nation. The government tried to encourage the drinking of beer instead of gin, and to this end allowed anyone of good character to sell beer on payment of two guineas a year. One youthful entrepreneur to take advantage of this was George Townsend, a young needle-maker from Alcester who moved to the little village of Hunt End near Astwood Bank, and started a brewing industry.

He made beer in a large black vat and the perry-making mill that he used is now in the Avoncroft Museum of Historic Buildings, near Bromsgrove. He made enough money to build a little public house, The Red Lion, which still exists, and in 1851 he opened a small needle factory employing sixteen men and two boys. Twenty years later he was employing 170 workers. He died in 1879, but his son, also George, took over and decided to try his hand at making bicycles.

The Townsends were typical stern Victorian employers. When one worker was off sick, George Townsend sent a horse and cart to bring him into work. In 1891, he decided to install underground boilers. He went bankrupt, quarrelled with his financiers, and left the company.

The financiers brought in two men to run the company. Robert Walker Smith, trained in the Wolverhampton engine sheds, was a brilliant designer,

The perry mill from Hunt End at Avoncroft Museum. Worcestershire was famous for its perry.
At one time, this perry mill belonged to George Townsend who founded Royal Enfield

and his inventions included the two-speed gears and the cush drive hub. The second was Albert Eadie, employed by a pen manufacturer and said to be the most brilliant salesman England has ever known. He was a large, jovial man, very popular, but unfortunately his methods were not always strictly legitimate. He was known for the Eadie Coaster Hub and made a small fortune out of it, but it was not his invention and it was patented in France. Financial support for the venture was provided by George Cartland, founder of the Edgbaston cricket club and brother of the romantic novelist, Barbara Cartland. In contrast to the Townsends, R. W. Smith and Albert Eadie looked after their employees, even building a social centre up the hill on the Evesham Road, now converted into residential accommodation.

The financial situation was in the balance. The needle rights were sold to Shrimptons and they concentrated on bicycles. The company was not on a sound financial footing until, in 1892, they received a contract for small gun parts from the Royal Small Arms Company in Enfield, Middlesex. To celebrate, the next new bicycle was called 'The Enfield', one of the first bicycles to be fitted with pneumatic tyres. The following year, in 1893, Eadie decided that if he added the word 'Royal' it gave the name a classy feel.

The Enfield Cycle Company prospered until Smith and Eadie decided to manufacture cars. Laws in England stated that a motorized vehicle was not to exceed 4 mph and had to be preceded 100 yards in front by a man with a red flag. Consequently, there were no engineers in England. The law was repealed in 1896, when R. W. Smith immediately clamped a little De Dion engine between two bicycles to produce a quadricycle. In 1901, they decided to go into four-wheeled vehicles and a year later they had built an 8 hp single-cylinder car, with the water-cooled engine at the rear. By 1906 the bicycles had supported the cars to the tune of £20,000 and the directors decided that it was time the cars were independent, and so the bicycles moved from Hunt End into the centre of Redditch, leaving the factory at Hunt End for cars only, now known as Enfield Autocar. By the end of 1907 a loss of nearly £20,000 was revealed. Albert Eadie said that he would put in £8,000 if the shareholders would match it, but they refused. The company was sold to Alldays and Onions for £18,000 and there were enough cars almost finished in the yard to cover that amount. The Hunt End factory closed down and Albert Eadie moved to BSA where he became managing director.

Fortunately, the bicycles continued to be very profitable and the motorbikes had been doing well since 1904, when Louis Hadley had won a race at New

Royal Enfield. Tony Knight enjoys a shandy with his restored
1951 500cc Twin outside the Red Lion at Hunt End

Brighton on a 2 hp Minerva engine in front of between 3,000 and 4,000 spectators. Under the control of R. W. Smith, the Enfield factory eventually grew to 30 acres. R. W. Smith passed away in 1933, but his son took over the reins – though it is said that after he died in 1959 the company seemed to lose its way.

Their best-known motorbike was the 350 Bullet type, developed from the 1930s onwards. All the designers had a hand in it – Reg Thomas, Ted Pardoe, Jack Hassall, John Smith and Charlie Rogers.

It was a sturdy bike, good in trials, easy to maintain, and it was the first Trials bike to have telescopic forks both front and rear to make a comfortable ride. Two brothers, John and Pat Brittain, rode the bike to victory again and again and won innumerable awards.

During the Indian/Pakistan conflict, the Indians needed a bike that could cope with rough terrain and they chose the Bullet. When hostilities ceased, the Indian government arranged to import the Bullet, on condition that their engineers could be trained to manufacture the bike in India. Although Royal Enfield motorbikes are no longer made in England, they are now imported from India.

————————————

MORGAN MOTOR COMPANY

Royal Enfield failed in their attempt to produce an early car, but one company in Worcestershire succeeded. Tucked way in the surburbs of Malvern Link is a worldwide car industry. Furthermore, the cars are all hand made. This is, of course, the Morgan Motor Company.

The company was started by the son of a local vicar, Henry Frederick Stanley Morgan, usually known as 'H.F.S.'. Born in 1881, as he grew older it became obvious that he was more interested in engineering than in theology and, encouraged by his parents, he attended the Crystal Palace Engineering College in south London. H.F.S. was desperate to buy a car, but unfortunately a hired 3 hp Benz ran away with him down a 1 in 6 hill between Bromyard and Hereford and the cost of £28 for repairs delayed his ambitions for many months. Eventually he was able to buy an Eagle Tandem – that is, a three-wheeler, water-cooled, with an 8 hp De Dion engine. In 1901 he was apprenticed to the great railway engineer William Dean at the GWR railway works in Swindon, where he subsequently worked for a few months as a draughtsman. In 1905 he joined a friend to open a garage in Worcester Road, Malvern Link, where he also ran Malvern's first bus service. A second garage was opened in 1906, adjacent to the Star Hotel opposite Foregate Street station, but this lasted for just a few years.

In 1909 he acquired a 7 hp twin-cylinder Peugeot engine and mounted it into a three-wheeled lightweight frame of his own design. Its unusually high power-to-weight ratio meant that it could accelerate as fast as any other car at that time. He was persuaded to exhibit two similar cars at the Olympia Motor Show in 1910, both with JAP engines, one an 8 hp twin and the other a 4 hp single cylinder. Sadly, he received few orders and his friend withdrew from the partnership. However, the managing director of Harrods took a liking to the vehicle and arranged to have one in his shop window. Soon after, the single-seater was entered in the London–Exeter reliability trial and achieved the highest possible award, a gold medal.

One of the reasons that the car was so unpopular was that it could only seat one person, and so H. F. S. redesigned it with a second seat. He also found time to marry a vicar's daughter, Ruth Day, who not only fulfilled all her wifely duties as a passenger in reliability trials (which involved bouncing on the car when going uphill and leaning out when it swung round corners) but also managed to produce four daughters and a son, Peter.

The car continued to win medals and trade boomed. The Morgan Motor Company Limited was founded in 1912 and by 1913 it had won more awards for reliability and speed than any other light vehicle. In 1913 a special racing Morgan won the Cyclecar Grand Prix in Amiens, France, against stiff opposition from many Continental cars.

By 1919 production had transferred to a new factory in Pickersleigh Road, Malvern Link, and a four-seater family model was introduced. Throughout the 1920s and 1930s, the Morgan was one of the most successful of all light cars.

In 1936 a fourth wheel was added. The car was known as the 4/4 – that is, four wheels and four cylinders. By 1939 they were selling 1,000 cars a year, with many going overseas to France,

Peter Morgan (son of the founder H. F. S. Morgan 1881-1959) who is standing, and his son, Charles Morgan (Peter's son and current head of the family firm) who is seated in the foreground. The picture is taken with a Morgan Plus 8 parked in the factory yard outside the Chassis Shop, the third row of the old factory workshops in Pickersleigh Road

Courtesy Morgan Motor Company.

The Morgan Plus 8. This is photographed at the entrance to the top paddock at Prescott Hill Climb near Gotherington, a few miles away from Tewkesbury

Russia, India, and North and South America. Success continued in the 1950s and 1960s with a larger, more powerful car called the Plus 4. 1959, however, saw the end of an era with the death of the founder, H. F. S. Morgan.

H. F. S.'s son, Peter, took over as chairman when his father died and successfully guided the company through some very difficult times as well as introducing another powerful new model in 1968: the Plus 8.

Peter's son Charles joined the company full time in 1985 and in the late 1990s developed the Aero 8 supercar. Sadly Peter Morgan died in 2003 but Charles has continued to innovate, with the latest new model being the re-introduction of a modern Morgan three-wheeler, similar to those that achieved so much success in the 1930s.

There are nearly 5,000 members of the Morgan Sports Car Club for four-wheelers worldwide and, in 2009, 3,200 three-wheeler Morgans converged on Cheltenham. They came from as far afield as the United States, Australia and New Zealand.

Shortly before he died in 1959, H. F. S. remarked, 'Looking back through the years, seeing both the errors and the triumphs in their correct perspective, I feel I have enjoyed it all. The motor trade has been, so far as I am concerned, a most interesting business.'

THE SHELSLEY WALSH HILL CLIMB

About 10 miles north-west of the Morgan factory is Shelsley Walsh where, on 12 August 1905, the Midland Automobile Club organized a hill climb and took out a ninety-nine-year lease on a steep hill there. Thus began the oldest motor sports event in the world to have been held on the same site and without a break except during wartime. Now, for several weekends each year, the tranquillity of west Worcestershire resounds to the clamour of as many as 30,000 spectators and the roar of 200 vintage cars.

The course is about 1,000 yards in length and rises 328 feet. The average gradient is 1 in 9.14 (10.9 per cent) and in parts is as steep as 1 in 6.24 (16 per cent)! The track sometimes narrows to a mere 12 feet. For nine years, until 2002, the record for completing the course stood at 25.34 seconds, but this record has now been broken several times. Morgan cars have often taken part, and in 1912 they achieved the fastest speed at an average 22 mph.

The Midland Automobile Club discovered, to their horror, that the lease was due to expire in 2005 and the owners of the land were asking for £1,000,000 to

The Shelsley Walsh hill climb is the oldest motor sports event in the world to have been held on the same site and without a break except during wartime

extend the lease for a further ninety-nine years. The MAC launched the Shelsley Walsh Trust, and the money was raised. The future of the hill climb is safe until 2104 and the site is now being developed.

_____

SANTLER MOTOR VEHICLES

The Morgan Company was not the first motor vehicle engineering enterprise to be established at Malvern. Charles and Walter Santler built one of the very first cars in England from a small workshop in Malvern Link.

Thomas Santler was a builder in Victorian times, with premises in Howsell Road, Malvern Link, that were first established in 1875 during the town's heyday. Thomas' sons Charles, born in 1864, and Walter, born in 1867, were two creative young brothers who attended the Lyttelton Grammar School in Great Malvern.

Charles then joined the Great Western Railway in Swindon as an engineering apprentice whilst Walter studied electrical engineering with Messrs. Goolding & Co. in London. During the 1880s the two brothers returned to Malvern and began working at their father's business but pursued their own particular interests. Walter concentrated on the development of early domestic electrical installations, complete with engines to drive generators, which could be fitted in private homes or public buildings. Charles, meanwhile, assisted by his brother, experimented with early motor cars before moving on to bicycle repair and construction, establishing workshops to build 'Malvernia' bicycles.

The petrol-driven engine as we know it is generally regarded to have been invented in Germany in the 1870s by Nikolaus Otto, whilst Karl Benz and Gotlieb Daimler independently developed motor cars, the Benz of 1886 being regarded as the first practical car. Charles had visited Germany and claimed to have helped Karl Benz in the development of his machine.

In their father's workshop in 1887, Charles and Walter built a four-wheeled chassis. At first, it was driven by steam, then by gas, but neither was powerful enough. After two years of experiments, they eventually used a single-cylinder petrol engine similar to that developed by Benz, mounted under the seat in the middle of the vehicle and driving the rear wheels. Known as the Santler 'Malvernia', it was able to achieve the remarkable speed of 12 mph. Unfortunately, the law only allowed them to drive at 4 mph, but they were able to test their vehicle over the private roads of the Madresfield Court estate.

These experiments had to be done in their spare time as the electrical and bicycle business was thriving. In 1896 the business moved into larger premises in Worcester Road, Malvern Link. Known as the Malvernia Works Cycle

Manufactory, the workshops undertook the repair and manufacture of both pedal cycles and, later, motor cars. Santler also helped H. F. S. Morgan by machining many of the components for the early Morgan cars when, becauase of the great demand for the car, Morgan's facilities were stretched to their limits.

Santler vehicles never went into full production and after the First World War the business went into decline. A final attempt was made to save the business by building a three-wheeled cyclecar called the 'Rushabout'. Sadly, this venture failed and the workshops eventually closed in 1922. Both the brothers died in their mid-seventies – Charles in 1940, and Walter in 1942. They have been honoured by a new retirement development in Malvern named Santler Court, which, ironically, has been built on the former site of the original Morgan factory in Worcester Road!

The Santler 'Malvernia', the brothers' first car, was ostensibly forgotten until 1938, when a veteran car enthusiast, John Mills, bought it for £5 and restored it. It has been resold two or three times, but is the only Santler car in existence – a rare example of an early petrol-driven car. Dr Alan Sutton of the Veteran Car Club carried out further research and restoration work and the car was sold at auction some years ago for well over £100,000. Its present whereabouts are unknown.

9

OTHER WORCESTERSHIRE ENTERPRISES

Two products have taken the name of the county right across the world: Worcestershire sauce and Worcester Porcelain. In addition, there are Worcestershire vinegars and Kays Catalogues.

WORCESTERSHIRE SAUCE

The traditional story of the discovery of Worcestershire sauce tells of an officer of the British Raj, Lord Marcus Sandys, ex-governor of Bengal, who returned to England in about 1834 with a sauce that had taken his fancy. Two brilliant

Worcestershire sauce. It seems to have been adapted from an Indian recipe but there are two versions of its origins

dispensing chemists lived at number 68 Broad Street, Worcester, John Wheeley Lea and William Henry Perrins, so Lord Sandys asked them to recreate this sauce for him. They analysed it and made the appropriate potion, but unfortunately it tasted terrible, so they bottled it and put it away in the cellar. Three years later they were having a clear-out when they came across the bottle. They decided to have a taste of it before throwing it away and, to their surprise, it had matured over the years to become a delicious sauce. The recipe is a secret.

The Sandys family were well-known and respected landowners in Worcestershire. The family fortunes rose in 1559 when Edwin Sandys was elected Bishop of Worcester, then Bishop of London in 1570, and finally Archbishop of York in 1575. He died in 1588, a year or two after he had arranged to have the tower added to Hartlebury Church. The Sandys family were lords of the manor of Wickhamford and another ancestor, Sir Samuel Sandys, married Penelope Washington whose coat of arms, the stars and stripes, is shown on her tomb in the local church, and is said to be the basis of the national flag of the United States. The church is much visited by American tourists.

Unfortunately, we have to spoil the story about the origin of the sauce to point out that Lord Sandys never visited Bengal. Also, the barony in the Sandys family had been revived in 1802 for the second baron's mother, Mary Sandys Hill, therefore in the 1830s Lord Sandys was actually Lady Sandys. According to *The World* newspaper, Mrs Elizabeth Grey (1798–1869), a well-known Victorian author, went to visit Lady Sandys at Ombersey Court, and Lady Sandys remarked that she wished she could get some good curry powder. Mrs Grey said that she had received a very good recipe from her uncle, Sir Charles, Chief Justice of India. Lady Sandys said there were chemists in Worcester and perhaps they could make it up for her. At first Lea and Perrins didn't know if they could get all the ingredients, but eventually they sent her a packet of the powder. Then someone thought that if it was diluted, it might make a good sauce.

We shall probably never know the truth of the matter but one fact is certain: Lea and Perrins realized that they had a wonderful new flavour on their hands, quickly bought the rights, and made a fortune. The company expanded into the current factory in Worcester in 1897, and was bought by Heinz in 2005.

WORCESTERSHIRE VINEGARS

Worcestershire also became famous for its vinegars. Two Worcester chemists, William Hill and Edward Evans, founded a vinegar works in 1830 which became one of the biggest in the world. The vat was 40 feet high and contained nearly 115,000 gallons. Another sauce and vinegar factory was founded by Hickin Bold in 1781 and was based at Stourport-on-Severn. In 1798 Charles Swann from Tenbury offered to finance its expansion. Two thousand tons of earth were imported from Pitchcroft in Worcester (now the racecourse) to build a platform between the River Severn and the River Stour for their new factory. In 1894 they built the three largest vats in the world. Each vat held 140,000 gallons of vinegar. In the 1940s one vat burst and flooded the cellars of the surrounding houses. The factory was taken over by British Vinegars in 1954, who used the trade name Sarson's. It was bought by Nestlé and closed down in 2000.

Another chemist or drysalter, William Skey, invented a process for manu-facturing sulphuric acid using a commercial process and built a large chemical works at Dowles. He was born in Upton-upon-Severn in 1726, apprenticed to a grocer in Bewdley, then set up as a grocer and drysalter. He may have been involved in the manufacture of saltpetre, or potassium nitrate, a powerful oxidizing agent, and although it has many innocent uses it is also an essential ingredient in the manufacture of gunpowder. Skey became very rich and bought 270 acres of land from Lord Foley in 1775, on which he built Spring Grove House in Bewdley Safari Park. The artist John Constable often called there as he was courting Maria Bicknell, a relative of Skey. The house was owned by the Skey family until 1871 and opened as a Safari Park in 1973.

WORCESTER PORCELAIN

By the middle of the eighteenth century the cloth trade was declining and, faced with the prospect of severe unemployment, the leading citizens of Worcester were looking for a new trade to replace it. At that time, porcelain was very popular but had to be imported as no one in England knew how to make it. Dr John Wall, who also founded Malvern spa, got together with a friend of his, William Davis, a Worcester apothecary, and together they worked on the problem. A company at Bristol, Miller and Lund, was making an acceptable imitation of porcelain, and within a year Dr Wall had co-operated with them and been given their secret recipes together with the necessary equipment.

Photograph supplied by Worcester Porcelain Museum

Worcester porcelain teapot hand-painted with the Cannonball pattern in about 1760

At the same time, Wall and Davis set up a company with thirteen friends as directors. Some of them were Quakers. Among the directors was the proprietor of the *Gentleman's Magazine*, which gave them free publicity, and Richard Holdship, whose wife was persuaded to sell some of her property to buy a soaprock mine in Kynance, Cornwall, to provide the necessary clay. They were joined by a master engraver, Robert Hancock, who trained the two well-known artists, Valentine Green and James Ross. At first they copied oriental designs, but soon developed their own style with exotic birds and flowers.

The first factory was in Warmstry House, next door to the bishop's palace, with a garden that stretched down to the River Severn where they could load the delicate cargo. But there were many problems to overcome. They needed to convert a private residence into

Breakfast cup and saucer from a Flight & Barr
Worcester service made for King George III in about 1807

a factory, and the soaprock contained traces of sulphur that exploded when heated, but by 1754 the porcelain was on the market. Within ten years they were employing nearly 200 people. Dr Wall died in 1771 and the company went into decline. Twelve years later, in 1783, their London agent bought the company for £3,000 for his sons.

Teapot from the breakfast service made by Chamberlains of Worcester for Admiral Nelson
in about 1805. Nelson visited Worcester with Emma but as they were enjoying an illicit
relationship they met with a cold reception!

A stroke of luck came their way in 1788 when George III visited Worcester for the Three Choirs Festival (see page 286) and asked to visit a local factory. He was shown round the porcelain works, ordered a quantity, and this gave it a Royal Warrant. George IV patronized the porcelain to the tune of £4,000.

In 1793, Martin Barr, an artist, had a shop in Worcester and was putting up the shutters one night when a dragoon officer, obviously very drunk, picked a quarrel with him and gave him a nasty cut on his head. When the officer sobered up he was appalled at his action that could have lost him his commission. Barr was given 'hush money' which he used to buy his way into the porcelain company which became known as 'Flight and Barr'. The Barr family were directors for many years. A Flight and Barr tureen recently went to auction with an asking price of £2,000.

The company had a serious competitor. Robert Chamberlain was born in Worcester in 1736 and claimed to be the first apprentice employed at the original works in 1751. He established a successful new porcelain factory in Severn Street. Many of his employees came from the Worcester School of Art and were craftsmen of a very high calibre. In 1840 the two rival companies combined.

They now needed larger premises. It so happened that six directors of Royal Worcester were also shareholders in a company set up to manage Worcester's Public Pleasure Grounds. The Pleasure Grounds went bankrupt in 1865, and so Worcester Porcelain was able to acquire the grounds for £8,500. This is where it remained until it closed in 2009. Although they no longer manufacture porcelain, a Worcester Porcelain museum and shop remains open.

KAYS CATALOGUES

The working classes may not have been interested in the spa, but another commercial organization was so popular, especially with the less well-off members of society, that it became a household name. 'Kays Catalogues' was one of the largest private company employers in Worcestershire. It employed over 27,000 people across the United Kingdom and in Worcester itself there were about 6,000 to 7,000 employees at its peak.

The founder, William Kay, was born in Portsmouth in 1856, but moved to Worcester to work as a jeweller's and watchmaker's assistant to a John Skarratt. This was an old-established company in St Swithin's Street, going back to 1794. William left Skarratt's in 1886 to go into partnership with a local architect, and they called their enterprise 'Kay'. In 1890 the architect left, and William employed two clerks and one errand boy and decided to change the name to 'Kay's of

Worcester'. Sales were strictly cash with order. In 1902 William began to publish a thick catalogue twice a year. In 1907 he was able to open impressive new premises at 23 The Tything. By the mid-1920s William Kay was nearly seventy, and so his sons stepped in to manage the business, combining, in 1927, with Great Universal Stores. William Kay died in 1929.

During the Second World War, the company began offering easy payment terms, whereby goods could be paid for on a weekly basis. This had a big impact on society. Expensive items such as engagement rings, which had been out of reach of the poorer classes, could now be acquired with the aid of hire purchase. Your furniture could be replaced and you could have a new suite every year. Your status was not now how much money you had, but how far you were prepared to get into debt.

Business boomed, and Kays (the apostrophe was dropped) opened new offices in Leeds and Glasgow. In 2003, Kays and Littlewoods were merged into one company, Shop Direct. In 2007, Kays ended its long association with Worcester by transferring to Liverpool.

10

TRAINING AND EDUCATION IN WORCESTERSHIRE

As late as the 1880s, only half the population of England could read. For the majority, there was no need. There were few newspapers, no road signs (only milestones), no need for letter-writing, no written instructions, and books were expensive. Education remained limited to a small and privileged male minority.

Nevertheless, Worcestershire was probably better served with schools than any other county. By 1800 some fifteen grammar schools and more than forty elementary schools had been established in the county. A gentleman by the name of Mr Oldham came to Bewdley in 1740 and said that he was surprised at the knowledge of Latin by the working-class tradesmen and mechanics, who quoted Latin proverbs and phrases at every opportunity. The Bewdley school was known as the Free Grammar School of King James, but old records show that it had been founded before his reign, thirty years previously, in 1577, when the chapel wardens had spent 2s 6d in putting the 'scholemaster's chambers' in order. Sadly, when Charity Commissioners later visited the Bewdley school in 1833, they found that the master had ceased to teach, although he was still drawing his salary, and the usher (the assistant teacher) kept a private boarding school. The school was closed and not reopened until 1864, and then only in a room in the High Street, described as unfit even for a ragged infants school. The Bewdley school struggled on, but was closed in about 1912.

SCHOOLS FOUNDED BY MONASTERIES

Formal education in Worcestershire probably began in the early monasteries. Worcester Monastery was the first to establish a school, closely followed by Pershore Abbey, with that of Evesham following shortly afterwards. The chantry priest was often the schoolmaster (see Chapter 3).

Monastic education was of two types. First came the education of 'oblates', the young lads presented by their fathers to be educated for the life of a monk. This was largely learning by rote and recitation, with discipline by the birch rod. The life of an oblate was only a little less severe than that of a monk – they slept longer and ate earlier. No other language except Latin was to be spoken on or near the school premises. The oblates were taught arithmetic, astronomy, geometry and music, and once they had completed their monastic education some went on to Oxford University where Gloucester Hall (later known as Worcester Hall) was established specially for the monks in 1291. Those who joined the monastery later in life also needed training.

A second type of education was given to the children of the poor. By 'poor' was meant the children of the gentry and middle classes. The working classes were never taught to read and write. It was of no use to them, and it might have given them ideas above their station.

The number of students in each school usually varied from year to year from about five to one hundred, depending upon the popularity and expertise of each schoolmaster and/or his assistant. Sometimes, the schools took in boarders, which boosted the accounts.

WORCESTER SCHOOLS

In 672, the Council of Churches divided England into five regions and the Bishop of Worcester was given responsibility for the huge See of Mercia (see Chapter 1). An early cathedral was built, St Mary's, and a monastery attached. A school was founded there within a few years, perhaps in 685, by the first Bishop of Worcester, Bishop Bosel.

Two schools now claim to have an early foundation, the Royal Worcester Grammar School and the King's School. Both once stood near the cathedral and are probably as old as the cathedral itself. Both claim royal charters. They are so old that the history has to be pieced together from a word here and there in ancient documents. It is now generally thought that the King's School developed from an expansion of Bishop Bosel's school into the Almonry in the tenth century, while the Royal Worcester Grammar School came from an offshoot of Bosel's school outside the monastery.

In the ninth century came the sporadic attacks of the Vikings up the River Severn. Buildings were destroyed, the monks were scattered, and education was disrupted. After Alfred the Great (of burned cakes fame) had defeated the Danes in 878, he decided to shake up education in Worcester. He wrote to the

Bishop of Worcester, Bishop Werfrith, telling him to re-establish the monastery school of St Mary's, saying that 'The youth of English freemen who are rich enough to devote themselves to it should be set to learning … until they are well able to read English writing then Latin'. The school gained such a good reputation that it was chosen to educate a future monarch, King Alfred's grandson, Aethelstan. He became a wise and well-loved ruler and reigned for fourteen years (924–39).

Priests sometimes also organized the training of children through an apprenticeship monitored by the Trinity Guild of St Nicholas. A fixed annual payment was made to a master craftsman in return for an apprenticeship over a certain period. When Edward VI came to the throne in 1547 a guild school was meeting in Trinity Hall in the city, with 100 scholars under the headmaster, John Oliver BA. Unfortunately, there was a misunderstanding over his salary, which should have been about £6 per annum as a schoolmaster, but the written agreement stated that this £6 was a pension for life unconditionally. Oliver moved away, taking the pension with him. There was no money to pay a schoolmaster and, to make matters worse, the guild was also responsible for keeping the town walls and bridge in a good state of repair, and they were in such a poor state of repair that the guild had to close the school during four years of Queen Mary's (1553–8) reign in order to provide urgent repairs. As soon as Queen Elizabeth came to the throne in 1558, the city took Oliver to court to retrieve their £6 per annum to pay a new headmaster.

There was a national scandal in 1848 concerning the neglect of cathedral schools and Worcester was cited as one of the worst. The master's salaries had been raised, paid for by reducing the scholarships of the boys. The scholarships were restored, but the masters' salaries were kept at the same level. There were then fifty-one boys in the school.

KING'S SCHOOL,

Previous names of this school include The College School, Free School and Cathedral School, sometimes with 'Grammar' added.

King's School stands by the cathedral, next to the River Severn, on a site that has played a leading part in the history of Worcester for over 2,000 years. It has been a Roman trading post, a cathedral, a monastery, a prison and various military strongholds, including a castle. As we have seen, a school was founded here as early as 685.

Part of King's School. Number 6 College Green is where Elgar took music lessons as a boy

Number 12 College Green now houses History, Politics and Economics for King's School, together with the chaplain's room and residence. It was once a canon's house

When Henry VIII was planning to close down the monasteries, Thomas Cromwell made a great survey of all the monasteries; this was known as the *Valor Ecclesiasticus*. He lists the Almonry School, but scribbled on the side of the page is a great surprise – a note that the school was set up by the ordinance of St Oswald and St Wulstan. This means that the school has a tenth-century foundation and the great Saint Wulstan himself was teaching fourteen Almonry scholars. Both Bishop Wulstan and Florence of Worcester, the monk historian of the early 1100s, were teachers in their early days at Worcester Monastery. Two or three of their young monks passed for Oxford every year.

By 1341 it was occupying the Almonry, which had been built about twenty years previously. It probably stood on the site of what is now 15 College Green. The almoner, who gave food and money to the poor, seems to have doubled up as teacher. The first name of a schoolmaster appears in 1397 when John Ekynton received a cloth tunic for his labours. It was probably still quite a small school, with about fifteen students.

At the dissolution in 1541, Henry VIII closed the schools in Worcester run by the monastery (by now known as a priory), and instead established a cathedral college with two separate schools in it – first a choir school and, secondly, a separate school of forty scholars that was the refounded Almonry School. The properties that had belonged to the monastery were given to the dean and

The old refectory of King's School. Inside is a huge relief by the eleventh century Herefordshire School of Sculpture

chapter so that the cathedral could run the school. The king himself appointed the first headmaster, so that the school became known as 'The King's School', but future headmasters were to be appointed by the dean and chapter.

The scholars had to be 'poor' and with no friends to help them, of 'native genius' and with an 'inborn aptitude for learning'. Most of them were the sons of local gentlemen. They were aged between nine and fifteen, although ex-choristers were given an extra year in lieu of time spent in the choir. The school moved out of the Almonry into College Hall, still in the cathedral grounds. The refounded school flourished and, only two years later, twelve of its pupils went to university. Originally, all scholars were free, but in later years fee-paying students were introduced.

By 1636, 200 boys were attending King's School and the cathedral authorities decided that they were a nuisance. For many years the boys had used the huge refectory, built in the twelfth century for the monks.

The authorities wanted to convert the refectory into a library with a door made into the cloister. The question was, where was the school to go? A chapel had been built in the early 1200s by William de Blois, Bishop of Worcester. It lay between the north (entrance) door of the cathedral and the dean's house opposite. Below the chapel was a cellar used to deposit 'the bones of the faithful'. By 1636, it had fallen into disrepair, the chapel was being used as a hayloft and the cellar was full of decaying bones. The King's School moved into this building. Fortunately, the old school was only in the chapel until 1641, when Parliament interfered because of the numerous complaints from parents of the stink of the bones. The school returned to the refectory.

From *The Victoria County History* (vol. 4, page 459) we have a description of life at the King's School in 1858:

> The head master, Rev W. H. Helm, was an old boy … son of a well-known lawyer who lived in the college precinct. His idea of teaching was to tell the boys to learn something. If they did not know it they got a severe caning on the hands … Arithmetic was taught by the second master, who also taught some algebra. The head took us in Euclid, and used to declare that he had no hope of getting us past the fifth proposition. The boys acted accordingly. He was also supposed to take us Monday afternoon in French. He would set us to work and book the time against us. The boys managed the games, which considering that we had to find and hire a field for ourselves, was decidedly good.

Incidentally, the Reverend W. H. Helm was only twenty-four when he became headmaster; he lived in College Yard to the north of the cathedral. He died very suddenly four years later.

By 1879 the school was known as the Worcester Cathedral Grammar School and was still part of the cathedral body. The boys were usually from the city and the surrounding area. Then a new headmaster arrived – the Reverend W. E. Bolland. There was a problem with the choir boys, whose frequent absences from lessons for choir practice disrupted the classes, so the Reverend W. E. Bolland re-established a separate choir school. After five years as headmaster, he was party to the biggest change in the school since the time of Henry VIII. The school was made independent of the cathedral. Governers were to be elected, rather than just being clerics of the cathedral, although the dean and chapter remained the majority of the board of governors. The New Scheme was approved by Queen Victoria in 1884.

The College Hall was in urgent need of repair. One Sunday evening a year later, as boys and masters were on their way to the chapter house for the Sunday evening service, they were narrowly missed by 20 tons of rubble falling from the roof of the College Hall Undercroft. The restoration work on the hall lasted for almost two years.

Four girls were admitted into the sixth form of this all-male establishment in 1971, beginning a move towards full co-education. In 1985 there were seventy-three girls in the sixth form, both day and boarding. The school was fully co-educational by 1995 and now has over 1,000 pupils.

THE WORCESTER FREE SCHOOL, LATER THE ROYAL WORCESTER GRAMMAR SCHOOL

When the first Bishop of Worcester, Bishop Bosel, was appointed, he founded a school in Worcester in about 685. It was outside the monastery and catered for the relatives of monks and children intending to enter the monastery.

A documented squabble in 1291 proves the existence of the school. The rector of St Nicholas' Church in the city laid on a special service for Worcester scholars at the Feast of St Swithins, when a boy bishop was elected for the day. Wax for the candles was expensive and the problem was: who owned the used wax, the rector or the scholars? The matter went to the Bishop of Worcester who decided that the wax belonged to the Worcester School and that the rector had to rely on the generosity of the scholars to get candle wax.

Headmasters were appointed by the Bishop of Worcester who generally chose well, although there was at least one disaster. In the 1420s, the bishop wrote that the school was at a low level 'through the negligence, carelessness, want of attention and idleness of Sir Richard, chaplain, or rather through his

Royal Worcester Grammar School now occupies several sites in Worcester. This photograph was taken in Upper Tything

deep fault and very bad and vicious government, which have rendered him, and still render him, notoriously utterly unworthy to keep the school any longer'. Strong words indeed!

The Bishop of Worcester, Sylvestro de Gigli, who rarely, if ever, set foot in Worcestershire, appointed Hugh Cratford as headmaster, and in 1504 stated that anyone who tried to set up a rival school in Worcester city to teach grammar would be excommunicated. Curiously, Cratford continued to be paid by the almoner as a schoolmaster, so it appears that the Almonry School survived and Cratford taught at both schools.

Queen Elizabeth refounded the school in 1561 as a 'free scole of the cyttie of Worcester' – that is, there were no school fees. A list was made of rules and ordinances. The school was to be an elementary or preparatory school to prepare its scholars for further education, governed by six eminent people known as 'The Six Masters'. The old school house, the Guild Hall, was sold, so a new house was bought, probably on the site of Lady Pakington's house in Worcester. An honest, virtuous, single man or a priest, learned in good 'clean' Latin literature, was to be appointed as headmaster. The school hours were 6 a.m. to 11 a.m. and noon to 5 p.m. Every Wednesday and Friday, at 9 a.m., the schoolmaster was to go to the parish church 'with his scholares before him in order', read a chapter from the Bible, sing a psalm, and pray for the queen and all the other founders who had given money for the maintenance of the school. Queen Elizabeth's portrait was hung in the old school hall and apparently decorated from time to time, hence in 1763 the entry in the account books read: 'Paid the Trinity Women for dressing the Queen, 7s 6d'.

The wealthy made several generous bequests. Thomas Wylde endowed two large areas of Pitchcroft in the 1500s which seems to have supported both schools. Thomas Morre of Worcester conveyed £40 6s 8d in 1626 for 'the bringing up of ten poor male children, all under the age of 12 years and above the age of four years', all 'lawfully begotten', whose 'parents are destitute of abilities and means to give them necessary food and raiment, much less to give them education fit for Christians'. They were to wear 'long blue coats of ancient cut'. These long blue coats were quite common as they were often worn by apprentices. They were to live near the school in 'William Shelton's house' and a man and woman were to be appointed to look after them. In the selection of boys, preference was to be given first to the 'blood of the founder', next to those of the parish of St Martin's, after that in the parish of Spreckley, and then to the parish of Suckley.

At first the school flourished, especially when the Cathedral School was moved to the charnel house! There were demands for the free school to become a rival grammar school and, for a few years, it rose in status.

When Charles II came to the throne, the Blue Coat Hospital (a residential school for orphaned children) was re-established. From 1687 to the middle of the nineteenth century, boys from the Blue Coat Hospital formed the nucleus of the school. By 1851 there were twenty-one boys plus six Blue Coat boys. It had again become an elementary or preparatory school. The pay for the schoolmasters was so poor that they were chiefly old men, who did not last long. The school was rebuilt in 1735.

Then, in about 1860, the dynamic headmaster Francis Eld arrived. He discovered the teaching to be out-of-date and below standard. He abolished classics lessons and replaced them with two modern languages. The classes in mathematics he took himself. He introduced science, along with a cabinet of geological specimens, followed by art and drawing. The Blue Boys were transferred to St Martin's National School. By now there were thirty places at the school for which he set an entrance exam. The school deserved better premises, and so in 1868 he rented White Ladies House, a red-brick building on the site of an old nunnery. The house is rumoured to contain hidden treasure, left there by Charles I during the Civil War. The following year, in 1869, Queen Victoria granted, by royal warrant, the school the title of the Royal Grammar School of Queen Elizabeth.

Scholars began to win open scholarships to Oxford and Cambridge. In 1877 a chemistry laboratory was provided. The number of pupils rose slowly from 75 boys in 1880 to 112 in 1899, and by 1904 it served 216 boys. Francis Eld retired in 1893.

In the early 1860s a bitter dispute arose between the headmaster of Worcester's King's School and the Worcester Royal School. John Meake had been a successful scholar at the King's School from 1613, had survived the Civil Wars and, after the Restoration of Charles II, decided, in 1655, to bequeath a substantial income to his former school to provide Oxford University scholarships from the 'Free Grammar School of Worcester'. For the next 200 years King's School sent a number of scholars to Oxford University. Then, in the early 1860s, the headmaster of Worcester Royal Grammar School said that those going to King's School were fee-paying and the phrase 'Free Grammar School' only applied to his own pupils. The dispute was so bitter that the Oxford University Commissioners decided to resolve it by refusing to take pupils from either school who had been awarded a Meake Scholarship!

Many of the present school buildings were paid for by James Dyson Perrins of the Lea and Perrins Worcestershire sauce factory who was an old boy, and the Perrins Hall, built in the Jacobean style, is named after him. In 2007 the school merged with the Alice Otley independent girls' school to become co-educational.

In *The Victoria County History* is the comment, 'It is remarkable that the two schools of Worcester have, after a century and a half of decadence and decay, thus blossomed out together in a growth far surpassing anything that either the masters or the governing body could have believed half a century ago.'

Prince Henry's Grammar School, Evesham

The old Evesham School porch

Evesham School has good reason to complain of the historians who have deprived it of its antiquity. Within the precincts of the great Benedictine Abbey was a school at which able local boys were taught Latin grammar and prepared for the priesthood. There is documentary evidence that the school existed in 1376 and perhaps before – even in the 1300s. Elfward was one of its early abbots. He moved away from the abbey and, when he was an old man, he asked to go back to Evesham Abbey to die. But the monks, remembering the flogging with which he had instilled grammar into them, said that if he did, they would leave.

The last Abbot of Evesham, Clement Litchfield, built a new school just outside the Great Gate of the abbey. A few years later, in 1539, the abbey was closed by Henry VIII but the school survived and the porch still stands in Merstow Green. A plaque identifies the building.

The school was never a wealthy one and was still struggling in 1605. The Vicar of Evesham, Dr Lewis Bayley, was determined to refound it more securely. Dr Bayley had been tutor to Prince Henry, the brother of the future Charles I. He still had important contacts at court and he managed to secure a new charter for the town, which included its school – hence the renaming of the school. Prince Henry was only twelve years old at the time, so it was unlikely that he had much to do with the decision. Sadly, the school lost its royal patron on his death in 1612.

The school continued to be poorly funded until the county council provided the present site in Victoria Avenue, by which time the school had become a co-educational grammar school. In 1973 it became a comprehensive high school, achieved grant maintained status in 1993, and became a Foundation School in September 1999.

WELL-KNOWN EARLY WORCESTERSHIRE SCHOOLS

For centuries education was thought to be wasted on girls, whose lives were to be spent in the home, looking after their families. Occasionally a school came into being that admitted girls, but their education usually centred around home crafts. A school was founded in Cropthorne in 1735 by Mrs Mary Holland where girls were admitted, then in 1815 Lady Apphia Appleton founded Peachfield Lodge School in Malvern. The girls were taught spinning and weaving, using the flax grown in the local fields. Wealthy young ladies were usually taught at home. Those who entered convents and nunneries usually continued their education, learning Latin and Greek, which were essential to those who were to work on the manuscripts in the libraries, copying and translating.

Wolverley Free Grammar School

One of Wolverley's early buildings, the Free Grammar School, still dominates the village. The school was founded in 1618 by William Sebright, who was born in Wolverley but became town clerk of London and acquired various properties both in London and Worcestershire.

There's a curious story that the school came to be founded because Sebright disliked London milk. He bought 20 acres of land in Bethnal Green where he could farm Worcestershire cows and, in his will of 1618, he left the money raised

Wolverley School

from the sale of this land for a school for the children of Wolverley, 'the place of my birth where I was bredd up'. It was on condition that the vicar should not be elected schoolmaster; this was probably not a personal vendetta, but possibly the vicar was a Royalist and Sebright was a Parliamentarian – certainly his grand-daughter became the wife of Oliver Cromwell. Over the years, the Bethnal Green investment has brought in a handsome income.

Sebright was interred in the Church of St Edmund the King, in Lombard Street. Some forty-six years later the church and his effigy was destroyed in the Great Fire of London, leaving the school in Wolverley as his only memorial.

The school has moved out of its wonderful building, but is still in existence as Wolverley Sebright VA Primary School.

Hanley Castle Grammar School

Many people believe that John Knottesford founded Hanley Castle Grammar School in 1485, but in actual fact he was only a trustee. The school can actually be traced back to 1326. The reason for the error is that Knottesford was allowed to erect a magnificent tomb in the church because, when the church was acquired by Henry VIII, Knottesford bought it from him for the parishioners.

In about 1589 a commission was set up to look into the abuse of charities, and one of its first investigations was into the mismanagement of Hanley Castle Grammar School. The rents from the land owned by the school should have been bringing in about £60 a year, but in fact they were only raising £8. Consequently, no schoolmaster had been employed and the school itself was employed in 'divers loathsome uses … by placing beggars and diseased persons in it'.

Hanley Castle Grammar School is best known to P. G. Wodehouse enthusiasts as Market Snodsbury Grammar School, attended by Bertie Wooster and his friend Gussie Fink-Nottle. The school features in several scenes in Wodehouse's writing, especially in the comedy in which Gussie gives a speech, having had his orange juice discreetly laced with gin.

By the mid-1900s Hanley Castle Grammar School had about 200 pupils aged eleven to eighteen but then, in 1969, it became a comprehensive. It now takes in pupils from Upton-upon-Severn and is one of three state secondary schools for children from Malvern; consequently, the number of pupils has grown to 900.

BROMSGROVE GRAMMAR SCHOOL OF KING EDWARD VI

Bromsgrove School's oldest building, commissioned by Sir Thomas Cookes around 1693

In Worcestershire, several of the old schools are named after a king or a queen. In most cases, the reigning monarch simply refounded an old school that is consequently much older than its name implies. For example, a grammar school at Rock (5 miles south-west of Bewdley) was attributed to Edward VI, but was founded in the first year of Henry VIII's reign by Sir Humphrey Connysbie, who donated lands to support a chantry priest and a free school.

Until the mid-1800s, it was assumed that Bromsgrove School had been founded by Edward VI, the son of Henry VIII. Then the headmaster, the Reverend Dr J. D. Collis, showed through his research that the school had existed during the reign of Henry VIII. In fact, a school at Bromsgrove was mentioned in the 1400s in the will of the local landowner, Humphrey Stafford, who founded a chantry in Bromsgrove Church. Endowments were made 'to fund a school-master, being a priest, who was not only bound to keep a school there but also to aid and assist the curate' (the spelling has been modernized). All that Edward VI did was to fix the payment of £7 per annum already made to the schoolmaster, and in return for rendering that meagre service, he took a lot of their land.

The school was put on a more stable footing in 1693 when Sir Thomas Cookes of Bentley bequeathed £50 annually, £20 of which was for a master to teach twelve poor boys living in Bromsgrove or adjoining parishes. Cookes also

Photograph courtesy of Bromsgrove School

Bromsgrove School. The former headmaster's house now accommodates
the administration offices and senior academic staff offices

rebuilt the school and the oldest part now dates back to that time. Three years later, Cookes gave £10,000 for a building at Oxford University, plus an endowment for its upkeep. The building was to be for boys from Bromsgrove and Feckenham, and especially for any of his own relatives. Gloucester Hall at Oxford was converted into Worcester College for this purpose. These rights were withdrawn in 1857, except for students of Bromsgrove School.

Throughout the centuries, Bromsgrove School has had its ups and downs and has even been closed occasionally. The period from 1816 to 1819 was perhaps one of the worst, when the Reverend Thomas Davies was appointed as master but was taken off to Fleet prison for debt. He was also found guilty of 'frequent inebriation in public as well as private' and 'the use of language not the most decorous'. The Bishop of Worcester was asked for help and managed to procure the Reverend John Topham of St John's College, Cambridge, who put the school on an upward curve. Among its famous pupils was the poet A. E. Housman, whose statue now stands in Bromsgrove High Street.

The county historian Treadway Russell Nash lived between 1725 and 1811 and wrote that, in his time, the school had only twelve boys who were taught, clothed and afterwards apprenticed. The school now has 1,500 pupils, aged from seven to eighteen!

Bromsgrove School have recently purchased Perry Hall, a seventeenth-century building, in the centre of the town. This was once the home of A. E. Housman, the poet

QUEEN ELIZABETH'S
GRAMMAR SCHOOL, HARTLEBURY

Once again, the name of the school is misleading and does not give the real age of the school. A school is mentioned at Hartlebury in William the Conqueror's Domesday Book of 1068, and the book of governors still exists, which goes back to the 'yere of our Lord God a thousand five hundredth fyftie and sixe'. The first building was a timber-framed hall where the younger children were taught to read and write, plus a small classroom where the headmaster taught Latin and Greek.

Bishop Edwin Sandys persuaded Queen Elizabeth in 1557 to grant the little school a royal charter. About ten years later, a list of statutes and ordinances was made; this has been preserved. One of these states: 'That the schoolmasters should take the profits of all cock-fights and potations commonly used in scools, and other gifts given to them by any of their friends or their scholars besides their wages, until their salaries should be augmented.'

We know that cocks were kept in the school because the order book, still kept by the trustees, has an entry in 1616 for the cost of 'the building of a brewhouse and Chamber and Cockloft over it, for Mr Pierce our head schoolmaster'.

The school fell into debt and was closed from 1841 to 1852. It was said that a question that the trustees could have settled in two days took the Court of Chancery eleven years to determine.

Stanley Baldwin, the Prime Minister, was chairman of the governors. In gratitude, the school presented him, in 1938, with a pair of gates for Astley Hall. Lord Baldwin's son gave them to the school in 1953 in memory of his father and they are still in use.

One morning in 1940, the boys arrived at the school to find it no longer existed as it had burned down overnight. Lessons were held in Hartlebury Castle until a new school was built.

The school had 120 boys when educational reforms came in during 1977 and it was merged with the two Kidderminster schools, King Charles I Grammar School and the Girls' High School, to become King Charles I School.

King Charles I Grammar School, Kidderminster

The Free Grammar School of Charles King of England in Kidderminster is the only school in England to bear the name of King Charles. This again is misleading as it was founded by the lord of the manor, Thomas Blount Esquire, in 1566. The school was renamed in 1636, during the reign of Charles I, when the charter to the town included the school. Until 1848, lessons were held, originally by the chantry priest, in a chapel at the east end of the parish church. The charge for learning writing and arithmetic in the mid-1700s was 5 shillings per quarter.

Lord Dudley supplied the funds for a new school in 1848. There was one large hall for the boys instead of classrooms, but the headmaster had a private room in the tower. The only playground for the boys was the churchyard. In 1851 an enthusiastic headmaster, John Shephard, took over the school and he sent several pupils to universities. Unfortunately he fell ill and, by the time he died in 1869, the number of pupils had dropped to six. Three years later the school was redeveloped and supplied with a new curriculum. By 1890, the number of pupils had risen to 86 and, in 1912, to 100 boys.

Kidderminster High School for Girls was founded in 1868 and moved to Hill Grove House in Comberton Road premises in 1912. In 1977, the school was joined by the Charles I School and by the Queen Elizabeth Grammar School in Hartlebury.

In 1868, a school for girls had been founded in Kidderminster and, in 1912, a school was built for them next to Hill Grove House in Comberton Road. The

Kidderminster High School for Girls

house was a splendid mansion, occupied in 1819 by William Boycott, a local draper, who was prominent in the town. It had a stone portico with columns, six large rooms downstairs, six bedrooms, plus servants' quarters and extensive gardens. The house passed through several hands until it was bought in 1919 by George Anton, a wealthy carpet manufacturer. George's widow died in 1948 and Worcestershire County Council were given the first option to buy the land, which they did, as the girl's school needed upgrading.

In 1977, Kidderminster High School for Girls merged with King Charles I School and Queen Elizabeth Grammar School in Hartlebury, so that they all now occupy the splendid premises of Hill Grove House.

EDUCATION AFTER 1800

Rowland Hill

Rowland Hill

The statue of Rowland Hill stands outside the Town Hall in Kidderminster. He is best known for inventing the present postal system, but he also helped to bring about changes in education. He founded the Hazelwood system, where younger pupils were taught by the older ones. He was born in Blackwell Street, Kidderminster, in 1795, one of six children, but when he was only a few years old the family moved to Birmingham. His father was an innovator in education and politics, and in his social circle were men such as Joseph Priestley and Tom Paine. They believed that education was a life-long process and that children should be given the skills to cope with life rather than being crammed with facts. Kindness, instead of caning, and moral influence, rather than fear, should be the predominant forces in school discipline.

The school was governed by a student council and science was a compulsory subject.

At the age of eleven, Rowland was appointed as a student teacher. In later years he set up a series of highly successful schools, first at Hilltop in Birmingham, then in 1819 at Hazelwood in Edgbaston, and at Tottenham in London in 1827. Teams of educationalists came from as far away as France to look at the schools and the chief French education officer placed his own son in a Rowland Hill school.

Rowland Hill died in Hampstead, London, in 1879 and is buried in Westminster Abbey. There is also a family memorial to him in Highgate cemetery.

Sunday Schools and Dame Schools

The children of the poor could learn the basics of reading, writing and arithmetic without payment through the Sunday School movement which began in 1757. Classes were held on Sundays (the only free day for many workers), local parishioners were employed as teachers, and the textbook was the Bible. Pupils were sometimes taught by those who could hardly read themselves! By the 1850s, in England, as many as 1.5 million children between the ages of five and fifteen were attending Sunday School.

Those who could afford a few pence each day might send their children to a Dame School. Almost anyone could put a few chairs in their front room, buy some slates and chalk, and call themselves a 'school'. In fact, some of the Dame Schools were little more than baby-minding establishments. William Avery, born in Redditch in 1800, remarks:

> As soon as I was old enough to be in anyone's way, my scholastic duties began. The first who commenced directing my enquiring mind was Mrs Biddle, in Evesham Street. When I was about six years old I went for a year to the finishing school kept by Mr (and Mrs) Henry James, in Evesham Street. The school was held in various houses. This was a mixed school, the terms ranging from fourpence to tenpence a week with an extra charge in winter time for fire. The style of teaching was one which would not, perhaps, be approved of by the present inspectors of schools, what was learnt was imparted on the stick principle, and was consequently remembered.

William Avery left school to become an apprentice needle-maker at the age of seven.

As the nineteenth century progressed there was an ever-increasing interest in education and it became a political hot-potato. Not only were the children of

England lagging behind those of the Continent in basic literacy, but manufacturers were having difficulty finding workers with sufficient expertise. The needle masters of Redditch complained that they had to buy their machines from Germany as there were no design engineers in England.

Victorian schools

There was a step forward in 1833 when, for the first time, Parliament became involved with education and a sum of money was made available annually for the building of schools for working-class children.

Schools mushroomed across Worcestershire. There was often bitter rivalry between the nonconformists, the Church of England and the Catholics; consequently, there was tremendous competition between the denominations to raise funds and build schools. In 1844 the Reverend G. F. Fessey, Vicar of St Stephen's in Redditch, wrote to the Anglican National Society (builders of the Anglican schools) warning them, 'The Wesleyans, always a powerful sect in this place ... are using every means to anticipate us in the establishment of a school.' Almost immediately the National Society gave a grant for a new school. The Reverend G. F. Fessey worked hard to collect the rest of the money required for the building.

Schoolrooms were added to, or converted from, existing church buildings, such as Worcester's St Peter's, Clent's St Nicholas, and Cropthorne's St Michael's. In Tardebigge, Lady Harriet Clive converted a public house into a school. She came to live at Hewell Grange in about 1819 and worshipped in Tardebigge Church every Sunday.

Opposite the church was The Magpie Inn, and the locals say that the vicar would set his congregation working their way through the psalms while he nipped across to The Magpie Inn for a quick pint! Lady Harriet hated The Magpie so much that one Sunday, as she walked past, she removed the pub sign. The ground drops steeply by the side of Tardebigge Church into the Birmingham and Worcester canal (see Chapter 10). Nearby is the start of the 580-yard Tardebigge tunnel where boats had to be taken through by leggers – that is, men lying on their back and 'walking' along the walls. The leggers used to wait for work in The Magpie, with the result that some of them began work in an inebriated state. When, in about 1820, one of the leggers fell into the canal and was drowned, Lady Harriet took the opportunity to close the inn and turn it into a school.

Twenty-three years later, Lady Harriet built two separate schools on the site, one for boys and one for girls. The old pub building was partly demolished and converted into living accommodation. The school and the house are still there, although the school has been modernized.

The building of a new church and Sunday School in Redditch reaped unexpected rewards. In the early 1800s Thomas Williams had a little needle-making factory in Evesham Street in the centre of Redditch. He was a Methodist, but he objected to all the rules and regulations, so he gathered a small group of needle-makers together and founded a branch of the Independent movement, later known as the Congregational Church. He bought 2 acres of land next to his factory and in 1825 a foundation stone was laid for a new church complex. Thomas died just eight weeks later, so he never saw any of his buildings completed. A church and a large Sunday School were built on the site. The ground floor of the school had many rooms and on the first floor was a hall and four large classrooms. The Congregationalists also owned the freehold of most of the shops and property on that side of Evesham Street. When the Redditch Development Corporation arrived to build the new town, they discovered to their surprise that the Congregationalists owned a large part of the town centre. The Congregationalists would only sell their land to the authorities on condition that they had a central church in return. This was an awkward request, but a compromise was made by way of the second-floor Ecumenical Centre.

The establishing of School Boards

The Forster Education Act of 1870 was of great importance. England was divided up into 2,500 areas and in each of these a School Board was elected by the ratepayers to look at education in that area. The various voluntary schools were allowed to continue unchanged, but if there were not enough schools, members of the School Board had the authority to build them with money provided by the ratepayers. The religious instruction was to be non-denominational, which did not please the various Christian groups. The Boards could charge a weekly fee not exceeding 9d and they could also apply for funding in the form of a government loan. Attendance of all children had to be guaranteed, so they were allowed to appoint 'Board Men', or School Attendance Officers, to visit the home of any child absent from school. 'The Board Man will be after you' was a common threat in many households. Quite incidentally, the Act was a first step towards women being given the franchise, as they were allowed to vote for members of the Board and sit on the Board themselves.

Most Board schools were built on a shoestring to avoid a sharp rise in the rates. Hume Street Board School in Kidderminster was opened in 1877 with two classrooms and unbelievably horrendous lavatories. The girls' lavatory consisted of two planks and a hole in the ground, while the boys' urinal had slate panels and only one toilet. Yet the infants from St John's School in Chapel Street were transferred here in 1925 when their building was condemned, so that must have been even worse! Hume Street School closed in the 1980s.

Droitwich was more fortunate. Two years after the passing of the 1870 Education Act, John Corbett provided his Stoke Works families with a handsome Gothic-styled Mission Hall and school. Situated in Shawl Lane, the establishment was one of the largest in Worcestershire. Its main building accommodated 500 girls and boys in a central area divided by a partition, girls on one side, boys on the other. It had playgrounds and other recreational establishments, all paid for by John Corbett himself. On Sundays the school became a Mission Hall.

The life of a Victorian schoolteacher was appalling. St John's Girls' School in Kidderminster was founded in 1862. The headmistress, Miss Starr, was straight from teacher training college and her only assistants in a school of about 130 girls were two pupil teachers and two monitors, one of them unpaid. The pupil teachers would probably have been about fourteen years of age and the monitors about twelve. Miss Starr would have had to teach the top class, look after the school as a whole as its headmistress, prepare the pupil teachers for their examinations to enter teacher training college, and apply for grants. Sometimes the vicar or a member of the local gentry would pop in to help.

The old St John's Girls School. This is actually the second school, the first has long since disappeared. The girls were in one part, the boys in another and the infants were in the chapel

There were two classrooms; the larger one had a gallery, while the smaller one was used for infants or special classes. A stove heated the larger room, but the winters of the 1860s were so cold that Miss Starr was obliged to march the girls round between lessons to keep them warm! There were no desks. Usually, work was done on slates that were taken home to be washed; only the older girls had paper and pencil. It was not until seventeen years after the school's foundation that a request was passed to the managers for the installation of drinking water.

The schoolmistress also had to keep accounts. Education was not free until 1891 and each girl was supposed to bring her pennies to school. If she didn't do so, Miss Starr had to send her home, but sometimes there was no money in the house and the girl failed to return.

Attendance was irregular. Children were often absent on Mondays and Fridays to help with the weekly washings or to look after the younger brothers and sisters. The school would sometimes be closed for days or even weeks on end because of a virus. The years 1886 and 1887, for example, saw one epidemic after another, of measles, conjunctivitis and scarlet fever. In most rural areas, allowances were made within the 1870 Act for schoolchildren to assist farmers with the harvest. Miss Starr makes a note in her log of 1862 that some pupils asked to leave early because the pig killer was coming. Many people kept pigs in their backyard and would have employed a man to kill them. There would have been much squealing, smell and mess, and obviously the children didn't want to miss the excitement!

Some of the young monitors had difficulty controlling their classes. An entry in the 1866 log book is a typical example: 'Sent part of 4th class into 5th and part to 3rd for the monitress could not govern them.'

Miss Starr left in 1865 after three years of hard work, and Miss Tustin arrived. She discovered that, in addition to her normal duties, she had to teach at night school! She should have been helped by the volunteer staff, but they were often absent and she was left on her own with as many as forty-seven girls, all at different stages. To make matters worse, boys were outside throwing stones at the classroom windows. She had to wait for three years until help arrived and a new mistress came to oversee the infants.

Compulsory attendance was not introduced until 1880; it was supposed to be from five to thirteen years, but children could leave over the age of ten if they had achieved a certain educational standard. Over the next few years the compulsory school leaving age crept up until, under the 1918 Education Act, it reached the dizzy heights of fourteen.

When free education arrived in 1891, Miss Ireson wrote in the log book of Crabbs Cross School, 'Free education! What a boon! No bother about school fees or attendance.'

FROM 1904 ONWARDS

In the late nineteenth century the schools were swept up in the patriotic fervour of the time. Queen Victoria's birthday fell on 24 May, and from 1904 onwards this became known as 'Empire Day'. Children would march round the hall, singing patriotic songs and waving Union Jacks.

During the First and Second World Wars, 1914–18 and 1939–45, there was little progress in education but in 1944, when it became obvious that England would be victorious, a great euphoria swept through the nation. The terror and shortages of the war were coming to an end and a glorious new vista was opening up and this included education. The 1944 Butler Education Act brought hope to all. Schools with substandard buildings were to be demolished. At that time, the educational standard of most schools was shockingly low. Pupils were admitted at the age of five and spent their entire education at the same school, leaving in their early teens. Under the Act, pupils were to enter a new system at the age of eleven. There would be a free grammar school for those children who passed the eleven plus but, if they failed, the secondary modern and technical schools provided an equally good education more suited to the non-academic child. As one Worcestershire mother remarked, 'If our Margaret doesn't pass for the eleven plus, it doesn't matter, she'll learn shorthand and typing at the secondary modern which might be better for her as a career anyway. In fact, I might not put her in for the eleven plus.' In the Act the school leaving age was raised to fifteen, then – in 1971 – to sixteen.

The Labour government of 1965 decided to combine grammar and secondary modern schools into comprehensive schools. In 1971 Worcestershire decided that it would adopt a three-tier system of education. The primary schools would be from five to nine years old, then pupils would move to the middle schools from nine to thirteen, and finally to the high schools from thirteen to eighteen. One Worcestershire headmaster has remarked that most education experiments in the county have been dictated more by the availability of buildings than by any educational philosophy.

11

TRAVEL AND TRANSPORT

❧ *Roads* ❧

The original stones of the Roman roads have long since disappeared, but amazingly, after 2,000 years, several roads still follow the same routes. In the first century, the Romans built a road from Gloucester to Littlechester near Derby. Today, the A38 from Worcester to Wall in Staffordshire follows much the same line, going north from Worcester through Droitwich, Wychbold, Bromsgrove, Longbridge and on into Staffordshire.

The following is an excerpt from Neville Billington's local history paper to the Worcestershire Forum Local History Day School in November 2008:

I think many Roman roads remained serviceable until around 1066, hereafter, they fell into serious disrepair. I think the main obstacle to proper understanding of the subject is that the word 'road' is a misnomer for the Medieval period. 'Ways' – or better still 'tracks' – are better words to describe the dire underfoot and underhoof conditions and the narrowness of passage.

Sadly, this is all that remains of part of the Roman road between Wixford and Alcester

There is some evidence that maintenance of ways in this period was a manorial responsibility. Parishes had no statutory responsibility in the era we are discussing but they may have occasionally become involved by necessity. Certainly the monasteries took a serious interest in the upkeep of ways on humanitarian grounds and built bridges to deal with the harrowing situations that arose in times of heavy rainfall. Swollen rivers could cause hundreds of wayfarers, many with children, penniless and desperately hungry, to be stranded either side of a fording place for days or weeks on end and it is easy to understand why monasteries strove to alleviate this plight. In many cases when a monastery built a bridge, it would even construct a chapel on it so that travellers could pause and worship when crossing. There was such a bridge in Droitwich. Today's bridge was built in the 1930s but it used to be called Chapel Bridge. In olden days carts and carriages crossed the river via a ford, but travellers on foot and on horseback had the option to go via the bridge and through the chapel. This meant that when the Salwarpe was in spate travellers caused serious interruption to worship. Eventually, on 27 May 1751 the Vicar of St Peter's, the Reverend Treadway Nash, and others applied to the Diocese for a faculty to demolish the chapel. Their application said: 'There is a common road through the chapel ... which is dayley made use of by travellers'. It went on to complain that 'during devine service travellers pass and re-pass the same on horseback' and went on to describe the situation as a 'great scandal to religion'.

One of the oldest original bridges in Worcestershire is the packhorse bridge at Shell on the Saltway between Droitwich and Worcester. The bridge is just wide enough to take a man and a horse

The problem of river crossing caused such difficulty that many bridges were built by local gentry. Such a bridge – of wooden construction just wide enough to take a horse – was built by Humphrey Pakington over the River Teme in the Worcestershire village of Stanford in 1548. In later years this was replaced by a stone bridge (which survived until a few years ago). For many years, a brass plaque was affixed to the parapet of this bridge which recalled the earlier structure. The plaque read: 'Humfrey Pakynton borne in Stanford … payd for yt workmanship and makyine of this brygge the whiche was rered and made the first day of may and in the furste yere of yt rayne of Kyng Edwarde.'

In 1555 parishes formally became responsible for repair of the ways but this was greatly resented. It brought no more than very patchy improvement for the traveller. Writing in 1586 William Harrison said: 'Now to speak generallie of our common high waies through the English part of the lie, you shall vnderstand that in the claie or cledgie soile they are often veerie deepe and troublesome in the winter half.'

In early Medieval times England was very much a land of wilderness with huge forested areas, moors and heathland making it very easy for travellers to become hopelessly and dangerously lost. Enclosure of many parts of the country started in the Tudor period, with fields and hedges gradually becoming an increasing feature of the landscape. The Enclosure Acts in the 1730s greatly hastened this, in so doing consolidating the spread of lanes that to an extent lessened the chances of getting lost. Nonetheless, enclosing did not happen everywhere. People routinely died of exhaustion, hunger and hypothermia miles from anywhere, causing the expression 'fallen by the wayside' to become an enduring expression in our language.

In an attempt to avoid people becoming lost, in 1697 a statutory duty was imposed on parishes to erect direction markers at significant points along the main ways in order that travellers might be guided.

For centuries there was a great diversity of people travelling the ways of the kingdom: packhorse trains, drovers, waggoners, tinkers, hawkers, minstrels, tumblers, preachers, messengers, pedlars, wounded soldiers and just plain wanderers. People would sometimes be simply destitute, roaming the countryside …. Ways were narrow and would frequently become waterlogged, largely impassable in winter.

Let's start our journey from Worcester and take the way northwards. We soon come to Droitwich and we cross the River Salwarpe just a few yards north of the Saltway crossroads. People carrying salt from hereabouts travelled to distant places from the earliest times and loads of this type would usually be conveyed by pack horse with the return journey carrying a different commodity (perhaps wood in this case).

Professor Christopher Dyer tells of an incident at Wychbold, the next village as we head north from Droitwich. It concerns a long-distance carrier named William

Part of the Saltway running between Droitwich and Alcester

de Bottebroc. He lost his life in the village in 1277 when his cart, loaded with a large barrel of wine, toppled over and fell on him. It is believed that the wine had been collected from the quay at Worcester and was on its way to someone in Coventry.

A short distance from Wychbold we come to Upton Warren. Betty Wright has recently been looking at parish registers for the village and we learn from her that in 1853, a baby named Noah Bury was baptized in the village. His parents were Thomas and Elizabeth, described as 'travellers from Farnborough'. They were camping in Holloway Lane.

Leaving Upton Warren the modern road snakes right and then left as it heads towards Puddlewarf Hill. If you look over the hedge to the left you can still see the line of the Roman road cut through the hill in the field, from whence it coincides again with the modern road at Rock Hill. It continues via Worcester Road dead straight to Bromsgrove High Street. Edward III and his court made an overnight stop in Bromsgrove during his journey on this route from Worcester to Lichfield in 1327. Kings in those days usually travelled on horseback but the carriage that followed him would have carried key female members of his court. The carriage was heavy and was drawn by three or four horses which were harnessed in-line owing to the narrowness of the ways. It was extremely ornate with tapestries hanging, unbearably hot in summer and bitterly cold in winter; dogs, birds and squirrels were carried as pets. The vehicle had no springs. At least a king and his entourage in those days had the reassurance of a company of archers to ensure safe passage from outlaws, thieves and brigands, hazards common wayfarers faced daily.

Roamers would sometimes tell hard-luck stories to get a night's rest and a bite to eat. On 30 December 1680 Thomas Ogden reached Bromsgrove 'from Whits-by in Yorkshire Coasts and was bound Bristoll Losing All he head by ship rack', a plight that earned him a night's rest in the town.

We are heading northwards and the road now takes us to Townsend Mill. From here the Roman road went as the crow flies to Lickey Rock and the latest satellite photographs of the field beside the modern A38 show the Roman foundations with remarkable clarity, albeit only for a few yards. So we will turn left and follow the way of later centuries to Lickey End where there used to be a toll house on the Worcester to Birmingham Turnpike (the way was turnpiked in 1727). It is from here that the road through Rubery to Longbridge was cut in 1830, which later became the route of the A38. So, from the days of the Romans to 1830, the only way north was over Lickey and this is the way we are going, in so doing following relatively closely to the footsteps of the Romans and tackling a gradual climb towards the summit of Rose Hill.

An incident reported in The Times on 9 February 1799 reminds us of the difficulties the weather could cause. Passengers in the Admiral Duncan Long Coach heading for Bristol were stranded in snow for hours at Lickey on this road while an operation involving no fewer than ten horses were engaged to free it.

The road now leaves Worcestershire and enters Staffordshire.

––––––––––––––––––––

TRUSTS AND TOLL ROADS

Roads began to be turnpiked in the eighteenth century. Small groups of wealthy local men formed Turnpike Trusts which were responsible for collecting tolls and using them to keep the road in good order. Each section of toll road had to be approved by an Act of Parliament. The first Worcestershire turnpike road was the Bromsgrove turnpike in 1726 on the Worcester Road, followed by the Hagley turnpike of 1753. A toll road from Birmingham was planned to reach Evesham to take the produce to the Birmingham markets, but the Trust ran out of money and the toll road ended at Dunnington crossroads.

There's still a tollhouse at Dunnington, now converted into residential accommodation. Trustees usually set up stones or posts stating the distances

From the 1750s, Acts required Trusts to erect milestones. This one is near Little Malvern by the Welland crossroads

from nearby towns. By the middle of the nineteenth century, between 400 and 500 miles of roads in Worcestershire were under the control of Turnpike Trusts.

Some of the tolls were used to build toll houses and pay for a tollmaster. On a busy road, tollkeepers worked long hours so that often the keeper and his wife would work shifts. Although today the tollhouses seem tiny, they were more spacious than most of the working-class houses of their day and large families were often reared in them. Many of these tollhouses have survived, and the Milestone Society have identified some at Stoke Prior, Hunnington, Droitwich (at the

The tollhouse at Dunnington

This tollhouse has been rescued by Avoncroft Museum of Historic Buildings.
It was built in 1822 at Little Malvern as part of Upton-on-Severn's turnpike road

beginning of the Saltway), Drakes Broughton, Pershore, Wribbenhall, Kidder-minster and Fairfield.

The old tollhouse is still there by the bridge at Stourport-on-Severn. Origi-nally, the tollhouse was one side of the bridge and the kitchen on the other, so that when the wife of the tollkeeper was on duty and cooking, she had to leave her saucepans to run across the road and collect the tolls. By 1893 the cost of the bridge had been paid for and so it was made free. Fifteen thousand people arrived to celebrate the festivities. A song was composed in honour of the tollkeeper:

> *Then a 'good word' for 'Peter Snider', he's a faithful servant been,*
> *For you always had to pay when you wished to cross the stream.*
> *No matter how impatient you was to get away*
> *He would always keep the gate shut till you'd pay*
> *And then he'd let you pass through – right away.*

The tollgate at Hartlebury had a particularly conscientious tollkeeper. In the late 1700s George III arrived with his splendid retinue to visit the bishop, but the toll-keeper closed the gate and refused to let them through until each and every one of them, including the king, had paid the appropriate tolls.

The old tollhouse on the bridge at Stourport-on-Severn

In the second half of the eighteenth century many Trusts experienced financial difficulties and closed.

HORSES AND COACHES

Scott Atkinson, who first promoted the nickel cadmium battery in England, was asked in the 1970s, 'What was the overriding memory of your childhood?' to which he replied, 'The smell of horse manure'. For thousands of years, most transport involved a horse. The first cars began to appear during the last few years of the nineteenth century, heralding a totally new way of life. Even today, many pensioners have an equine tale to tell. David Wilson from Hunt End near Astwood Bank, says, 'My grandfather was Herbert Morris. He used to keep cows and had a horse and a milk float. Every morning he would get up early, milk the cows and do his milk round, but on the way home he would spend all his money in the pubs. Then he would go to sleep in the float and the horse would take him home. My grandmother would throw the pots and pans at him, but he never changed.'

Because of the depression and rationing, horses were still being used in the 1950s.

Farm wagons in the Transport Section of Worcestershire County Museum in Hartlebury Castle

HIGHWAYMEN

At the close of the Civil War, stagecoach services appeared. The slow, cumbersome vehicles were easy prey for robbers and from about 1650 to 1750 highwaymen were a menace to travellers, and today feature prominently in Worcestershire folklore. The notorious forger, thief and highwayman Captain Thomas Dangerfield (1650–85) kept a diary and in it he notes that he spent a night at The Angel in Pershore.

Then there was Captain James Hind (1618–52), a Royalist who had a reputation for courtesy and it is said that he robbed the rich to feed the poor. When he held up Parliamentarians, he gave them a lecture on the way that they had treated the king. He fought in the Battle of Worcester, but managed to escape to London where he changed his name and worked as a barber. He was betrayed and arrested in 1651, and finally sent to Worcester to be tried. Highwaymen were only hanged, but Hind was said to have helped Charles II to escape and was therefore tried for high treason, which carried the greater penalty of being hung, drawn and quartered. Parts of his body were displayed in different parts of the

Holy Trinity Church on the Lickey Hills. The highwayman Captain James Hind is reputed to come here, looking for his head

town and probably later wired together and hung from a gibbet. However, his head, which was placed on Worcester Bridge gate, was buried in a Worcestershire churchyard – though no one knows which one. According to Worcestershire folklore, Hind visits the county looking for his head. A retired engineer moved to a modern bungalow in the Lickey Hills near Monument Lane in 1979, and says he had not been there long before he began hearing strange stories from the locals. One evening he heard a clippity clop outside his bungalow, and rushed out just in time to see a headless rider drifting through his hedge with his head under his arm.

With the coming of well-armed mail coaches, and later, the railways, the highwayman petered out.

_____

PASSENGER COACHES

By the 1800s, roads had improved and coaches became more comfortable. A double-bodied postcoach was advertised in 1808 as taking passengers and running from Worcester to London three days a week, starting from Worcester at noon and arriving in London at 8 a.m. the next morning.

By 1841 four coaches a day (except on Sundays) were running from Worcester to London several times a week and to all major Midland towns plus places as far afield as Liverpool, Leeds, Carmarthen, Aberystwyth, South-hampton and Bath. Horses were changed every 10 or 15 miles so that coaching inns developed, such as The George in Bewdley, The Angel in Pershore and Ye Olde Talbot Hotel in Worcester.

Although the stagecoach has captured the public imagination, it only lasted for fifty or sixty years as the main form of public transport in this country.

Worcestershire County Museum at Hartlebury Castle has a collection of vehicles through the ages, and although they don't have a stagecoach, they do have a four-in-hand coach from about 1830, used by the Heygate family to travel from Southend to London.

THE ROYAL MAIL

The Royal Mail's origins go back to 1516 when Henry VIII, frustrated at the non-delivery of his personal post, created a Master of Posts. Even before the Civil War, postmasters were settled in all the important towns of England. Post boys

The Angel Inn and Posting House at Pershore. The infamous highwayman,
Dangerfield, wrote in his diary that he stayed here

were introduced nearly a century later, in 1719, and although they were called 'boys' they could be any age from sixteen to sixty. The post went to a central depot, and from there was taken out by the post boys either on horseback or by mailcarts. The landlord of The Angel in Pershore, early in the 1900s, said he could remember seeing a row of beds in the stables where the post boys slept. They were filled with straw and looked like a row of coffins.

The post boy was supposed to travel at 5 mph, but rarely achieved such a speed. Stagecoaches were much faster, but it was illegal for them to carry post. Then it was suggested to the Postmaster General that the mail should be carried by a dedicated stagecoach, and the first 'mailcoach' ran in 1784 between London and Bristol.

The Royal Mail revolutionized travel in England. The coach had to run to time, so the roads needed to be improved. An operating timetable was laid down and a fee per mile agreed. Passengers took second place; only four per coach were allowed, and if they were late they were left behind. All postmasters and postmistresses had to have their post for collection sealed and ready to be picked up, hanging on a cleft stick for the guard to grab as the coach thundered past. The post to be delivered was thrown off the coach to be taken round locally by the post boys, now known as postmen.

The mailcoach was exempt from tolls, so there was no stopping at the toll gates. The guard blew a horn when approaching a toll gate and keepers were to open their gates when the coach was not less than 250 yards away. This was at

The George Hotel in Bewdley, another of Worcestershire's posting houses

any time of the day or night as the mailcoach often raced through the night. Horses had to be changed every 6 to 8 miles. Aloft was the guard, a Post Office representative. He carried a brace of pistols, a cutlass and a blunderbuss and was usually an ex-soldier. Both he and the coach driver were immaculately turned out with scarlet coats and tall hats.

A coaching inn would keep a dozen or more horses in readiness. Two minutes was enough to change the coach horses, and sometimes it could be done in fifty seconds. The driver or guard might be changed at the coaching inn, or a passenger would alight, and a large staff of cooks, waiters, waitresses and kitchen maids would be in attendance.

ROWLAND HILL

By 1830, 261 mailcoaches were operating under royal licence. Postage was paid by the recipient according to the number of pages used and the distance travelled; consequently, the post was only used by the wealthy. Then in 1837, Rowland Hill (see also Chapter 9) published a pamphlet recommending various postal reforms. He had been born in Blackwell Street, Kidderminster, in 1795. His family had been wealthy landowners since the thirteenth century, but the French wars ruined his father's company that manufactured a coarse weave of cloth known as Kidderminster stuffs. When Rowland was only about five, the family had to leave Kidderminster, and move nearer to Birmingham.

Rowland suggested that there should be a uniform rate of postage at one penny per half ounce prepaid by an adhesive stamp. This was greeted with derision by Royal Mail officials, and the Postmaster General said that he had never heard of such an extraordinary scheme. Nevertheless, the idea received popular support and the 'Penny Post' was accepted by Parliament in 1839.

William Avery, the Redditch diarist, writes:

> The year 1840 was one of great importance … as being the year in which the postage of letters was reduced to a penny. The post office resources must have been taxed to the very utmost, for I believe that almost every man who had a friend made an excuse to send a letter, and those who had not a friend sent an unpaid missive to an enemy, leaving him to pay the postage, which was double.

By 1841, only a year after the Penny Post had been introduced, the Post Office at 49 Foregate Street, Worcester, was open from 7 a.m. to 10 p.m., with several deliveries and collections to and from different destinations every hour, both day and night.

Rowland Hill was appointed Chief Secretary to the Postmaster General in 1854 and he was made a KCB in 1860. He died at Hampstead in London in 1879, and two years later a statue of him was erected outside Kidderminster Town Hall.

✥ *Rivers and canals* ✥

The three main rivers of Worcestershire are the Severn, the Teme and the Avon. The Severn is the greatest – the Romans called it 'Sabrina' – and it was once the second busiest river in Europe. It rises as an insignificant stream high on Plynlimon, and finally empties into the Severn estuary below Gloucester. It travels through Welshpool, Shrewsbury, Bridgnorth, Bewdley and Worcester.

The Teme rises in the Kerry Hills, flowing through Powys, Shropshire, Herefordshire and Worcestershire to meet with the River Severn near Worcester. It has never been made navigable, with the result that it is a completely natural river, winding through green banks, running shallow in some places and deep in others.

The River Teme at Shelsley Beauchamp

The River Avon below the Cleeve Hill escarpment

The River Avon begins at Naseby and is said to rise in the garden of the manor house opposite the church, where wording on a cast-iron cone states 'Source of the Avon 1822', but there has been no water here within living memory.

It passes the magnificent abbeys of Tewkesbury, Pershore and Evesham, the battlefields of Evesham and Naseby, the castles of Warwick and Kenilworth, and Shakespeare's birthplace – Stratford-upon-Avon. It finally joins the Severn at Tewkesbury.

North of Tewkesbury, the River Avon forms the boundary between Gloucestershire and Worcestershire for about four miles. Nearly halfway along this stretch of river is the little village of Twining Fleet, once a popular destination for holidaymakers who could hire boats or take trips from Tewkesbury and visit the church or The Fleet Inn.

There were two ferries here: a small one for passengers, and a larger one, capable of carrying animals, carts and wagons across the river. In the spring of 1875 it took on board a two-horse dray, loaded with several casks of beer. As the boat neared the bank, the horses started to panic and got out of control. They jumped into the river, pulling the driver and the dray after them. The ferryman managed to pull the drayman out of the river, but the two horses were drowned.

Cropthorne Mill and weir. Most of the mills in Worcestershire were powered by water wheels. The River Avon has been diverted to enable boats to avoid the weir

The Avon was one of the first natural rivers to be made navigable. In the reign of Charles I, in 1635, William Sandys of the wealthy Worcestershire family was granted the authority to improve the Severn through Worcester and Gloucester to Warwick, so that it would take barges of up to 30 tons. He completed the work in three years, but unfortunately the Civil War followed. Bridges were blown up and much of his work destroyed. By 1725, when the novelist Daniel Defoe passed through, the river was navigable again for heavy goods.

The river transport, though, was unable to compete against the railways, and by 1874 the Avon was derelict. It was saved in 1949 by Douglas Barwell. He bought the defunct Lower Avon Navigation Company and formed a Trust, and by hard work and dedication they managed, in 1962, to open the river for boats as far as Evesham. This was the first successful restoration of a river by a voluntary organization and was a great inspiration to others. The Upper Avon Navigation Trust was formed in 1965, with the result that the river from Tewkesbury to Stratford was opened for craft in 1974.

Canal mania and a new Worcestershire town

One of the first canal complexes was built in Worcestershire. Francis Egerton, 3rd Duke of Bridgewater, was only in his twenties when, after an unhappy love affair, he became obsessed with a scheme to combine the four great rivers of England: the Trent, the Mersey, the Thames and the Severn. To raise the finances he lived like a hermit in his stately home. He employed James Brindley, who had already worked with him on canals that ran from the duke's coal mines at Worsley to the markets in Manchester.

James Brindley was born in 1716, and even as a child was building toy water mills, so it was almost inevitable that he would one day become a millwright. He was a meticulous man, always dressing carefully in a smart snuff-coloured coat and white cravat. He married the daughter of his colleague when he was forty-nine and she was nineteen. The novelist Arnold Bennett was a descendant.

The duke asked Brindley to survey for two canals, the Trent and Mersey, and the Staffordshire and Worcestershire. On 14 May 1766, an Act was passed authorizing both canals. There had been a problem with the latter – where should

Stourport-on-Severn

it join the River Severn? Brindley had decided on a sandy waste, known as Lower Mitton, by the Severn in the flat Stour valley. To everyone's amazement, the sandy waste grew into a town known as Stourport-on-Severn. Dr Treadway Russell Nash (1725–1811) wrote:

> About 1766 where the river Stour empties itself into the Severn below Mitton, stood a little alehouse called Stourmoth: near this place Brindley has caused a town to be erected, made a port and dockyards, built a new and elegant bridge, established markets, and made it the wonder not only of this county but of the nation at large … Thus was the sandy barren common at Stourport converted, in the space of thirty years into a flourishing, healthy and very populous village.

After Birmingham, Stourport-on-Severn became the busiest inland port in the Midlands. By 1783 it had brass and iron foundries, vinegar works, tan yards, worsted spinning mills, carpet manufacturers, barge and boatbuilding yards, wharves, warehouses, shops, inns and houses, and by 1795 it had about 1,300 inhabitants. Inspired by its success, canal mania began and between 1790 and 1797, fifty-six canals were constructed; many others were proposed and turned down by Parliament.

The former central warehouse in Stourport-on-Severn, dated early nineteenth century

Brindley was also surveying for other canals, and his hard work and dedication undermined his health so that in 1772 when he was only about fifty-six, he died from diabetes and a kidney infection. Sadly, he never saw his wonderful new town completed.

As for the Duke of Bridgewater, his dream was realized in 1790 when the Birmingham/Fazeley/Fradley/Coventry/Oxford line was finished. The canals were very profitable and he made an enormous fortune, but he never married and on his death his fortune passed to a cousin.

Many of the buildings in Stourport-on-Severn were on a 200-year lease, a fact that had been overlooked until, in the late 1900s, shops and family businesses discovered that they didn't own the ground on which they stood. One of the victims was the Methodist Church. The owners offered to sell the freehold to the congregation, but they could not afford it and the church was closed. Fortunately, the building was listed and no one would buy the site for development, so after three years it still had not been sold and the asking price for the freehold was reduced. By that time, the Methodists had managed to raise enough money to purchase the freehold so they were able to move back into their church.

————————————————

PRESERVING AND IMPROVING THE CANALS

One of the worst battles in Parliamentary history occurred in 1842 over a Bill to improve the waterways so they could take larger boats. It was finally decided that the River Severn was to be dredged and deepened, and locks were to be constructed at Holt, Lincombe, Bevere and Diglis. When Lincombe Lock was built in 1844, the depth of the water between Worcester and Stourport increased by 5 or 6 feet.

George Cadbury is famous for his chocolate – less well known is the fact that he saved the Staffordshire and Worcestershire canal from closure. By the 1920s the docks at Stourport had fallen into disrepair. George Cadbury took over as chairman of the governing body, persuaded the company who ran the docks to lower their charges, modernized boats and facilities, and mounted a publicity campaign. By 1938 the canal was profitable again and all debts had been cleared.

There's a plaque on the wall of the canal at Stourport to boat-builder Holt Abbot, who saved the inland waterways. In 1947 he was forced to give up his work as an engineer owing to a collapsed lung. He had already built one narrow boat so he decided to convert his hobby into a business by boatbuilding, and founded Canal Pleasurecraft Ltd. Then, in 1954, Holt read in the papers that the council had decided to cut off the River Severn from one of Stourport-on-

Severn's basins and turn the basin into a charabanc park. This would mean that the basins were cut off from the River Severn. Holt was devastated and began a campaign to keep the canals open. As a result, £500,000 was allocated to stop the decline of the canals and in the following year, 1956, Parliament voted another £5,500,000 to the regeneration and preservation of the canal systems.

A year before Brindley died, he designed the Droitwich Barge canal to carry salt from Droitwich to the River Severn north of Worcester at Hawford. Almost at the end of the canal-building era, in 1854, another small canal, the Droitwich Junction canal, was completed, which connected the Barge canal with the Worcester & Birmingham canal. Commercial traffic finished in 1916 and the canal was closed. Some land was sold off to private landowners and the M5 motorway cut through it in the 1960s.

Then, in 1973, a group of volunteers gathered at Droitwich, determined to reopen the canal. A Trust was formed and grants were applied for. Derelict locks and bridges had to be rebuilt and a new tunnel created under the A449 Worcester to Kidderminster Road. The canal ring was opened in July 2011 after a three-year regeneration plan costing £12.5 million. The Droitwich canals will now link the Worcester & Birmingham canal to the upper reaches of the River Severn, forming a cruising ring of about 22 miles, known as the 'mid-Worcestershire ring'.

_____

RIVER SEVERN BOATS AND THE PEOPLE WHO WORKED THEM

In the early days, both the River Severn and the canal were very shallow and only three types of vessels tended to be used: the narrow boats, the barges and the magnificent trows. Although the trows were flat-bottomed boats, they could be as long as 100 feet and a mast could be as high as 80 feet. Where the river ran shallow, teams of bow'olliers (boat haulers) would drag the boat through the muddy, shallow stretches. A trow has been preserved at Gloucester docks.

The cargoes included pig iron, rod iron and iron wares, coal, fruit, spices, tobacco, wool, fish oil for lamps, leather products, glass from Stourbridge, pot clay from Amblecote, rolls of carpet from Kidderminster, porcelain from Worcester, and salt from Droitwich.

Entire families were born, worked and died on the boats. Bill and Bert Hughes are the grandchildren of Joby Clarke who worked as a boat carrier for the LMS Scottish Railway. They said, 'Our grandmother was a proper boat lady. She had thirteen children and they all lived on the boat. There was a cabin at the front for the children and one at the back for their parents. It was a rough, tough life; if a wife hit the side of the lock with the barge or made some clumsy manoeuvre her husband would smack her ear'ole.'

An Act of 1877 limited the number of people who could live on a boat and another of 1884 made schooling compulsory for canal boat children. The Black Star in Stourport-on-Severn dates back to the 1700s and is three buildings combined. The section nearest the road was the original pub, the middle section could have been a chapel, and the section furthest away is thought to have been a school for waterways children.

PASSENGER BOATS AND STEAMERS

A delivery service from Stourport to London was in place by 1800 and, two years later, a regular service was in place for passengers as well as cargo. It was a pleasant, noiseless ride; the only trouble was that it took between twenty and twenty-five days.

It is still possible to catch an old steamer in Stourport-on-Severn but the steam engine has gone, so has the grand piano

The advent of steam power brought steam-powered boats. In the summer of 1821 the Severn Steam Yacht Company built and launched two steam-powered passenger boats. One was *The Sovereign*, intended to carry 500 passengers and light parcels between Stourport-on-Severn and Gloucester each day. To celebrate the launch, a twenty-one-gun salute was planned using a small cannon, but unfortunately the cannon exploded, killing the gunner. The boat only ran occasionally and was withdrawn twelve months later.

Thirty years later steamers were carrying passengers to and fro between Worcester, Holt Fleet, Upton-upon-Severn, Stourport and Tewkesbury almost as a bus service.

However, the age of steam-driven motorboats was rapidly coming to an end by the mid-1900s, replaced by petrol, petrol paraffin and diesel, although the old boats were still known as 'Steamers'. The *River King* was a steel-hulled diesel-powered vessel built in 1931 and there is a rumour that, in the Second World War, she was one of the boats making the dramatic rescues at Dunkirk.

Partly because of the river and the boat trips on the 'steamers', Stourport-on-Severn became a great holiday town. Bob Blunt, the founder of Blunt's Shoes, remarks, 'The steamers used to ply up and down the river, these were the lovely old steamers with varnished wood and polished brasses. They had a piano on board with the pianist playing by ear, he rattled out the music beautifully.' One retired resident, Fred Rimmel, remembers, 'Trains used to arrive from all over the Midlands, Dudley, the Black Country and other places. It was the only place for an outing in those days. When one of the trains disgorged, the street were solid with people advancing to the riverside. You had to battle your way through to get to the other side of the town.'

STOURPORT-ON-SEVERN'S REDSTONE CAVES

Across the River Severn from Stourport are the Redstone caves, where the remains of an ancient monastery, first recorded in 1160, are built into the cliff face. The river was shallow here and John Speed's 1610 map of Worcestershire shows that the only other Severn crossings were the bridges at Worcester and Upton-upon-Severn. This was one of the main routes from Worcester to Wales. The funeral cortège of Prince Arthur, Henry VIII's older brother, probably came this way from Ludlow for Arthur to be buried in Worcester.

The monks probably helped travellers cross the ford when it was first founded, but as time went on the monks became greedy so that by 1553 Bishop Latimer described the hermitage as being 'able to lodge 500 men and ready to

Across the River Severn from Stourport are the Redstone caves, the remains of an old hermitage

lodge thieves as true men'. He added, 'I would not have hermits master of such dens but rather that some faithful men had it.' Perhaps the monks charged travellers for helping them across the ford, then charged for indulgences, and again for accommodation.

THE WORCESTER & BIRMINGHAM CANAL

In 1791, nearly twenty years after Brindley's death, work began on another canal – the Worcester & Birmingham canal – going north to Birmingham from Worcester. This time some of the steepest hills of the county had to be negotiated. One of the main problems was how to raise the level of the water at the long incline at Tardebigge. At first, a canal boat-lifting mechanism was used, designed by the engineer John Woodhouse. The boat went into a lock and the whole lock, complete with boat, was lifted into the air to be joined to another canal on a different level. In the end it was considered that the lifting installation contained too many moving parts and would be liable to frequent breakdowns. The engine was dismantled, and instead England's longest flights of locks for narrow boats

A barge passes through England's longest flight of locks for narrow boats near Tardebigge

were built, with fifty-eight locks in total. Thirty locks are in the Tardebigge flight alone, achieving a rise of 217 feet. A 580-yard tunnel starts by Tardbigge Church and finishes on the other side of the B4096.

To take the canal across the Wast Hills, it was necessary to build one of the longest tunnels in the country – 2,726 yards in length, it runs from the edge of the Birmingham conurbation to surface just north of Hopwood Park Services on the M42. This canal was not completed until 1815.

The Worcester & Birmingham canal still runs from the centre of Birmingham to the Severn at Diglis, just south of Worcester, although commercial traffic ceased in 1961.

BEWDLEY

For thousands of years, as far back as the Iron Age, Bewdley was the main river port connecting the Midlands and central Wales to Bristol and the outside world.

In Medieval times and until 1544, Bewdley was a sanctuary town (see Chapter 11). There's an old legend about the caves at Blackstone Rock near Bewdley, across the river from the town. A beautiful young lady by the name of Alice was to be married in Birmingham to Sir Harry Wade. As she made her way to the wedding, a young man on horseback snatched her and carried her off. The wedding party was in hot pursuit and when they started gaining on him the young man threw the lady into the River Rae at Deritend where she was drowned. He carried on to seek sanctuary in Bewdley. Grief-stricken, Sir Harry became a hermit in a cave at the Blackstone Rock, hearing confessions. Many years later, a middle-aged man came to confess to Sir Harry, saying that in his youth he had admired a lady, but was too shy to confess his love. He could not bear the thought of her marrying another, so had snatched her on her wedding day. With a cry of rage, Sir Harry leaped at him and pushed him over the edge of the cliff to be drowned in the Severn.

The arrival of Tickenhill Palace, built by Henry VII for his son, Arthur, brought much prestige and trade to the town.

The first bridge, made from timber, was built in about 1447 when John Carpenter, the Bishop of Worcester, devised the cost-effective policy of granting indulgences of forty days to all those who helped to build the bridge. A second bridge was built in 1483. The present bridge is the fourth and was built to Thomas Telford's design in 1798.

Disaster came for Bewdley in the 1700s, when the building of Stourport-on-Severn took away their trade. Some 400 donkeys stood idle in the streets, and so many workers were unemployed that the poor tax rose to ten shillings in the pound.

The River Severn at Bewdley

THE SHRAWLEY CAVES

About 6½ miles downstream of Bewdley are the caves at Shrawley, with their
heart-warming tale recorded by the Reverend J.L. Molliott of Abberley:

> In the parish of Shrawley, in the banks of the Severn, there are some curious
> caverns, called Red Rocks, anciently the abode of hermits, and it is reported that
> they occupied their leisure time in fishing out of the river certain baskets,
> pitched on the outside, containing children supposed to have been launched on
> the surface of the stream from Bewdley Bridge. These children in Christian
> charity were baptised and nurtured, giving them the name of the river, and if
> they seemed in good condition, educated them and settled them for life.

They were all given the name of Severne, which first appears in Shrawley in the
sixteenth century.

⇀ *The railways* ↽

The first passenger steam railway in England is said to be the Liverpool and
Manchester, opened in 1830. Five years later, a group of wealthy businessmen
met at The Star Hotel in Worcester to discuss the possibility of sponsoring a
railway line from Birmingham to Gloucester. It received royal assent the
following year and was open and running two years later. The merchants were
only interested in trade between these two towns, and if Worcester had been
included, the track would have been diverted. The rail authorities offered to build
a branch line to Worcester, but as this would have cost £60,000 and as Worcester
city would have had to foot the bill, they declined. The nearest the railway came
to Worcester was to Spetchley, where passengers were met by a horse-drawn
omnibus. One passenger complained that it was an hour's bumpy ride to the city.

By 1844 trade was declining, sales of gloves, porcelain and metal goods were
all falling, and a group of tradesmen felt that a railway would revive old trades
and bring new ones to the town. They called a meeting and agreed to build a line
from Oxford through Worcester, Stourbridge and Dudley to Wolverhampton.
Three companies tendered – the Great Western Railway (GWR), Tring from

Hertfordshire, and an Oxford, Worcester and Wolverhampton railway, known as the OW&WR. This last company was chosen.

Right from the beginning, the work of the OW&WR was unsatisfactory and it became known as the Old Worse and Worse. Unfortunately, the OW&WR used a broad gauge of 7 feet, whereas Tring was already building lines (such as the one from London to Birmingham) in a narrower gauge of 4 feet 8½ inches. This meant, of course, that one line could not link up to another. A Royal Commission made a careful study of the two lines in 1845 and decided to recommend the smaller, narrower, gauge. An Act was passed the following year making the narrow gauge compulsory for all new railways, but the GWR used broad gauge. The Act was one of the factors confusing and delaying the work of the OW&WR.

Five years later no line had appeared. The Commissioners called for a report on the line in 1849, but the only reply was that there was still a lot of work to do. In charge of the Great Western Railway was one of the great engineers of the nineteenth century, Isambard Kingdom Brunel. The Commissioners wanted the work handed over to him, but the OW&WR refused. Instead, they made agreements with other railway companies. GWR went to court and had the agreements made void.

A disagreement in 1851 was so severe that it has been described as the last great battle on English soil between two private armies. The OW&WR were

The railway bridge over the main road outside Worcester's Foregate Street station bears the arms of the GWR

building Campden tunnel, 3 miles from Honeybourne (Worcestershire) and near Mickleton (Gloucestershire). The contractor for the Old Worse and Worse was Mr Marchant. GWR was helping with the finance under Isambard Kingdom Brunel. Marchant complained that the Old Worse and Worse owed him a great deal of money. Brunel decided that a new company, Peto & Betts, should finish the work, but each time the new navvies arrived, they were driven away by Marchant's men. Brunel decided to take matters into his own hands, and on the night of Friday 10 July 1851, he gathered about 200 men ready to take over the works at the Worcestershire end of the tunnel, in the early hours of darkness on Saturday. Marchant had been warned and the magistrates were waiting. Brunel was persuaded to leave. He returned later, but found himself facing three dozen policemen armed with cutlasses together with soldiers from the Gloucester regiment. He hastily retired.

Everyone appeared to have gone home, but Brunel quietly gathered 2,000 navvies from his works at Birmingham, Oxford and Warwick. At 3 p.m. on Monday morning, under cover of darkness, they entered the tunnel but were faced with Marchant brandishing pistols, backed by his men. The two sides set upon each other. Three men had fractured skulls and several had broken arms or legs. While the magistrate was reading the Riot Act, more fighting broke out on the embankment. Several men had broken limbs, one was nearly trampled to death, while another had his little finger bitten off.

Work stopped for two weeks, then finances were sorted out and Peto's men were employed by GWR.

The OW&WR's main line between Oxford and Wolverhampton was ready in 1853, and by 1860 there was a connection to Hereford. A station was not built for passengers until 1865 and travellers had to wait until 1880 for a waiting room – but what a waiting room! On platform 2b, the Victorian ladies' waiting room is a Grade II listed building. Inside are cast-iron features from the nearby Vulcan Iron Works, while outside are unusual 'majolica' ceramic tiles, made by Maw and Company of Broseley. Worcester's second station at Foregate Street is better known because its adjacent bridge, bearing the coat of arms of the GWR, straddles the main High Street.

————————

THE LICKEY INCLINE

The main line between Birmingham and Bristol was built in about 1840, passing through Barnt Green and Bromsgrove to Ashchurch. Blocking the line were the western aspect of the Lickey Hills. Tunnel-building was a long and difficult

The infamous Lickey incline

process and accidents were common. Consequently, it was decided to tackle the Lickey Incline. No other track in England had been built at this gradient (1 in 37.7 – that is, 2.65 per cent) for this length (2 miles) and it is still the longest, steepest mainline railway.

Banking engines, known in the United States as 'Helpers', were imported from Philadelphia to push trains up the incline. Later, the railway companies were able to build their own powerful engines and the Bromsgrove Works built a large 0-6-0ST in about 1845. Later, in 1919, 'Big Bertha' from Derby, a massive 0-10-0, was the star of the line. Trains descending the bank had to have all their brakes pinned down if they were loose-coupled. Often, the first few wagons nearest the engine were brake-fitted, which meant that only the second or third loose-coupled wagon had to have its brakes pinned down. The person in charge of the shunting walked alongside a slow-moving train and had a special pole to pin down an adequate number of brakes. Once the brakes were pinned down, the train was difficult to start and difficult to stop. The line had to be cleared as far as Stoke Works.

The Lickey Incline had to be taken parallel to the road linking Bromsgrove to Finstall. There was, on this road, a Chapel of Ease dating back to 1773 and the railway blocked its entrance, making it inaccessible. The problem was solved by building a footbridge over the line. However, from time to time the services would be interrupted by a thunderous clattering as a train passed by, and the whole building would rattle and shake. Finally, a new church was built further away, and St Godwald's of Finstall opened in 1884. The Chapel of Ease was only used as a mortuary and for an occasional wedding. It became a ruin and was pulled down in 1970.

The early steam trains used cutting edge technology and there were several fatalities. Thomas Scaife was killed on 10 November 1840 and is buried in St John's churchyard, Bromsgrove. A second tombstone stands next to it for Joseph Rutherford who died in the same accident. There's a verse on each gravestone; Scaife's reads as follows:

Gravestones in the churchyard of St John Baptist in Bromsgrove to the memory of Thomas Scaife and Joseph Rutherford

My engine now is cold and still,
No water does my boiler fill;
My coke affords its flame no more.
My days of usefulness are o'er.
My wheels deny their wonted speed,
No more my guiding hands they heed;
My whistle, too, has lost its tune,
My shrill and thrilling sounds are gone;
My valves are now thrown open wide,
My flanges all refuse to guide.
My clacks, also, tho' once so strong,
Refuse to aid the busy throng,
No more I feel each urging breath,
My steam is now condensed to death.
Life's railway o'er, each station past,
In death I'm stopped and rest at last,
Farewell, dear friends, and cease to weep,
In Christ I'm safe, in Him I sleep.

These were two young men working on the recently opened Birmingham to Gloucester railway. Rutherford was works foreman and Thomas Scaife was a bank engine driver on the Lickey Incline. A tank engine, rather aptly named 'The Surprise', was standing over an ashpit at Bromsgrove station. The train driver was John Henshaw (sometimes written as Inshaw), working with his son, Paul. John Henshaw had built the engine. There had been some kind of technical problem that day, so Scaife and Rutherford asked if they could take a look at the engine. Henshaw and his son stepped out of the cab and Rutherford and Scaife climbed in. Suddenly, without warning, the engine blew up. Scaife was blown 25 yards and died immediately. Rutherford was blown against a wall of brass rods, three of which were broken by the force of his body. He died later from scalds. Paul Henshaw was thrown up in the air and over the rails, but he lived. The chimney was blown 100 yards and the furnace was thrown over the station. An inquest attributed the explosion to sediment in the boiler, plugs left in the boiler by the makers, and the thinness of the boiler wall.

Four months after the Bromsgrove accident, in March 1841, a banking engine blew a plug and scalded the American driver, Mr Donahuy. A month later, on 7 April, another engine blew a plug and badly scalded three men on the foot-plate, including William Creuze who died the next day.

WILLIAM CREUZE

In 1840, William Creuze was the locomotives superintendent of the Birmingham and Gloucester Railway Company. Born in London in 1810 of French parents, he had a Cambridge degree in mathematics and had also won a prestigious prize for literature. He was one of England's first mechanical engineers. During the first winter, the Noris banking engines from Philadelphia were finding it difficult to cope with the Lickey Incline and it was touch and go as to whether they would succeed. If they failed, the line would have to be closed. Creuze was celebrated as a hero when he managed to keep them running.

On the night of 7/8 April 1841, the locomotive *Boston* was descending the Lickey Incline, tender first, when it was subject to a violent escape of steam. With Creuze were Edward Carter, who was driving the engine, William Walworth, foreman of the Bromsgrove Depot, and his wife. Walworth and his wife managed to jump clear, their fall broken by the steep embankment. Creuze died from his injuries.

A descendant of William Creuze, his great-great-grand-nephew, Warwick Sheffield, lives in Australia but came over in January 2010 for the commemorations of the bicentenary of the birth of William Creuze, organized by the Bromsgrove Society with the help of local railway groups and district and county councils.

BARNT GREEN TO ASHCHURCH

The line from Birmingham to Redditch was completed in 1859 and the following year plans were submitted for a railway branching off eastward, via Alcester, to the terminus at Honeybourne. This would have given the opportunity of through trains to London. The proposal caused uproar in Evesham as irate residents realized that their town was being bypassed. New plans were submitted for a line from Evesham to Redditch via Alcester, with a tunnel under Mount Pleasant. It received royal assent in July 1863.

This called for the major engineering feat of a tunnel under Mount Pleasant, running from the end of Redditch station and emerging at (what is now) Tunnel Drive. Work began in 1863, but a worker was badly injured by the collapse of scaffolding, then a fatal accident occurred when James Bishop was too near to the rock-blasting, and a few weeks later another worker was injured by a landslip. These accidents and investigations delayed the work so that the line was not opened until 1868.

The new line was a great advantage because, if a rail company didn't want to send their train up the Lickey Incline, it could go through Redditch and it would still reach the Oxford, Worcester and Wolverhampton line. To celebrate Redditch's elevated status, a new and better station was built, a quarter of a mile from the old, leaving The Railway Inn without a station.

As well as the technical difficulties, a new railway line had a whole range of problems, much to the entertainment of the local press. Redditch historian Ian Hayes writes:

> The Redditch railway and the local newspaper, the *Redditch Indicator*, both arrived on the scene in September 1859 … Although at first guardedly supportive of the railway, W. T. Heming, proprietor and editor of the newspaper, soon took to showing the enterprise in a rather poor light, this in spite of the large advertisement that was taken each week. No aspect of the railway's activities was immune; 'The second general meeting of the shareholders was held on 27 September. There was a scant number attended, an unmistakable proof of confidence in the directors.' One of the main problems in the first year was to be the train timetable. The first arrival from the Birmingham direction was 11.00 a.m. The following editorial comment appeared in the *Redditch Indicator* for 15 October: 'A person on

Thursday being asked, "Did you come by train?" replied "No, I could not spare the time, I walked". In May 1844 an advertisement appeared in the *Indicator* giving through day return fares to Droitwich including admission to the baths. Third class bargain was about 1s 10d. Heming pointed out that the only third class train of the day left Redditch at 5.15 p.m. with no return facility.

During the following months the *Indicator* was not short of copy regarding the railway: 'Serious Accident: The train being rather longer than ordinary some delay occurred in shunting the engine to push it up the station platform and the passengers, many of them impatient, loudly demanded to get out. The ticket collector yielded to this clamour, and the train was emptied before moving up. It was very dark away from the influence of the gas lights, and Mr Hill, who had no idea of the distance to step down, in taking the last step fell with his leg doubled under him' (*Redditch Indicator*, 21 December 1859).

Some further incidents were coming to the attention of Heming:
'An accident occurred on the train leaving Birmingham at 1005 a.m. on Monday. It was a mixed train, immediately following the engine and tender were four heavily loaded coal waggons. At a point a mile beyond Alvechurch the train left the rails. It was found that the wheels of the third coal truck had come off. The axle had fractured and was found some distance away. The engine and two waggons remained on the rails, but the remainder of the train was derailed. The driver took those passengers having urgent business through to Redditch' (*Redditch Indicator*, 10 May 1863).

This made interesting comment on railway practice at the time!

Richard Heming went on to see his newspaper flourish, he was also to become the local insurance agent, and captain of the Redditch fire brigade. He died in 1879. The line between Redditch and Ashchurch was closed in the 1960s.

WHAT THE RAILWAYS DID

By the 1880s, GWR had built a network of railways across England. The railway was faster and safer than wagon or barge. It was able to carry heavy goods such as large metal products from the various forges, and quarry-stone from the Lickey Hills at Barnt Green, Bromsgrove and Rubery. Several companies moved their entire factory to be near a railway line. One example was William Blizzard Williamson who moved the Metal Box Company from Wolverhampton to Lowesmoor in Worcester.

John Corbett, who owned the salt works at Stoke Prior near Droitwich, developed his own railway depot in the 1870s. When the Birmingham and

Gloucester Railway arrived at Droitwich in the 1840s, there was a goods depot near Stoke Works, so a branch line was taken into the industrial area. Corbett later bought the industries and purchased two locomotives, one for each side of the canal. He also bought 400 wagons and built a workshop to service them.

Evesham was an important station and farmers were able to get their produce quickly to town markets; in fact, Evesham had two stations. The present Evesham station was built by the Old Worse and Worse, while across (what is now) the car park stood another station on the line from Ashchurch to Barnt Green. In the autumn, the trains would be crammed with hop-pickers travelling to Evesham, Pershore and Worcester or to those stations along the Herefordshire side of the county – Kidderminster, Stourport-on-Severn, Newnham Bridge, Tenbury Wells, etc. (see Chapter 8).

The line from Worcester to Hereford and South Wales was intended to bring coal to the Midlands, but it had a great impact on Malvern's tourist industry. Although the first train brought coal to the Midlands, over the next year 3,000 visitors flooded into the town.

Lady Foley, the main Malvern landowner, led a campaign to bring the line through her town, which meant boring a tunnel 1,567 yards long through some of the hardest rock in the world. Three railway companies pooled their expertise: the Worcester and Hereford Railway, the Newport Abergavenny & Hereford Railway, and the Old Worse and Worse. They amalgamated in 1860 to form the West Midlands Railway, then joined the Great Western Railway (GWR) in 1863.

Great Malvern station

Two subcontractors went bankrupt, but the line was completed under the supervision of a local engineer, Stephen Ballard, and opened in 1861. The tunnel starts at King Edward's Road near the Worcestershire golf course and finishes near the station at Colwall. As time went by, trains became larger and the tunnel was too small, so a second one was built alongside and opened in 1926. The old tunnel was closed, but during the Second World War it came into use as a storage depot for the navy's torpedoes.

Like Worcester, Malvern has two stations: a small one at Malvern Link and a larger station in Great Malvern. The latter is one of the most spectacular of Worcestershire's stations; the original Victorian design has been preserved and each column supporting the platform roof is decorated with a unique design ranging from acorns to spiky chestnuts. The original clock was destroyed in a fire, but fortunately a factory at Redditch, Washford Mills, was being demolished at the same time so their identical clock was transferred to Malvern. Next door was the Imperial Hotel, which has been converted into part of Malvern Girls College. A covered walkway went from the station to the college, known locally as 'The Worm'. This was recently renovated.

DR BEECHING ARRIVES

After the end of the Second World War, on 1 January 1948, railways were nationalized. In 1962, British Rail became an independent statutory corporation as the British Railways Board, which gave way to privatization between 1994 and 1997. Dr Beeching wielded his axe on the rural branch lines in the 1960s.

THE SEVERN VALLEY RAILWAY

Fifty years ago, a group of steam enthusiasts were certain that they could reopen the line from Kidderminster to Bridgnorth and make it pay as a tourist and leisure attraction. Today, the Severn Valley Railway operates throughout the year, running from Kidderminster, through Bewdley tunnel to Bewdley, across the Severn to Upper Arley, then to Highley Engine House, Hampton Loade and Bridgnorth. The Victorian station at Upper Arley is often used for films and television programmes, such as the BBC's *Oh, Doctor Beeching!* To reach the main part of the town, you need to cross a footbridge, erected in 1971 to replace a ferry that had been in operation for over 600 years.

Today the steam train runs from Kidderminster to Bridgnorth, a total of 16 miles

Vehicles on the M5 about to cross the river Avon at Bredon

12

EARLY SPORTING WORCESTERSHIRE

THE SPORT OF KINGS

The great Medieval sport throughout England was hunting, and there were few counties more suitable for a hunt than Worcestershire.

William the Conqueror loved hunting so much that when he became king in 1066, he declared huge areas of Worcester as 'Forest' so that no one could hunt there except him and those who enjoyed the king's favour (see Chapter 2). In the early 1200s King John visited Worcestershire almost every year of his reign and spent most of his time on horseback, hunting. He built lodges at Feckenham, Kinver and Hanley Castle. The deer (hart) was a favourite quarry, but boars, wolves and hares also lived in Worcestershire forests and were hunted. Fox hunting was made illegal in 2005, bringing to an end one particular incarnation of a sport that has taken place for thousands of years.

Hunting was so widespread throughout the county that it has become part of Worcestershire folklore. Who was the mighty Callow, who has given his name to Callow's Hill near Hanbury, Callow's Leap at Alfrick, and Callow's Grave near Tenbury?

The Norman tympanum over the doorway of Ribbesford Church is badly worn but you can just make out a hunter with his bow and arrow. Presumably he is shooting Leviathan, a monster sometimes representing the devil

The legend of the Jovial Hunter of Bromsgrove has been incorporated into the town's coat of arms as the head of a boar. It comes from a ballad written in the time of Henry VIII, and could refer to Sir Humphrey Stafford of Grafton Manor, whose body lies in Bromsgrove Church. The Staffords' coat of arms shows a boar. One of the earliest versions of the ballad states that Sir Ryalas, the Jovial Hunter (perhaps a pseudonym for Sir Humphrey), went into the forest and was met by an elderly woman who told him that her husband and thirty of his men had been killed by a wild boar. Sir Ryalas blew his trumpet to all four points of the compass, out from the forest came the wild boar and, after a fierce four-hour fight, Sir Ryalas managed to cut off its head. Instead of being pleased, the woman flew into a rage and said that the animal was her son, whom she had changed into a boar so that he could kill Sir Ryalas. With that, he recognized her as a witch and chopped her in two.

Harry-ca-Nab is said to haunt the Lickey Hills. Some say that he was a poacher who lived 600 years ago in Feckenham Forest and did something so terrible during his lifetime that after death he was condemned to hunt for ever as the devil's huntsman. Tradition says that he appears on stormy nights on a winged horse or a bull.

Another ghostly huntsman is said to be Peter Corbett, from Chaddesley Corbett, who died in about 1300. The story goes that his pack of hounds were kept in a great stone pit near Harvington Hall – not the present hall, but the old one in the village. He discovered his daughter was secretly in love with a gentleman from Wolverley and, because he disapproved of the match, he arranged for the young man to be torn to pieces by his hounds. His daughter, on hearing the news, threw herself into a nearby pool and drowned. Filled with remorse, Sir Peter then threw all his hounds into the pool.

The effigy of a knight in Saint Peter's church, Upper Arley

Medieval jousting at Avoncroft Museum of Buildings. The two opposing
knights were divided by a wooden fence and fought over the top

In his youth, the future Henry VIII was regularly sneaking off from court to go
hunting. He was a great athlete and loved a game of tennis, which was quite
different from today's lawn tennis. The racquets were not the same shape and the
game was played off various markings on the walls. Real tennis is still played, but
it is a minority sport. Hewell Grange, near Bromsgrove, had a Medieval tennis
court until the building was taken over to become Her Majesty's Prison.

The injury to Henry VIII's leg that hastened his death was brought about by
jousting. We know that Worcestershire knights took part in tournaments
because in Upper Arley Church is an effigy of a knight, thought to be that of the
unfortunate Walter de Balun, who was killed in a tournament in 1270 on his
wedding day.

COCK-FIGHTING AND BULL-BAITING

Other sports enjoyed by Henry VIII were those of cock-fighting and bull-baiting.
Cock-fighting is thought to have been introduced by the Romans and became
very popular; most towns – and even villages – had a cockpit behind a hostelry,
and sometimes the stable yard was used.

The word 'cockpit' was so common that it was later used to describe part of an aeroplane. Cock-fighting and bull-baiting lasted well into the 1800s. William Avery, the needle-maker, was born in Redditch in 1800 and often watched fights that he describes as follows:

> Another favourite amusement of the neighbourhood was cock-fighting. The most celebrated cockpit was one kept by Joseph Lewis at Crabbs Cross. It was made of gorse kids, with the sods turned up for the ring. People came from all parts to see the 'mains' fought in this pit, and as many as five hundred persons at a time would pay their penny entrance to witness the 'sport'. There were three ways of fighting, the 'long main' which generally continued for a week, the 'short main' which was finished in a day or two, and the 'battle royal' in which all the cocks were down at once and the last cock left was the victor.

Made illegal in 1849, cock-fighting continued illegally and, to this day, the RSPCA still brings an occasional cock-master to justice.

Bull-baiting was also a popular amusement across Worcestershire. Originally, it was considered essential that beef used for public consumption should be killed in public view so that everyone would know if the meat was fresh. William Avery reports that there were three bull pits within a few miles of Redditch town centre. He continues:

> A 'berrod' was appointed who looked after the animal and saw fair play. The bull was fastened to the ring by a cord several yards long, and then the dogs were loosed at him. The true bulldog made straight for the nose, and if he caught in any other place would keep changing his grip till he got hold of the desired point, but other dogs would rush at the nearest part, tail or nose being a matter of no difference to them. Often times the dog would be sent whirling in the air and then all hands would run to the rescue and catch him ere he fell. Sometimes the bull would inflict great injuries on the dogs, in fact it was an unusual thing to see a good dog with all his bones in their normal condition.

ARCHERY

In the Middle Ages and up to the sixteenth century, one 'sport' was compulsory – that of archery. Henry III passed a law in 1252, stating that all Englishmen between the ages of fifteen and sixty had to equip themselves with a bow and arrow. These were turbulent times. Then Edward III, who was frequently at war

The deep grooves in the stonework of the outer wall of St Andrews Church at Cleeve Prior are said to be caused by the sharpening of countless arrowheads

with France, carried the law still further and in 1363 decreed that every Englishman should practise his skill at archery, especially with the longbow, every Sunday afternoon. During the practice, the men had to respond to the commands used in warfare, such as, *Mark! Draw!* and *Loose!* If you accidentally killed someone with your arrow in target practice, you were not prosecuted. Special areas were assigned for practice that had to be at least 200 yards long. An arrow fired from an ordinary bow could reach 200 yards, whereas a longbow could reach 400 yards. The target area was known as 'The Butts', and this is how the road behind the Crowngate Shopping Centre in Worcester, known as 'The Butts', got its name.

Barefist boxing

Barefist boxing was the customary Saturday night sport. The workers would sit around drinking, then when boredom set in, one of them would throw his cap on the ground, everyone would throw in some cash, those interested in fighting for it would be paired off, and the overall winner would take the cash.

Pitchcroft Common, now the Worcester racecourse, has long been the site of many national sporting contests, and in 1824 over 30,000 spectators turned up to see the barefist boxing match in which the Irish champion, Jack Langan, was defeated by Tom Spring in about the eighty-fourth round. Tom Spring was born at Woodhope in Herefordshire in 1795; his real surname was Winter, but he changed it to Spring when he became a professional. The purse was 300 sovereigns, equivalent to more than £25,000 in today's money. The floor was flooded and a temporary wooden boxing ring had been built 2 feet off the ground. Spectators climbed the masts of the boats on the nearby River Severn to get a better view, two of the masts collapsed, and some spectators were injured.

Among Worcestershire's well-known boxers was Mr Batten, who lived in Beoley. The Earl of Plymouth decided to utilize his talent and employed him as a gamekeeper at Hewell Grange. Unfortunately, one night he drank too much ale at the Hall, quarrelled with the footman, and injured him so badly that he was dismissed.

Barefist boxing – also known as bare-knuckle boxing – was made illegal in about 1882. However, no magistrate was able to halt a popular centuries-old activity. The traffic island at Crabbs Cross on the borders of Worcestershire and Warwickshire is known as Boney's Island, it is said, because illegal barefist boxing went on there. Spectators arrived from across the two counties, and carts, carriages and horses were lined up for a quarter of a mile in every direction. If the magistrate from Warwickshire arrived to stop the fight, the pugilists had only to step a few yards over into the next county to be out of the arm of the law; and, similarly, if the magistrate from Worcestershire arrived, a slight shift in location and the fight could continue. Occasionally, both magistrates would arrive together and stop the fight.

Quoits and Ninepins

Two games that were once common in all towns and villages were those of quoits and ninepins. The former was an outdoor game, where metal discs were thrown at an iron pin about 20 yards away. Sometimes the metal discs would be replaced by polished horseshoes which gave a satisfying ring as they revolved round the target. Ninepins was usually played in a skittle alley where the wooden pins were knocked down by a wooden ball, a game that is now usually known as 'skittles'. The early skittles was a similar game, but the pins were heavier and knocked down by a cheese-shaped disc.

Courtesy of The Fountain Inn.

A game of skittles at The Fountain Inn in Clent

Some pubs in Worcestershire still have their skittle alleys. Perhaps The Bell Inn at 35 St John's, West Worcester, is best known as it stands on a historic site known as Church House, where a court was held to run the annual fair, collect tolls and settle disputes among traders. The cellars were used as the local lock-up. Other skittle alleys in Worcester are at The Goodrest Inn, Barker Street and The Gun Tavern, Newtown Road.

There are at least two skittle alleys in Malvern, one at The Express in Quest Hills Road and another at The Bluebell on the Guarlford Road. Among the other pubs with skittle alleys are The Kingsford in Wolverley near Kidderminster and The Fountain Inn, Adams Hill, Clent.

FISHING

Like many other occupations, fishing was originally a subsistence activity, a means of providing a tasty meal. Monasteries and large private houses kept their own fishponds where they bred fish for the dining table. In the grounds of Middle Battenhall Farm at Whittington are the remains of a network of Medieval fishponds so complex that fish must have been supplied to Worcester city commercially. The old fishponds of Evesham Abbey are now set in a series of monastic gardens, including an eighteenth-century garden featuring herbs and other delicate plants. In Redditch's Bordesley Abbey meadows, the remains of the abbey fishponds still attract a variety of birdlife.

As time went on, fishing became more of a leisure activity. As noted earlier, fish-hooks have been made in Redditch since 1776 and the town became the centre of fishing tackle supplies throughout England. There were at least eight large factories and innumerable small manufacturers. Samuel Allcocks of Standard Works in Clive Road was the largest fishing tackle manufacturer in the world, and by 1920 it was employing at least 1,000 people.

A young man who likes to be known as 'Mushy' caught this pike in 2009 in Twyford,
in Evesham & District Country Park

Sprite hooks are still made in Redditch by Vince Green. Originally the making of fish-hooks was a cottage industry, and even in the factories they were still made by hand. Vince builds his own machines, based on Victorian drawings. He comments that the hooks could have been mass-produced in the 1800s, but labour was so cheap that the masters didn't bother to build the machines.

Vince has spent a lifetime fishing in Worcestershire waters:

I used to go fishing with my father. He worked at Samuel Allcock's, the fishing tackle manufacturers in Redditch, and they owned a long stretch of water at Hillborough on the Avon near Bidford. There used to be works trips at the weekend on Hardings coaches. Sometimes we called in to a country pub; there was a famous one at Temple Grafton. We used to tramp in with our wellies and fishing gear. I think we would be out of place there now!

In the canal we fished for gudgeon, bream and perch, and in the Avon and the Arrow we fished for roach and chub. We threw the fish back but I must confess we did take one or two home and put them in the garden pool but they were bottom feeders so the only time we saw them was when we cleaned the pool out.

All along the River Avon, the yellow water lily, *Nuphar lutea*, known locally as Pandox, had a long floating root, often as thick as a broccoli stalk. It clogged up the rivers and would catch your lines while you were fishing. In the closed season we used to clear the river with drag lines attached to chains and cutters attached to the end of bamboo poles fifteen feet long. Sometimes, two of us would go into the river on a raft to work. We would cut through the runners underwater and either pull the plants out or push them into the centre of the river so that they would float down into somebody else's stream.

Worcestershire has produced several famous writers on fishing. Dick Orton, in addition to his literary career, was chairman of the Angling Foundation, a non-political, non-profit-making body which advised on angling and fish welfare issues. Captain Terry Thomas lived near Alvechurch and was well known for his television appearances as well as his books. Courtenay Williams wrote several books, his most famous being a *Dictionary of Trout Flies*.

––––––––––––––––––––

HORSE RACING AND PITCHCROFT

No doubt ever since men climbed on to the back of a four-legged beast, they have raced one another. Horse racing, steeplechasing and the breeding of appropriate horses became a popular pastime for the gentry and yeoman farmers in Worcestershire from about 1837 onwards. Competitive events began to be held at Tenbury Wells, Upton-upon-Severn, Malvern Wells, Redditch, Bromyard, Crowle and other villages.

One of England's oldest racecourses is at Worcester on the old meadow by the side of the River Severn known as Pitchcroft. This is where the whole history of England hung in the balance in 1651, for General Leslie and all the Scots cavalry stood here during the Battle of Worcester, refusing to join in the fighting. Had they done so, Prince Charles might have won.

Since that time, the field had remained a common meadow. Many people think that when a piece of land is described as a 'common', it doesn't belong to anyone. In fact, all land is owned by somebody, and a common is a piece of land on which people (usually the locals) have certain rights. On Pitchcroft, the freemen of the city had grazing rights, but these were limited to a certain period of the year. Other people, such as the yeomanry, also had rights and all these privileges sometimes conflicted. In the early 1800s the editor of *Berrows Worcester Journal* remarked that he remembered a time when he struggled with a heavy roller to prepare the ground for a cricket match, but when the team

Horse racing on the historic Pitchcroft course

arrived later they found that the cattle and artillery guns had ruined the pitch.

The freeholders could enclose the lands provided that they did not interfere with the footpaths. This meant that the meadow was criss-crossed by banks and hedges, making the field one of the finest jumping courses in England.

The first official race on Pitchcroft was held on Friday 27 June 1718. The race was open to any horse, mare or gelding, and the prize was a saddle and bridle valued at £3. There were to be three 2-mile heats and the winning horse was to be sold for £7. Those who wished to enter their horses had to notify the licensee of The Crown in Broad Street. Additional entertainment was included in the form of a race for the men round Pitchcroft with a prize of a pair of silver buckles, and a race for the young women across the course with a 'fine hat' as first prize. From that time onwards, the event was held most years.

In the early days only one race took place and entries were few. However, by 1749 the prize had risen to 50 guineas and it was supported by a number of eminent people. Lord Byron entered his chestnut called Lightning in 1755 with the odds of three to one. The following year Lord Foley donated a purse of £50 and that same year Sir John Pakington won with his bay gelding called Forrester. When, in 1754, a race was held for five- or six-year-olds or 'aged' horses, mares or geldings, the Marquis of Buckingham's bay came second and Lord Craven's grey mare came third. By 1822 the Gold Cup had been introduced and 1837 saw the introduction of two events a year, flat racing in the summer and steeplechasing in the autumn.

From 1853 onwards the event became increasingly popular. The Earl of Coventry was a great patron after he came of age in 1858 and he presented the Coventry Cup. In 1870 there were fourteen races in two days and seventy-eight horses competed for £730 in prize money. A grandstand had been built with two galleries, one for the ladies and one for the gentlemen.

Racing at Worcester was a sport for the wealthy. *Berrows Worcester Journal* of 1856 reports, 'The company at the Balls at the Town Hall last night was exceeding grand and numerous. There will be a ball again there tonight and tomorrow night, and a public breakfast at Digby bowling green where there was a very grand appearance this morning.'

The hedges were removed in 1880 to make a figure-of-eight course. The landowners agreed to sell their land to the council in 1893 on two conditions – first that the yeomanry were able to hold their annual training on the common each year and, second, that for twelve days each year the land was closed and handed over for the organization of racing and tournaments. Two years later the council had acquired 150 acres. In the early 1900s the land was fenced and leased for racing purposes to a committee of townspeople.

The course has been changed many times, and the 1880 figure-of-eight course has long gone. Flat racing was discontinued in 1966, but summer jumping started at the course in 1995 as a result of winter fixtures being lost to flooding.

Horse racing gave everyone an opportunity to indulge in one of the nation's favourite pastimes – that of betting. The amount of money that changed hands was enormous. The Why Not Inn at Cookhill was built with the winnings from a horse of that name. The Townsends of Hunt End built a pair of semi-detached houses in Enfield Road with their Derby winnings.

Landowners loved betting so much that they would sometimes let a property on a number of lives. The lessee would be asked to choose say, three people, and they could rent the property for as long as one of those three people were still living!

At the east end of Pershore Abbey are the tombs of the Hazlewood family who owned Wick Manor. About 250 years ago their estate passed to the Hudson family. The late Charles Hudson said there was a story in his family that the property had changed hands because of a 'mega' game of cards. Then one day a member of the Hazlewood family knocked on his door and asked if he could look round the house as his family had once owned it. The same story had gone down his family, so it looks as if there may have been some truth in it. Mr Hudson said that they could look round the house with pleasure provided they didn't ask him to play cards!

A big gamble: Wick Manor is said to have changed hands as the result of a huge bet

CRICKET

Driving through Worcestershire on a weekend summer afternoon, many a flat green field near a village is dotted about with figures clad in pure white. This may look innocent enough, but there is nothing like the village cricket match for a bit of skulduggery. For example, the pitch can be laid out to favour the Home Team, with the Away Team placed to face the setting sun in the final overs. The ball can be tampered with. Either side can have a secret weapon on their team, such as the local strong man who can easily whack the ball across the boundary line!

The County Cricket Club goes back to 1865, when there was a meeting in the Star Hotel in Worcester to found a county cricket club and find a suitable ground. In the chair was the Lord Lieutenant of Worcestershire, Lord Coventry (1839–1930). One of his sons played for Worcestershire, and another went out with the first cricket team to South Africa. Lord Coventry was also keen on horse racing.

Another well-known family who were great cricket enthusiasts were the

Lyttletons of Hagley Hall. In August 1867 they played against Bromsgrove School, and the entire team was made up of the Lyttleton family; there was Lord Lyttleton, two brothers, and eight sons. The two youngest Lyttletons were only ten and twelve years of age. They won by ten wickets.

Although that great cricketing legend Dr William Gilbert Grace (1848–1915) was a member of the Gloucestershire county team, he played for Worcestershire several times, according to the *Victoria County History*. W. G. Grace was a qualified doctor, but cricket was his real career. Between 1880 and 1899 he played test cricket for England. He is still the fifth highest-scoring player of all time and the sixth highest wicket taker of all time. In one season alone he scored 2,000 runs and took 100 wickets. He popularized the game, and so many people turned out to see him play that cricket became one of the major sports of the summer.

One of the great mysteries of Worcestershire cricket is how Malvern College, which had such unpromising grounds, managed to turn out so many fine batsmen between 1892 and the end of the century. The grounds were not flat, but terraced, and during each summer the earth dried out and became lumpy. Seven members of the Foster family emerged from Malvern College, and were so well known for their cricketing skills that the county was nick-named 'Fostershire'. All the Foster brothers went to Oxford after leaving Malvern College. One of the brothers, Reginald Erskine Foster, was a right-handed middle-order batsman and captained the Oxford team. In the 1900 season, he scored 930 runs at an average of 77.5, a record in university cricket. The following year he was named Wisden Cricketer of the Year. His business interests usually prevented him from going abroad, but in 1903 England was desperate to find a captain and R. E. Foster was persuaded to take on that responsibility. Although he was out of practice, he managed to score 287 in the very first Test at Sydney. This was the highest score in Test cricket until 1930. He captained England in three Test matches in 1910.

R. E. Foster not only played cricket for England, he also represented the country in international football. He was one of the few double internationals and the only man to have captained England in both sports. Between 1900 and 1902 he played five matches for England, and in his second game against Ireland, he scored two of the three goals that led to victory. Unfortunately, he died of diabetes in 1914 at the age of thirty-six, only a few years before the discovery of insulin.

The Worcester Cricket Club now meet at Norton Barracks, renamed the Gordon Jones Memorial Ground after their late president.

FOOTBALL

Until a century or so ago a pig's bladder or an ox bladder was a great prize for any schoolboy because it could be cleaned, blown up and fastened to become a first-class football.

As the game became popular, it was obvious that a national ruling body was required. The Football Association was established in the north in 1863, followed by Birmingham in 1875. Organized football in Worcestershire may have been introduced to Kidderminster by men from the Black Country arriving in search of work. The first recorded game of football played in Worcestershire goes back to 1878 between Cookley and a team from Birmingham; Cookley lost by six goals to two. The following year the Worcestershire Football Association was formed under the authority of the Birmingham County Association.

The Earl of Dudley was president on the first committee. The secretary was a teacher from Feckenham, John Lewis, who served for twenty-one years, while twenty-three-year-old Joseph Pritchard, an architect, was chairman for fifteen years.

The football betting coupon put in an appearance in about 1913 and the secretary of the Worcestershire Association, in his annual report, emphasized its great evil and told the clubs to discourage its use, especially among the junior clubs. He went round the football meetings speaking against it.

An organization existed in 1928 known as the Worcestershire Sports Fellowship, with high-flying members such as Stanley Baldwin, Earl Beauchamp KG, the Earl of Coventry, the Earl of Plymouth and Lord Cobham of Hagley Hall. The secretary of the Worcestershire Football Association, Percy Harper, was summoned to Hagley Hall by Lord Cobham. Apparently, the latter was in touch with another football association known as the Worcester County Sportsmanship Brotherhood, but this was not the English Worcester, but the town of that same name in Massachusetts in the United States. Lord Cobham wanted to know if the Worcestershire Association would be interested in providing teams to play against the Massachusetts Brotherhood. The local council gave its support and Percy Harper and Frank Bullock were in charge of the organizing committee. Matches were played at Stourbridge, Evesham, Worcester and Kidderminster. An invitation was issued for a return visit, and a party of twenty left Liverpool in September 1930, and were away for five weeks. Both tours were a great success, but there was only one downside – no mention was made of who was paying for the trips. The Worcestershire Sports Fellowship was financially embarrassed for many years afterwards.

Percy Harper, the Secretary, was a well-known referee and had the great honour of being asked to referee the Football Association Challenge Cup Final between Arsenal and Newcastle United in 1932. Unfortunately, Harper has gone down in history as one of the referees making a catastrophic error of judgement. He allowed a goal for Newcastle after the ball had gone out of play. He later protested that his decision was correct and the ball had not gone out of play, despite photographs showing otherwise. Arsenal lost 2–1, but it should have been a draw. However, this does not seem to have affected his career and he was also appointed to referee the Welsh FA Cup Final in the same year.

Bad behaviour from players or spectators is not a modern phenomenon; in fact, the behaviour of certain junior clubs in 1893 was one of the worst on record. The Worcestershire Association disciplined its players by giving suspensions, but in 1900 they received a circular from the Birmingham Association telling them that they did not have the authority to do this. Only the Birmingham Association could suspend players. It was finally decided that twelve local Associations could give suspensions provided they notified the Birmingham Association.

One of the members of the Worcestershire Association who should be remembered is Captain Knight-Coutts, who served on the committee for over sixty-five years. He joined in 1906 as the junior club representative from Prince Henry's Grammar School in Evesham and remained a member until he died in 1971. During the Great War of 1914–18 he was made captain and awarded the Military Cross. When he returned to the committee after the war he reorganized the structure of the committee. He was presented with a medal in 1966 to commemorate sixty years of serving on the council.

A major change in recent years is that the Football Association has been joined by women's teams.

WORCESTER RUGBY CLUB

Worcester Rugby Club was founded by the Reverend Francis John Eld, headmaster of Worcester Royal Grammar School from 1862 to 1883. Members had to pay a small subscription and each member was asked to find a friend who lived within three minutes of the city. The first match was played against Worcester Artillery in 1871. They wore white shirts bearing the city's coat of arms, and blue knickerbockers. Since then, the club has had its ups and downs, closing completely during the First and Second World Wars. During the 1920s so many joined that it became necessary to have an A team and a B team. It reopened in

1945, after the Second World War, when fifty-three players turned up, after which it went from strength to strength, becoming known as the Worcester Warriors. In 1980 the club toured Canada, and in their possession is a letter from the Prime Minister, Margaret Thatcher, congratulating them on their initiative.

Down the years, the club's main problem has been that of finding premises. It has had to move at least a dozen times, before in 1975 it was able to settle at its present site at Sixways, near Warndon. Twenty years later the club was identified as suitable for establishing a centre of excellence for Youth Rugby and was able to obtain grants for £2.5 million through the Sports Council and the National Lottery. The 65 acres at Sixways now has a stadium with a capacity of 12,024. The game went professional in 1996 and Worcester followed suit.

13

THE ARTS AND WORCESTERSHIRE

✤ *Music* ✤

─────────────

SIR EDWARD ELGAR

Perhaps the most famous of all Worcestershire's artists, the statue of the composer, Sir Edward Elgar, stands in Worcester High Street opposite the cathedral

Very occasionally, an apparently quite ordinary individual rises from an obscure background to become a star to outshine all contemporaries. Such a person was the composer Edward Elgar. He was born in 1857, the fourth or fifth child of the family, in a modest red-brick cottage in the little country village of Lower Broadheath, about 3 miles west of Worcester. He left school at fifteen and had no formal musical education. This was a time when there were sharp divisions in society. The study of music was largely confined to the upper-class Protestants, and Elgar was not only working class but a Roman Catholic.

The only factor that set him apart was that his parents ran a music shop where he learned the violin and piano and was allowed to play with the various instruments on sale. His father played the organ at St George's Catholic Church in Worcester and Elgar sometimes went with him. There is no doubt that Elgar was inspired by the local countryside, especially by the magnificent Malvern Hills.

When Elgar was two, the family moved to Worcester. Tragedy struck twice. He was about seven when his brother died of scarlet fever, and two years later another brother, Henry, died of TB. We can only guess as to how this must have affected both the family and Elgar's music.

Elgar's birthplace at Lower Broadheath has been converted into a museum by his daughter. It holds such memorabilia as Elgar's writing desk set out ready for work, his birth certificate and various manuscripts. His earliest known work was written when he was only ten. At eighteen he was playing for the local music group. He went to London for violin lessons with one of the finest violinists of the day, and by 1884 he was playing the violin in the Three Choirs Festival under Antonín Dvořák. The following year he took over from his father as organist of St George's and was there for four years.

All this time he was composing, but he had tremendous difficulty in getting his music accepted – although this was partly his own fault as, no doubt feeling socially inferior, he tended to be rude and brusque to those who would have helped him. He had to earn a living by teaching part-time at the local preparatory schools, and taking private pupils. He even became music director to the County Pauper and Lunatic Asylum when he was about twenty-two.

He was nearly thirty when Caroline Alice Roberts arrived for piano lessons. Three years later, in 1889, they were married. Her father had been a major-general with the British Army in India and was not at all pleased at the thought of his daughter marrying a penniless music teacher with no prospects. The couple rented a room in Malvern, then moved to London for two years, hoping for fame and fortune; however, their only success was the birth of their daughter, Carice. Elgar loved plays on words and the name is compiled from his wife's Christian names.

Although several of his works had been performed at important venues, he had to wait until he was forty-two to achieve national fame. The *Enigma Variations*, conducted by Hans Richter, was premiered at St James Hall in London in 1899. He may have been stiff and awkward with his superiors, but with his friends he was relaxed and full of impish humour. Each variation represents one of his friends and he gives a clue to the identity of the friend in the title. Usually this is simply the friend's initials, but the ninth and most popular variation is named after a legendary biblical hunter, *Nimrod*, and dedicated to his friend A. J. Jaeger whose name, when translated into German, means 'hunter'. Another success was the *Dream of Gerontius*, illustrating Cardinal Newman's poem about the journey of the soul through to the day of judgement and beyond.

Music poured out of him. He wrote symphonies, violin concertos, chorus works, piano quintets, cello concertos and operas, and created settings for poems and ballets. In 1901, when Elgar was about forty-four, he told his friends,

'I've got a tune that will knock 'em flat! … a tune like that comes once in lifetime.' It turned out to be *Land of Hope and Glory* in the *Pomp and Circumstance* marches.

He was knighted by Edward VII in 1904 and later made a Knight Commander of the Victorian Order. Other honours followed. During the First World War he volunteered as a Special Constable but, by 1916, he was having health problems. His wife died in 1920, but Elgar lived on until 1934. He is buried with his wife and daughter in St Wulstan's Roman Catholic Church at Little Malvern.

Hans Richter was one of the greatest conductors, and he once began a rehearsal of Elgar's work by saying, 'Gentlemen, let us now rehearse the greatest symphony of modern times, written by the greatest modern composer – and not only in this country.'

Elgar's works now feature prominently in Worcester Cathedral's Three Choirs Festival. Within the cathedral is a plaque to Elgar, together with a memorial window to the *Dream of Gerontius*, while in the centre of the town is a life-sized statue of the great man himself.

In June 1999 he received one of the greatest accolades the government can bestow, in that he was selected to feature on the back of a £20 banknote, together with a view of Worcester Cathedral. These notes were in circulation for eleven years and were only withdrawn in July 2010. Few other counties have an individual who has received this honour.

WORCESTERSHIRE'S MUSICAL TRADITION

Worcestershire has a great musical tradition, going right back to the time of the monasteries. Worcester Cathedral library has the best collection of Medieval music manuscripts in England. The Three Choirs Festival is one of the world's oldest classical choral music festivals, and was being publicized in the reign of George I in 1719. It began in Hereford, but was soon rotating between the three cathedral cities of Hereford, Gloucester and Worcester. Usually held in August, it lasts for a week and the organist of the host cathedral becomes musical director and conductor for the event. Kings and queens sometimes attended. George III was staying next door to the cathedral in the bishop's palace for the Festival when, in a bout of madness, he climbed out of his bedroom window, down the ivy, and was running about the town in his nightshirt!

The content of the Festival has changed over the centuries. Originally, it was dedicated to sacred music, with Purcell and Handel dominating the programme. In 1800 Haydn's *The Creation* was introduced, then – for nearly a hundred years

– from 1840 to 1931 Mendelssohn's *Elijah* was performed at every festival. Sometimes works were specially commissioned, such as *De Profundis*, by Sir Charles Hubert Hastings Parry, first performed in 1891. Over the last few years the Festival has tended to concentrate on British composers, such as Ralph Vaughan Williams and Worcestershire's Edward Elgar.

————————

THOMAS TOMKINS

One of the most renowned organists of Worcester Cathedral was Thomas Tomkins, born in 1572 and a scholar and chorister at Worcester's King's School across the College Green. An anthem written by Tomkins was played at one of the most tragic events in history – the funeral in Westminster Abbey of Prince Henry, elder son of James I. The prince was destined to be king, but died of typhoid at the age of eighteen. Tomkins was afterwards appointed as organist at Windsor's Chapel Royal. He is, however, remembered more for his jolly music than for his sad and moving works, as he composed dances for the court of Charles I. One of these, *Lady Folliott's Galliard*, was a very quick dance and produced breathless couples for centuries afterwards! In 1640 he had a new house built on College Green which escaped the destruction of the Civil Wars of 1641–51 to become the headmaster's house. On retirement, Tomkins moved to Martin Hussingtree on the northern side of the city where he died in 1656 at the ripe old age of eighty-four.

————————

MUZIO CLEMENTI

Eighteenth-century Bengeworth, near Evesham, became home to the Italian composer Muzio Clementi. Born in Rome in 1752, he was an infant prodigy and an accomplished organist by the age of nine. When he was eighteen, an English MP persuaded him to live in Georgian England. Clementi achieved worldwide fame. He gave concerts in London and in 1777 he conducted the Italian Opera. The pinnacle of his career came when he and Mozart were both summoned to the court of Emperor Joseph II in Vienna. The emperor wanted to hear them both playing so that he could decide which one was the best. The result was pronounced a draw.

Clementi laid the foundations of modern pianoforte playing. He composed no fewer than sixty piano sonatas and his collection of studies, *Gradus ad*

Parnassum, is still used. Many of his compositions were inspired by Evesham and its customs, such as the traditional May Day celebrations.

There's a curious story about Clementi, told by local artisan Will Dallimore, who says he did some decorating for a lady by the name of Liz who had recently moved into a house in Elm Road, Evesham. She was studying the pianoforte, but each evening as she practised she heard rustling coming from just beyond her garden fence – but when she investigated, no one was there. Will says: 'Recently we returned to do some more decorating for Liz and discovered that she still gets her "visitor". She said she's usually noticed when she was practising from her book of piano studies, *Gradus ad Parnassum* by Muzio Clementi. The name rang a bell, so we looked him up in a musical directory. We found that during his time in Evesham he lived at the Elms, a house, believe it or not, whose garden would have then run down to the far side of Liz's fence.'

VESTA TILLEY

From about 1850 to the end of the 1930s the music hall (a variety show) was the most popular form of public entertainment, and Vesta Tilley has been described as 'the queen of the music hall'. She was born in Commandery Road, Worcester, in 1864 and was the second of thirteen children. Her real name was Matilda Alice Victoria Powles, but she took the name of Vesta Tilley when she was eleven, by which time she was performing in London.

Her father was a comedy actor and an occasional theatre manager and Tilley first appeared on stage when she was only three. The Victorians loved male impersonators and Tilley began her career as a male impersonator at the tender age of six. Her most popular role was that of poking fun at the English 'toff'. She made famous a song about Burlington Bertie, which is still quoted today. Burlington Bertie is a homeless gentleman who sleeps in an arcade, but puts on airs and graces. Each of the covered shopping aisles in Birmingham, London and Bournemouth were known as the 'Burlington Arcade'. The song begins: 'I'm Burlington Bertie/I rise at ten-thirty/And saunter along like a toff./I walk down the Strand with my gloves on my hand/Then I walk down again with them off.'

Tilley married Walter de Frece, a songwriter who owned a chain of music halls across England. She toured Europe and the United States, performed at the first Royal Variety Performance, and became rich beyond her wildest dreams.

Unfortunately, in 1914 she was caught up in the patriotic fervour of the time and her whole show was designed to encourage men to enlist. She dressed in khaki uniform, and gave voice to heart-stirring songs about England. The young men who failed to sign up were given white feathers, the symbol of cowardice, as they left the theatre. The mounting death toll in the following years brought about a feeling of bitterness against the music hall, and especially Vesta Tilley.

After the war Tilley's husband was knighted for his wartime service and he entered politics. She retired from the stage to help her husband in his political campaigns, and died in London in 1952 at the age of eighty-eight.

FRANCES RIDLEY HAVERGAL

Perhaps the work of Frances Ridley Havergal is known to more people than that of any other Worcestershire poet or composer. She wrote seventy-one hymns, among them 'Take my life and let it be', 'Who is on the Lord's side?', and 'Lord speak to me that I may speak'. She was born in Astley (near Stourport-on-Severn) in 1836, the year before Queen Victoria came to the throne, and was the youngest child of Canon W. H. Havergal. Some of the tunes for the hymns were written by Frances; others by her father. This was a time of religious revival and Frances was a totally committed Christian. She wrote the line 'Take my silver and my gold' after sending all her jewellery to the Church Missionary Society. When Frances was only eleven, her mother died.

St Peter's Church, Astley

Astley church. The heads probably date back to about 1160

Frances was an exceptionally clever child. She could read at three years of age and was writing verses by the age of seven. She knew Latin, Greek and Hebrew, spoke several modern languages, and was a gifted pianist with an exceptional singing voice. When Frances was about nine the family moved to Worcester, as her father became the incumbent of St Nicholas's Church in Worcester. He remained there for fifteen years before he had to move to Staffordshire because of his health. Frances sometimes worked as a governess to her sisters' children in Bewdley and Stourport.

She moved to Swansea in 1878 because of her poor health and died there the following year, rejoicing that she was going to meet her Lord. She lies in Astley churchyard with a biblical text on her tombstone more appropriate to sinners than saints, but which was evidently her favourite text: 'The blood of Jesus Christ His Son cleanseth us from all sin' (1 John 1:7).

Astley is only a tiny village, yet a great hymnwriter was born there and a famous statesman, three times Prime Minister, Stanley Baldwin, spent his final years there.

❧ *Applied arts* ❧

THE BROMSGROVE GUILD

There is one arts organization, founded and based in Worcestershire, of which the county should be extremely proud. This was the Bromsgrove Guild of Applied Arts. It was in existence for nearly seventy years, from 1898 to 1966, during which time it engaged over 200 top-quality artists and craftsmen and their work went across the world as far afield as China, Egypt, India and the United States.

The Guild was the brainwave of the dynamic Walter Henry Gilbert. Gilbert was born in Rugby in 1871 and learned his skills at Birmingham School of Art. In 1893 he was appointed art master in Rugby Technical School, moving to Harrow, then finally to Bromsgrove. The following year Gilbert married Margaret Alexandrina (known as Ina), who had been a fellow art student from

Dodford Church, built by the Bromsgrove Guild and described by the authoritative Nikolaus Pevsner as 'the best church of its date in the county'

the Birmingham School of Art and who had won several prizes for her work. They had two children, a boy who became an artist in his own right, and a girl.

He was about twenty-seven when he was appointed headmaster of the Bromsgrove School of Art, and within a year he had persuaded the school's governing committee to found a centre of excellence, gathering together the best skilled craftsmen in the Midlands and finding them commissions. The aim of the organizing committee was to create and market hand-made goods in such fields as metal casting, wood carving and embroidery and to teach those skills to young people through craft apprenticeships. There was a feeling among some artists, critics and writers that mass-produced products were destroying the nation's appreciation of crafts and hand-made articles. They were inevitably cheaper than those made by craftsmen.

At first it was agreed that members would not use their own names, but simply sign work 'The Bromsgrove School', although this practice seems to have died out.

A new purpose-built school had been erected in New Road, but the Guild used whatever premises were available. Guild members often worked from their own individual workshops. A wood carving shop was run by Richard Tapp at Moat Mill on the corner of the Worcester and Charford Roads in Bromsgrove, while an enamelling shop and plaster workshop were run by Henry Ludlow and George Bankart at Stoke Heath. Bankart was a particularly fine craftsman. He had been trained as an architect, but had become a specialist in ornamental plaster and lead work and it was a great loss when he resigned in 1902 as he felt standards were falling. The head office where Gilbert co-ordinated the work was the metal-working department in Station Street, Bromsgrove. Many of the craftsmen were former teachers or students from the Birmingham School of Art. Hewan Crichton was one of them; he became the Guild's chief modeller and was responsible for all the modelling of medals, medallions, figures and memorials beween 1919 and 1937. A small lead figure by Michael Crichton sold recently for £10,000 even though it was missing a thumb.

Their reputation was such that craftsmen from overseas came to join them, such as Louis Weingartner, a metal-work designer from Switzerland, and Celestino Pancheri, a woodcarver from the Austrian Tyrol.

One of the Guild's first important commissions was for the communion table, pulpit, choir stalls, carved wooden figures and light fittings for a new Unitarian Memorial Church at Wallasey in Cheshire. A few years later, in 1908, they were asked to design and supply fixtures and fittings for another church, that of the Holy Trinity and St Mary at nearby Dodford. The priest-in-charge was Walter Whinfield, who had inherited a large sum of money and decided to use it building a new church in the Arts and Crafts style. This lovely, simple church has become an icon of the Arts and Crafts movement. Built in 1907–8, the architect was Arthur Bartlett and he designed a church with no aisles but with a two-bay-long transept and a tower rising on the outer bay.

In 1900 Gilbert resigned as head teacher of the Bromsgrove School of Art to concentrate on the Guild. By the end of 1902 there were representatives in London, Glasgow, Edinburgh, Liverpool, Newcastle-upon-Tyne and the West Midlands. Among their prestigious commissions was an ornamental silver and gold trowel used by Edward VII to lay the foundation stone of the Royal Naval College at Dartmouth. They were asked to make several copies for similar functions. The gates of Buckingham Palace are among their best-known works. Cherubs encircled the keyhole; one of them, peeping through the keyhole, is said to be a copy of Gilbert's newborn daughter. Unfortunately, a cherub was stolen and so the rest were removed for safety. How a small town managed to obtain such an important commission is a mystery, but was probably something to do with Lord Windsor of Hewell Grange. Other well-known commissions include the copper Liver birds in Liverpool, the statue of Hygiela at Chequers, and the gates and sculpture at the Phoenix Assurance Building in Glasgow.

In 1912, an important commission arose in Canada. It was decided that a sculptor and his wife should visit the site, and Leopold Weisz was chosen. He was a jeweller based in Birmingham and he had been working for the Guild for about seven years. A French polisher, Frederick Snelus, should have been travelling with them to work in the Canadian branch of the Guild, but his wife became pregnant so he cancelled his ticket. Weisz and his wife sailed on 10 April 1912 on a White Star Line ship known as the *Titanic*. The wife of Weisz survived, but her husband was one of those who let women and children get into the lifeboats before him. This story has a happier ending than it first appears as Mrs Weisz was met by the Guild's Canadian agent, Mr Wren, and is said to have married him.

Finance was always a problem. Right from 1900, the survival of the Guild was touch and go. Gilbert realized that they needed a wealthy backer and turned to William McCandish, the resident secretary of the Scottish Widows Fund Mutual Life Assurance Society in Bristol. His wife was the daughter of the MP Lewis Fry and together they were able to provide sureties for overdrafts. McCandish and his wife were persuaded to move from Bristol to Bromsgrove in 1913.

In 1918, Gilbert resigned to take up the post of assistant manager of a sculpting and decorating business in Cheltenham at a much improved salary. He carried on doing a little work for the Guild until a dispute arose over the work for the new cathedral in Liverpool. It was said that he obtained the commission for the Guild, but then shared it with his new employer in Cheltenham. He died in London in 1946.

One week in 1916 the bank refused to lend the Guild any more money and the committee was unable to pay anyone a week's wages. In 1919 the Guild's Lead and Plaster Department went into liquidation. To make matters worse, its manager, Henry Ludlow, was knocked down and seriously injured by a car. In 1921 the Guild became a limited company.

During its final twenty years the Guild was managed by George Whewell, a talented Birmingham artist who began as an office clerk, became secretary, then director, and finally manager. He struggled to keep it going, but after the Second World War the type of work supplied by the Guild went out of fashion. The great craftsmen had left, employees dwindled, and much of their work was subcontracted. The company closed in 1966.

STAINED GLASS WINDOWS:
A. J. DAVIES AND ALBERT LEMMON

Stained glass windows by the Bromsgrove Guild were supplied to churches throughout the British Isles and beyond. If you go into the west cloister of Worcester Cathedral you will see six tracery windows showing the history of the English Church with special emphasis on Worcester and the cathedral. These were designed and made by a member of the Guild, Archibald John Davies. A. J. Davies was born in London, the third of eight children. When he was about seven years old, the family moved to Birmingham. A clever lad, he went to King Edward VI Grammar School for Boys at Camp Hill then went to the Birmingham School of Art. He taught for several years before he joined the Guild in 1907, setting up his own studio in later years. Among his many works of art are the First World War memorial window in St John's, Bradley Green and the Grape Harvest, in St Leonard's Clent. Both these windows were installed in 1920. He was also responsible for the glass in Holy Trinity and St Mary's at Dodford.

Assistant to A. J. Davies was Albert Lemmon who joined the Guild in about 1911. In 1915, when he was twenty-five, he joined up and saw the worst of the fighting in France and Belgium. He was awarded the 1914–15 Star, the 1914–18 British War Medal and the Victory medal. Everywhere he went he carried watercolours, pencils and paper. After the war came a demand for memorial windows to commemorate those who had lost their lives and Lemmon was able to draw on his experiences and sketches. He worked with Davies for nearly ten years before he set up his own studio, first in his home at 45 Birmingham Road, then finally in a studio at 155 Bromsgrove High Street. He was joined by his son, Peter, and between them they made over sixty stained glass windows and a range of other items. His work went as far afield as All Saints Church at Taradle, New Zealand. Most of the work from his studio is signed; look for the signatures AEL and PEL.

WORCESTERSHIRE CHURCHES AND THE ARTS

Worcestershire is a county of hidden treasures. With its strong Christian foundation, it has a great cathedral, four abbeys and innumerable village churches, many of these housing priceless works of art. The best piece of Anglo-Saxon art in the county is at Cropthorne, part of a beautifully carved preaching cross with birds and beasts set in a pattern. The cross is thought to date back to somewhere between 825 and 850 and was probably here before the church was built. Perhaps the Bishop of Worcester himself preached to a crowd at its base.

One of Worcestershire's great treasures. The Cropthorne Cross with its rich carvings may commemorate a visit from King Offa, one of the kings of the Dark Ages. He died in 796

In about 1125–30, Oliver de Merlimond, the patron of Shobdon Church in Herefordshire, went on a pilgrimage to Santiago de Compostela. He brought back either a sculpture or drawings of the carvings from the churches along his route. This probably inspired the Herefordshire School, which combined the French carvings with traditional designs – Celtic, Anglo-Saxon and Viking.

Their work spread across the Midlands, with many fine examples in Worcestershire. The carved doorways with their hideous beakheads at Rochford, Ribbesford and Romsley are theirs, together with the dragons on the font at Chaddesley Corbett, the chancel arch at Rock, corbels at Astley and Hagley and carved panels at Eastham and Stockton. The seated Christ above the south doorway of Rous Lench church also dates from this period – that is, about 1140 to 1150.

The misericords in some of the ancient churches are, indeed, hidden treasures for they are only visible when the seat is propped up vertically. The story

The dynamic font in St Cassian's Church at Chaddesley Corbett is unmistakably Herefordshire School

goes that the seats were designed in this way so that if a member of the choir fell asleep, his seat would tip down with a loud clatter. These fine carvings often portray scenes from everyday life.

Ripple Church has one of the best collections, dating from about 1450 to 1480. They show rural activities for each of the twelve months – hedging, ditching, sowing, reaping and the killing of a pig. Another four depict the four elements – light, darkness, heat and water. The July misericord shows a dispute over the weight and quality of some bread loaves! Worcester Cathedral and Malvern Priory also have misericords, and some of those at Malvern go back to 1350, including an amusing version of a sick man being attended by his doctor.

At a time when money determined your social status, the tomb of a deceased relative was one way in which the family could flaunt their wealth; consequently many Worcestershire churches contain works by some of the finest sculptors in England. In Elmley Castle are the tombs of William Savage, his son Giles and Giles's wife Catherine (who was actually buried in Great Malvern). William Savage never saw the baby in Catherine's arms as he was born after Giles had died. The baby is holding a golden purse and at their feet are four kneeling children. On the east wall is a spectacular memorial to the 1st Earl of Coventry dated 1699, with an interesting story behind it. Designed to be placed with the other

Two entertaining misericords from Ripple Church. These two are from a set of twelve showing the labours of the month. This one is for November and shows two pigs about to be slaughtered

family memorials in Croome d'Abitot, the 2nd Earl of Coventry refused to give it wall space because the 1st Earl of Coventry had married again and his widow (stepmother of the second earl) had made false claims about her ancestry.

Another magnificent memorial is in St Giles, Bredon. This was one of the most important of Worcestershire's Medieval churches; its spire rises to a height of 161 feet, while the entrance still consists of layers of Norman carving. The south chapel is dominated by an alabaster memorial to Sir Giles Reed who died in 1611 and his wife, Catherine Greville, the daughter of the great Warwickshire landowner, Sir Fulke Greville. The memorial is by Samuel Baldwin of Stroud. The

Bredon Church's memorial to Sir Giles Reed and his wife

effigies are on a chest between black columns, while above are cherubs, obelisks and a black eagle. The children are ranged either side.

The little village of Besford has the only timber-framed church in Worcestershire. In his book *Worcestershire Churches*, Tim Bridges writes: 'Hidden away in the narrow lanes north of Defford, this remarkable church is too little known … The interior is dimly lit and full of atmosphere.' It has a rare Medieval gallery with thirteenth-century carvings of quatrefoils, rosettes and vines and an alabaster effigy of Richard Harwell of Besford Court who died in 1576, aged fifteen. However, the greatest treasure is in the nave of the church. Richard evidently had brothers and sisters who died in their infancy and are commemorated by a triptych (a picture with two wings) of rare church paintings. As they are 400 years old it's only to be expected that they have suffered some damage, but you can still see that on the outside of the two end panels are shields held by angels while the inner wings show Father Time and a representation of Death. In the centre are badly damaged paintings of children. When opened, the triptych shows a kneeling figure with smaller figures and other scenes. Above was once a Christ in Majesty on a rainbow, below a child playing. In the strip of wood below there used to be the body of a child and two small naked boys, one with a flower, the other blowing bubbles. Unfortunately, these have not survived the passage of time.

There are also Medieval painted panels at St John the Baptist in Strensham, a village situated between junctions 7 and 8 of the M5. The church closed in 1991 and has been in the care of the Churches Conservation Trust ever since. Inside is a reconstructed gallery dating from the late 1400s, which has twenty-three panels with a painted figure in each panel. Christ is in the centre and on each side are three archbishops and nineteen saints. The panel with St John the Evangelist shows the devil emerging from a communion cup! However, unlike the paintings at Besford, these are not totally original, having been restored in 1875.

A visit to Worcestershire's stately homes will bring you face to face with other great works of art. Hagley Hall has Medieval tapestries together with paintings by the great English artist, Sir Peter Lely. Worcestershire has two spectacular Baroque murals – the first is in Hanbury Hall and dates from about 1710. Behind and above the grand staircase are larger than life figures from Greek mythology by Sir James Thornhill (1675–1734). On the ceiling is a portrait of Sacheverel about to be torn to pieces by powerful gods. This is a political comment; Sacheverel was a clergyman who, in 1719, spoke against Queen Anne's Whig government. As a result, he was suspended for three years. Thornhill also painted two ceiling panels in the Long Room or Dining Room.

The other unforgettable Baroque mural is at St Michael's at Great Witley. Witley Court was developed by the wealthy Dudley family, but the original house

St Michael's Church at Witley Court, consecrated in 1735

had been built by the Stourbridge ironmaster, Thomas Foley, in 1655, and it was the Foley family who were responsible for the present church (see Chapter 8).

Thomas Foley's grandson planned to build a Baroque church, rather like a Roman temple, but he died before work had begun and his widow paid for a Baroque church to be completed. Their son then heard that the Duke of Chandos at Edgware in Middlesex had gone bankrupt and the Baroque church interior at his house, known as Canons, was to be sold. He bought the paintings and medallions by Antonio Belluci, the colourful stained glass windows made to the designs of Sebastian Ricci, and the organ with its ornamental case. The organ is said to have been played by the great German composer, George Frederic Handel. The architecture of the church had to be altered to take the new purchases.

The font is not from Canons, neither is the sumptuous memorial to the first Lord Foley and his family. Carved by a Dutch sculptor, Michael Rysbrack, it is thought to be the largest in England.

MALVERN PRIORY

Much of the stained glass in Worcestershire was smashed by the Puritans in the 1600s, but a few bits and pieces have survived. Some of the oldest windows are in Malvern Priory; they date back to somewhere between 1440 and 1506 and are more complete than any other Medieval glass windows in England. Although they chiefly show religious scenes, the window high up in the north chancel clerestory tells the story of the founding of the abbey and the martyrdom of Saint Werstan (see Chapter 3). When they were first installed they were for viewing by the monks only, as this was the monastery church and the townsfolk were not allowed within its walls.

ALL SAINTS CHURCH IN WILDEN

All Saints Church in Wilden (near Stourport-on-Severn) is the only church in England with glass by Sir Edward Burne-Jones (1833–98) and William Morris (1834–96) in all its windows. From the outside this looks like a plain, small Victorian church, but open the doors and you are hit by a blaze of colour. It comes as a great surprise to find such an outstanding church in so humble a village. Wilden was not always the quiet hamlet it is today; on the other side of the road from the church was the huge iron factory of the Baldwin family (see Chapter 8). The ironmaster, Alfred Baldwin, married one of the famous MacDonald sisters. Of the five sisters, the eldest was the mother of the author Rudyard Kipling, the next married the Pre-Raphaelite painter, Edward Burne-Jones, while the husband of the third sister controlled the Tate, the National Gallery and the Royal Academy. The fourth sister married Alfred Baldwin, while the fifth stayed at home and looked after her parents. The sisters sometimes feature in Pre-Raphaelite paintings – for example, in Burne-Jones's 'King Cophetua and the Beggar Maid' the second sister poses as the maid. Alfred Baldwin's son was Stanley Baldwin, the three times Prime Minister.

All Saints Church in Wilden

DROITWICH – THE SACRED HEART

The Roman Catholic Church in Droitwich, the Sacred Heart and St Catherine of Alexandria, has the finest example of Byzantine-style art in the country with walls covered in glass mosaics. The church was built in 1921 and was one of the few Roman Catholic churches to be built since the time of Henry VIII. It was meant to symbolize a new golden age; consequently, the choice of glittering mosaics was very appropriate. The mosaics are made from about two million pieces of Venetian glass, altogether weighing 8.5 tons, and took two craftsmen twelve years to complete. They were designed by Gabriel Pippet who spent most of his life working on the mosaics.

Pippet was one of England's great religious artists. He was born in Solihull in 1880, one of sixteen children. His father was a church interior designer, four of his sisters became nuns, and one of his brothers was a priest and a canon of Durham. Pippet trained as a priest in Durham where he won a prize – not for art, but for athletics. He went to Italy to study Byzantine art and the church is in the style of a Roman basilica. He visited France, fell madly in love with a French girl, married her, and they remained a devoted couple all their lives.

Courtesy of the Presbytery

A few of the mosaics in Droitwich's Roman Catholic church. Designed by Gabriel Pippet,
they took two craftsmen 12 years to complete

The mosaics feature a variety of religious scenes. Pippet was frequently in trouble at school because of his artistic talents and his ability to draw cartoons of his teachers, and there are some caricatures in the mosaics. He was able to get his revenge on a priest who often criticized his work by depicting him as the executioner in the Martyrdom of St Catherine.

Making full-sized drawings on paper, Pippet then traced them on to the walls. He was assisted by Maurice Josey, who was in overall charge, and Fred Oates, who began as a teenage apprentice in 1922, but by the time the work was completed in 1934 he was well into his twenties!

Pippet loved telling little stories. He was working high up in the roof when an elderly gentleman called in to see how things were going. Pippet called out, 'Take your hat off when you enter church and put your cigarette out.' Thinking he was hearing the voice of God, the man turned tail and fled. Another of his stories was about the time that he was travelling back from Birmingham (presumably to Durham) when he found himself in the same carriage as an old man who had been to Birmingham for sentimental reasons. They began talking. It turned out that the man had been a guard on the trains before he retired. Pippet asked him for his most outstanding memory. The man answered, 'I was about to leave Birmingham when a mother asked me to look after her two boys who were going to boarding school for the first time. I took them into the guard's van and they were so delighted that they gave me half of the cake that their mother had baked for them to take to school. They were very well-behaved. I often wonder what became of them.' Pippet answered, 'I was one of those two boys.'

His greatest disappointment in life was that, although he worked on many other projects such as religious books and small murals, this was his only great work.

He died two days after his beloved wife in November 1964 and is buried in the shadow of the churchyard in which he worked.

❧ *Poetry* ❧

ALFRED EDWARD HOUSMAN

A. E. Housman was one of the most popular poets of the last century. His poetry combines the beauty of nature with a sense of impending doom, especially appropriate during the dark days of the First World War. Bromsgrove honoured him in 1985 with a statue in the High Street where he is shown as an adult wearing a walking cap and with a walking cane. In actual fact, he moved away from Bromsgrove in his late teens – to Oxford, then to London.

More copies of *The Shropshire Lad* have been sold than any other book of poetry. Here is an excerpt:

> *Loveliest of trees, the cherry now*
> *Is hung with bloom along the bough,*
> *And stands about the woodland ride*
> *Wearing white for Eastertide.*
>
> *Now of my threescore years and ten,*
> *Twenty will not come again,*
> *And take from seventy springs a score,*
> *It only leaves me fifty more.*

Curiously, he rarely, if ever, visited Shropshire. He was born in Bromsgrove in 1859, the eldest of seven children and the son of a solicitor who lived at Perry Hall in the centre of the town. He was also the grandson of the vicar of Saint Michael's Church at Catshill, north of Bromsgrove, who lived just over a mile away at the Clock House, Fockbury. Housman's father was a great patron of the inn across the road from Perry Hall, then known as the Shoulder of Mutton, and when his liquor ran short he would bombard their tin roof with stones.

Housman attended a Dame School in Bromsgrove which was founded and run by two minor poets, John Bird, and later John Crane. No doubt they had a great influence on the lively young boy. In 1870, when he was eleven, he won a scholarship to the prestigious Bromsgrove School. Tragedy struck on his twelfth birthday when his mother died from a form of breast cancer. His grief-stricken father went bankrupt and so the family moved to the parental home, the Clock House. Housman had a 2-mile walk to school each day and the tale is told that he entertained himself by vaulting over hedges using his mother's washing line prop as a vaulting pole. The unhappy teenager became a dedicated solitary walker, exploring the hills nearby at Lickey, Waseley and Clent.

His education continued at St John's College, Oxford. He visited his home town regularly, staying at the house of his brother and sister-in-law in Tardebigge.

Although a respected Latin scholar, Housman failed his degree, but after a brief spell teaching at his old school, he returned to Oxford for a term to take a pass degree. He then worked as an accountant in London, but was all the time writing scholarly articles so that, in 1892, he was offered the post of Professor of Latin at University College.

In 1911 he was offered the prestigious post of Kennedy Professor of Latin at Cambridge University. He died there in 1936. His ashes are buried in the county of his imagination, in St Laurence's Church in Ludlow, where his grave is marked by a cherry tree.

WALTER SAVAGE LANDOR

Born in 1775, the poet Walter Savage Landor's early years were spent at his mother's estates at Ipsley Court near Redditch and Tachbrook near Leamington Spa. He was repeatedly in trouble because of his hot temper, and was sent down from Trinity College, Oxford. Banished by his family, he went to live in Wales where he found inspiration for some of his best poetry. He married in haste, and settled in Bath for a while before he went off to raise a force for Spanish Independence. The great love of his life was Llanthony Priory, set in the Black Mountains of Wales. He bought it in 1806 and spent seven years designing and planting its valley, but quarrelled with the locals and went off to the Continent, leaving his mother to sort out his affairs. He travelled round France and Europe, but had to leave Como in Italy in a hurry after writing a lampoon on the authorities. He then lived at Fiesole near Florence where he quarrelled with his neighbour. He died in Florence in 1864, depressed, disillusioned and in poverty, and is buried in the local Protestant cemetery. Ipsley Court was partially restored by the Redditch Development Corporation in about 1970.

Despite his volatile personality he was capable of writing fine poetry, acclaimed by contemporaries such as Southey and Swinburne. He celebrated the countryside around his Worcestershire home in the following verse:

In youth 'twas there I used to scare
A whirring bird or scampering hare
And leave my book within a nook
Where alders lean above the brook
To walk beyond the third mill pond.

OTHER POETS ASSOCIATED WITH WORCESTERSHIRE

Wyston Hugh Auden spent three years as a popular teacher at the Downs School in Malvern in the 1930s and some of his poetry was written there, including a long poem called simply 'The Malverns'. Auden was born in York in 1907; he began writing poetry at thirteen, and by the time of his death in Vienna in 1973 he had written over 400 poems and 400 essays. Some of them were used on film and television. He collaborated with Benjamin Britten in the well-known film *Night Mail*, made by the GPO Film Unit between the First and Second World Wars. He moved to the United States in 1939, where he became an American citizen in 1946.

Alexander Pope often visited Hagley Hall and in the library of the Hall is a portrait of him with his favourite dog. William Shenstone lived at the Leasowes (near Hagley Hall), now in Dudley Borough. Just over the Worcestershire border in the direction of Henley-in-Arden was Barrells Hall, where Lady Luxborough, estranged wife of Lord Catherlough, was banished after her husband had accused her of having an affair with a music teacher. She spent her days designing her garden and gathering a circle of poets around her, including William Shenstone, William Somervile, Richard Jago and Robert Graves.

✦ *Literature and writers* ✦

FLORENCE OF WORCESTER, LAYAMON AND WILLIAM LANGLAND

The great traditions of Worcestershire literature has its roots in the days of the monasteries. Three of the great Medieval books were written by Worcestershire monks – that is, Florence of Worcester, Layamon and William Langland.

Florence of Worcester was one of the monks scratching away with his quill pen on parchment in Worcester monastery (next to the present cathedral) in the twelfth century. He produced a work of the utmost importance and one upon which the author of this book has relied heavily in the first chapters. He collected material to produce an early history of England, known as the *Chronicle of Chronicles* (see Chapters 1 and 2).

Stourport-on-Severn is so proud of its literary giant, Layamon, that it has named several roads after him and his work. There are, for example, Layamon Walk, Galahad Way and Hafren Way. Hafren was an old hermit and Sir Galahad was one of the knights of the Round Table. Layamon rescued the tales of King Lear and King Arthur from oblivion and, at a time when French was the

Areley Kings Church, home of Layamon

language of the court, he translated them into Anglo-Saxon poetry. This was the first great literary work in the English language. He was a source for Shakespeare, Malory, Tennyson, and many lesser writers.

Layamon was a young scholar of the cathedral's Priory School, becoming a monk. He seems to have been exiled as priest to the remote parish of Areley Kings, on the other side of the river to Stourport-on-Severn, round about the late twelfth or early thirteenth century. To be exiled to such a lovely place would have been no hardship; the little church sits on a rise with spectacular views.

Another monk, William Langland, has given us a well-known religious poem about the vision of Piers Plowman. He lived so long ago that the details of his life are uncertain, but he probably lived from about 1330 to 1400 (see Chapters 2 and 3). Langland seems to have been born in Cleobury Mortimer in Shropshire. His father could have been a tenant of lands held by the Despencer family at Hanley Castle. He became a monk or minor priest, probably at Great Malvern Priory, but was barred from further progress in the Church as he was married. He probably became a ploughman in the monastery fields. When a young man, he seems to have moved to London temporarily and earned a living by chanting dirges at funerals. This suited his gloomy disposition; a tall morose figure, he was generally known as Long Will.

The fifth line of *Piers Plowman* reads (with slight adjustments):

But one May morning in the Malvern Hills,
I met with a marvel that seemed made by magic:
I was weary with wandering, and went to rest
Under a broad bank by the side of a brook;
And as I lay, and leaned to look into the waters,
They sounded so sweetly that I sank into sleep ...

What follows is a description of life at that time with an imaginative and depressing satire on the corruption of the Church, the state and society. It was written just after the Black Death and against the background of the Hundred Years War at a time when the English forces were not very successful. Nevertheless, there are touches of humour and memorable descriptions of the Worcestershire countryside.

FAMOUS NOVELS FEATURING WORCESTERSHIRE

Down the centuries, several novelists have set their work in Worcestershire. Henry Fielding's *The History of Tom Jones, a Foundling* was published in 1749 and was one of the earliest novels ever written. In 1963 it was made into a film that won many awards. Fielding was born in Somerset in 1707 and died in Portugal in 1754, but somewhere along the way he became familiar enough with Upton-upon-Severn to place the final climactic scene of Tom Jones in The White Lion. Tom Jones and the love of his life, Sophia, are both staying there: Tom in the Wild Goose Room and Sophia in the Rose Room. The hotel now has two such rooms.

Then there was the Reverend Sabine Baring-Gould, a wealthy vicar who inherited an estate in Devonshire. He was born in 1834, his family were always on the move, and he went to Warwick Grammar School for a few months. He is best known as a collector of folk tales and songs. Among his many books are two about Worcestershire. *The Shadow of Raggedstone Hill* tells the story of a monk who offended the established Church and, as a punishment, was made to climb Malvern's Raggedstone Hill on his hands and knees every day for a year (see Chapter 3). A second Worcestershire book featured *Nebo the Nailer* and is an account of the Bromsgrove nail trade. Baring-Gould also wrote a third book about Kinver, just over the north-western border of Worcestershire. Entitled *Bladys of the Stewponey*, it tells how the licensee decided to marry off his daughter, Bladys, to the winner of a game of bowls. Unfortunately, she was claimed by the local hangman. The Stewponey has now been demolished.

FRANCIS BRETT YOUNG

Halesowen was part of Worcestershire when Brett Young was born there in 1884. Both his parents were in the medical profession and he too went to Birmingham University to qualify as a doctor. He met his wife Jessie Hankinson, a professional singer, while a medical student in lodgings in Birmingham. His career began in medical practice on board a steamship to the Far East, from where he returned in 1907 with enough money to buy his own practice. He was invalided out in the First World War and suffered with ill health all his life. Too sick to practise as a doctor, he turned to writing. A series of Mercian novels, inspired by the construction of the Elan Valley Reservoirs, were wildly successful. They are set in the Midlands, and linked by recurring characters. Worcester, Kidderminster, Ludlow and Shrewsbury are all there, while other Midland towns are given fictional names – for example, the hamlet of Cold Harbour is modelled on Wassell Grove near Hagley.

The couple travelled worldwide, but in 1932 they settled in the village of Fladbury, near Pershore, and bought the dilapidated Craycombe House which they renovated. One of the novels of which Brett was most proud was *They Seek a Country*, completed in 1937 in Craycombe. He says in the introduction that the book was the fruit of more than twenty years' thought, research and meditation.

Brett Young needed a warm climate for his health, so the winters were spent in Capri. In 1939, Craycombe House was requisitioned by the Red Cross as a convalescent home for the armed services. Brett suffered a serious heart attack in 1944 and had to move to South Africa for his health, where he died in 1954. His ashes were brought back to the county he loved and scattered in the precincts of Worcester Cathedral.

MRS HENRY WOOD

Unfortunately, times have changed and the books of one of the best-selling Victorian novelists, Mrs Henry Wood, are no longer read for two reasons: first, her books are extremely long, written for a society without radio or television, and second, these are real weepies, littered with abused children (usually at the hands of a drunken father) and tragic deaths. Her most famous book was *East Lynne*, in which a mother abandons her family then, years later, returns to the family home disguised as a governess to be near to her children. During the last fifty pages both she and her son suffer lingering deaths.

Mrs Henry Wood was born in Worcester in 1814 as Ellen Price. She had five brothers, all of whom went to King's School, four of them being choristers. Until the age of seven, she was raised by her grandparents. At thirteen, she was diagnosed with curvature of the spine so she had to spend much of her time lying on a special board and never grew taller than 5 feet. In 1836 she married Henry Wood, head of a large banking and shipping concern, and for the next twenty years she lived in France, where she had at least five children. Sadly, a small daughter died from scarlet fever.

In about 1856, her husband's business failed and the family had to return to London to live in a rented flat. She had already been writing short stories, but now she needed to earn a living. She must have been forty-six when, in 1860, she answered an advertisement by the Scottish Temperance League for a book to encourage temperance. *Danesbury House* won a prize of £100, and Mrs Wood had discovered her vocation. *East Lynne* appeared the following year; this achieved extraordinary success and was even performed as a Victorian melodrama. After another four books she serialized her stories in a magazine, *The Argosy*, of which she was editor and proprietor. In all, she wrote over 30 novels and 100 short stories. Many of her books feature Worcester, which she sometimes calls Helstonleigh. In *East Lynne*, she refers to a local sermon preached in Worcester Cathedral. She died in 1887 and is buried in Highgate cemetery in London.

GEORGE BERNARD SHAW

The foot of the Malvern Hills was selected for a Winter Garden complex that included the Malvern theatre. Many famous names were involved. The first Malvern Drama Festival in 1929 was planned by Sir Barry Jackson (later director of the Shakespeare theatre at Stratford upon Avon), presided over by J. B. Priestley (a prolific English author) and featured the first performance of George Bernard Shaw's drama *The Apple Cart*. Shaw was born in Dublin in 1856 of an alcoholic father, but moved to England when he was about twenty and worked as a journalist. He wrote over fifty plays, all of them with a political message. His outspoken remarks, particularly his tirade against the First World War, often made him unpopular but attracted theatre-goers. Two more of his plays were premiered at Malvern. He lived to be ninety-four and, in 1956, when he would have been 100, Malvern held a Shaw Centenary Week.

***

C. S. LEWIS

Clive Staples Lewis arrived in Malvern in about 1911 as a desperately unhappy young teenager. He was born in Belfast in 1898, but his mother died when he was ten and the grieving boy was sent to an appalling school in England where the headmaster was later committed to a psychiatric hospital. He returned to Belfast but, not surprisingly, developed breathing problems and was sent to Malvern for the pure air. Here, he blossomed. He went to Cherbourg House Preparatory School then, in 1913, to Malvern College. He developed a love of poetry, especially for the works of Virgil and Homer, and mastered French, German and Italian. In 1916 he won a scholarship to University College, Oxford. He enlisted and was sent to the Front, where he was wounded at the Somme. His best friend was killed, so he 'adopted' his friend's mother. In 1956 he married Joy Gresham, who was dying with cancer, and adopted her two sons. He died in 1963 and is remembered particularly for the Narnia series, which includes *The Lion, the Witch and the Wardrobe*, and for the *Screwtape Letters*, one of his many books about Christianity.

***

J. R. R. TOLKIEN

C. S. Lewis introduced John Ronald Reuel Tolkien to Worcestershire and the Malverns. Tolkien had been born in South Africa in 1892, but his father had died when he was four years old and, with two young children to support, his mother had returned to the West Midlands. Tolkien spent his childhood at the old Sarehole Mill in Hall Green south of Birmingham, now a museum. A brilliant scholar, he attended King Edward's School and became an Oxford academic and a specialist in early Anglo Saxon and Scandinavian writing.

C. S. Lewis invited Tolkien to Malvern to meet a former pupil of his, George Sayer, who was then Head of English at Malvern College. A plaque on the outside of the old Unicorn Inn in Belle View Terrace states that this was their customary meeting place.

The Unicorn Inn, Great Malvern

The three of them would walk together across the Malvern Hills. Excerpts from *The Hobbit* and *The Lord of the Rings* were recorded at Sayer's home in Malvern in 1952. Tolkien found the hills a great inspiration. Sayer later wrote Tolkien's biography in which he said that Tolkien would recite sections of his book as they walked, and he compared parts of the Malvern Hills to the White Mountains of Gondor.

There's a story that, one evening, Lewis, Sayer and Tolkien were walking home from a Malvern pub

The plaque on the outside of the Unicorn Inn

when it started to snow. They saw the light from a street lamp shining through the snow. C. S. Lewis turned and said, 'That would make a very nice opening line to a book.' There it is, in *The Lion, the Witch and the Wardrobe*, when the characters enter the kingdom of Narnia.

14

WORCESTERSHIRE AT WAR

THE WORCESTERSHIRE REGIMENT

On the northern outskirts of Worcester, where the A449 Barbourne Road meets the A38 Droitwich Road, is Gheluvelt Park, a small park watered by Barbourne Brook. The red-brick shell of the old Victorian waterworks is here, dating back to 1858, but the building has now been converted into a Community Environment Centre known as 'The Pumphouse'.

The park was opened on 17 June 1922 to commemorate the part played by Worcestershire Regiment's Second Battalion in the First World War Battle of Gheluvelt, near Ypres in Belgium. When the park was opened by Field Marshal John French, 1st Earl of Ypres, he said, 'On that day, the 2nd Worcesters saved the British Empire'.

Gheluvelt Park

In 1914, Germans invaded France and tried to get hold of the Channel ports. The British Army were fighting at Ypres, holding a battle line that kept the Germans at bay. At the entrance to Gheluvelt Park is a plaque to Captain G. E. Lea that states:

> At dawn on September 15th 1914, the 2nd Battalion of the Worcestershire Regiment took up a position on the Tilleul Heights to support the Highland Light Infantry. All day long the British positions were heavily shelled and there were many casualties. Captain G. E. Lea, one of the best officers of the Regiment, was wounded and died later in the day. The loss of Captain Lea was deeply felt. A man of very charming personality, a fine soldier and a graduate of the staff college, he would have gone far had he survived.

The village of Gheluvelt had been taken by an enormous German contingent who were occupying a large chateau. This was of great importance as it meant that the line was broken and the Germans could get through to the ports. The 500 men of the Worcestershire Regiment's Second Battalion were the only reserve for Gheluvelt area and they were resting in Polygon Wood when, on 31 October, orders came through for a counter attack. The village was hidden by a ridge and the top of the ridge was lined by enemy guns. 'A' Company took up a position on a railway embankment overlooking the village, while the rest of the Battalion made ready to attack. The only way of getting through the gunfire was by a quick dash. Over 100 men fell, but the remainder charged up and over the slope. The Germans were taken by surprise, and although they far outnumbered the English, they surrendered. The Battalion were able to link up with the South Wales Borderers who were still holding out. Ypres was held and the Channel ports were saved. In his despatch, the Commander in Chief, Sir John French, singled out the Worcestershires for special praise.

The original park contained twelve houses for men who were crippled or disabled in the service of their country.

The Worcestershire Regiment is over 300 years old, dating back to 1694 when, during the wars with France, William III needed more troops and ordered a new regiment to be formed. Since that time it has taken part in almost every major conflict. They were in the United States between 1746 and 1807, and one night in 1746, while they were eating their meal, they were attacked by the Native Americans. For the next 100 years it was the custom to wear their swords during each meal. The Regiment was at the heart of the unfortunate Boston Massacre. Private Hugh White was guarding the customs house in 1770 when a mob began harassing him and tried to force their way in. He shouted for help and Captain Thomas Preston arrived with nine soldiers.

Two of the soldiers were knocked down by the mob and someone in the crowd shouted either 'Fire' or 'Why don't you fire?' The soldiers took this to be an official command and opened fire. Three were killed and eight wounded; of these, two died later. The people of Boston demanded that the soldiers be put on trial, but they were exonerated.

The Worcestershire Regiment has taken part in most major offensives since that time. They have fought in the French Revolutionary Wars, the Peninsular War, wars against the Sikhs and the Indian Mutiny, the Spanish Wars of Succession, and the Boer War. By the time the First World War broke out in 1914, there were four Regular Battalions which were expanded to twenty-two. They fought in the Dardanelles, Salonika, Mesopotamia, Russia and Italy. In 1915 they were fighting in Gallipoli with heavy losses. The next year, in Katia, the Worcestershire Yeomanry suffered heavy losses. The Worcestershire and Warwickshire Yeomanry then combined to make a heroic cavalry charge near Gaza, which enabled the Allies to advance on the Middle East.

Some 13,000 officers and men went off to fight in the First World War and 9,000 of them never returned.

In the Second World War battalions from the Worcestershire Regiment were at Dunkirk, Eritrea, Tobruk and Arnhem, and suffered heavy losses. In the

Gheluvelt Park war memorial. Each plank represents a battle and the length of the plank is according to the number killed

Regimental Museum is a lacquered bowl, presented by the people of Shwebo to the Second and Seventh Battalion for liberating them from the Japanese. The Second Battalion covered 400 miles in six weeks, arriving at Shwebo just after the Seventh Battalion, who greeted them with a table laid out for a meal – the tablecloths were made from parachutes.

After the war, in 1947, the Second Battalion was disbanded, then twenty years later the Seventh Battalion was reduced to one company which became part of the Mercian Volunteers.

In 2004, the army was restructured and on 15 December the Secretary of State for Defence announced that the Worcestershire and the Sherwood Foresters Regiments (29/4 Foot) would become the Second Battalion of the Mercian Regiment, along with the First Battalion Cheshire and the Third Battalion Staffords. This was a sad finale to companies that had, over the centuries, given so much to protect their homeland.

❧ *The First World War* ❧

The headmaster of King's School in Worcester complained in June 1915 that, of a class of twenty-one fourteen-year-olds he had taught in 1911, three had already died on campaign, a dozen held commissions, and the remainder except one were also serving. This meant that, contrary to War Office regulations, young men were being sent to the front before the age of nineteen.

The War Office in 1914 gave a payment of between 2/6d and 5 shillings to anyone 'who brings a Recruit to a Recruiter or to a

Kidderminster war memorial, outside St Mary's Church. The sculptor was Alfred Drury (1856–1944). The figure represents the angel of peace, she holds a child (the future) while she raises an olive branch as an emblem of peace. The memorial is for both the First and Second World War

At the base of the pedestal is a plaque showing a fallen soldier being crowned by Immortality.
At his feet stand his widow and child with the gift of remembrance

Military Barracks', and so friends of friends flooded in, lying about their age. So many skilled workers enlisted that a lack of suitable manpower was one of the factors leading to the shortage of weapons.

Unfortunately, higher military command was in the hands of cavalry officers who gained their military experience in the Boer War. No one foresaw the static war of the Western Front. County newspapers including *The Redditch Indicator, Berrow's Worcester Journal* and *The Kidderminster Shuttle* published regular listings of the dead and wounded, and throughout Worcestershire its churches became all too frequently the scenes of memorial services. On the home front, the enthusiastic golden glow of the early months of the war faded away, especially as it was accompanied by food shortages and long queues. An elderly gentleman from Astwood Bank remembers:

> The food situation was terrible. We had more dinner hours than dinners. We had to queue for everything. I remember queueing for four hours for 6 lb of sugar. I would often miss school because I would be sent to stand in a queue, then I would get the cane when I arrived at school the next day.

Another gentleman remembers that he had to wear clogs as you couldn't get shoes.

The work of a Worcestershire vicar caught the public imagination and became a symbol of the trenches. 'Woodbine Willie' was, in fact, the Reverend William Studdart-Kennedy and he earned his nickname from his habit of carrying cigarettes to hand out to soldiers on the front line. (Smoking was an acceptable habit at that time.) He was born into a large family in Leeds in 1883, and decided to become a minister of the cloth. His first post brought him to Worcester in 1914 as vicar of St Pauls, then he volunteered to become a Chaplain to the armed forces on the Western Front where he impressed everyone with his personality and bravery in ministering to those on the front line. He was awarded the Military Cross in 1919 for his action on the Messines Ridge, where he insisted on running into No Man's Land under fire to comfort the injured. His experiences during the war led him to become a leading campaigner for peace, and as he was a great orator, he spoke to packed halls across the country. In 1922 he moved to London where he lived for seven years before he died.

Peace came in 1918, at the eleventh hour of the eleventh day of the eleventh month. The situation after the war is described here by Vic Bott, who lived in Redditch and died just before his hundredth birthday:

I was demobilized from the First World War at the age of 20. After four years of voluntary active service at a shilling a day, a grateful nation's contribution to our resettlement was a pitiful gratuity of £30 and a poorly-made demob suit. We had no job and no skills and we were thrown into a mass of redundant munition workers whose generous pay and skills created a 'them and us' situation. It was a complete disaster.

The Labour Exchange was in the centre of Redditch where Shipways is now, and the queue to sign on stretched for several hundred yards right down Ipsley Street.

I became one of the million or so servicemen looking for work and finding that none was available. Four years of warfare did not provide us with the skills necessary for a job in civilian life. We were given a month's furlough with pay to get rehabilitated, then we had to let three days lapse before we signed on in order to get some money. When we received our money, it was only ten shillings and it was an impossibility to keep a family on that amount.

A momentous occasion in 1921 was the formation of the Redditch branch of the British Legion. Its aim was to help ex-servicemen in distress, and it was very much needed. It was managed by the Smith family. Major Smith (Managing Director of Royal Enfield) was the President, his younger brother, Gilbert, was the Treasurer, and the youngest, Stanley, was the Chairman. R. W. Smith owned a Masonic Lodge down Easemore Road and he let the British Legion have the use of it for a peppercorn rent.

At that time there were three main charities in Redditch that aimed at relieving the grievous poverty of the day – first the British Legion, secondly, a charity run by the Church, and thirdly, Redditch Civic Aid, which was rather like a local national insurance scheme run by employers in which all employees were stopped so much a week. Of these three charities, the British Legion was, I am sure, the liveliest. At its height it had about 180 members and we raised thousands of pounds over the years. I was one of a fourteen-strong concert party who went all over the county giving concerts. I used to do a Rolf Harris-type act, making lightning sketches in charcoal to such songs as 'The Village Blacksmith'. I led such an active life outside work that my wife said that she was going to get my portrait taken and stick it on the wall so that she would see me sometimes.

Vic Bott eventually found a menial job at Royal Enfield and rose to become one of its senior managers.

The first Poppy Day was held by the British Legion on 11 November 1921. The red poppy became their symbol after a poem written in 1915 by John McCrae. Some of the fiercest fighting took place at Flanders and Picardy. The poem begins:

> *In Flanders fields the poppies grow*
> *Between the crosses, row on row,*
> *That mark our place, and in the sky*
> *The larks, still bravely singing, fly*
> *Scarce heard amid the guns below.*

⟼ *The Second World War* ⟻

Evesham war memorial in the Abbey park. The sculptor is Henry Poole, 1873-1928

Sunday, 3 September 1939 was a beautiful day, bright and sunny, but the dark clouds of war hung over the nation. The British had demanded that German forces should come out of Poland and at 11.15 a.m. Neville Chamberlain announced on radio, 'I have to tell you now that no such undertaking has been received and that consequently this country is at war with Germany.'

Worcestershire was of great importance. Few people know that it was one of the places chosen to be a place of refuge for the royal family and the government in the event of invasion. Madresfield Court (near Great Malvern) was generally earmarked for the British royal family, Spetchley Court for Winston Churchill, Hindlip Hall and Bevere House (all close to Worcester) for the Cabinet, and the Abbey Hall Hotel at Malvern for the Admiralty.

If that sounds improbable, one should remember that Croome Court (west of Pershore) was used by the exiled queen Welhelmina of the Netherlands, while Ribbesford House, near Bewdley, was the headquarters of General Charles de Gaulle, head of the Free French Forces. Branches of the Air Ministry occupied both Hindlip Hall and King's School in Worcester.

Croome Court – home to the Coventry family since the sixteenth century.
The gardens were designed by Capability Brown

'THE WAR WAS WON ON THE PLAYING FIELDS OF MALVERN'

On 16 July 1940 Hitler issued Directive No. 16 in which he said, 'Since England, in spite of her hopeless military situation, shows no sign of being ready to come to an understanding, I have decided to prepare a landing operation against England and, if necessary, carry it out.' Over 2,800 aircraft and a large Armada of vessels including 2,000 barges were assembled across Western Europe, ready to pounce on England. A battle in the air, known as the Battle of Britain, started on 13 August and continued until 7 September. The RAF aircraft were outnumbered by four to one but, despite the loss of hundreds of planes, they managed to keep the enemy at bay.

Their success was partly due to their early warning radar system. As early as 1920 scientists had the ability to counter an air attack by using a series of observatories on the ground and sound locators. This information was passed to a central control room where the operators were able to use wireless to give directions to the pilots and to those manning the guns. Unfortunately, by 1930 planes became too fast for the locators to pick up their speed, and the research lapsed. A few years later someone noticed that planes caused interference on a short-wave radio, and radar was born.

Early warning ground-controlled radar at the Battle of Britain was so successful that the government decided to expand the research to include airborne radar. The RAF had difficulty finding targets when flying over Germany in the dark, and most bombs fell in open fields; in fact, one wit asked why the English did the Germans' winter ploughing for them. Churchill asked Lord Cherwell, his personal scientific adviser, to solve the problem and Cherwell contacted the radar scientists.

The first radar laboratory, known as the Telecommunications Research Establishment, or TRE, was at Bawdsey near Felixstowe; from there it moved to Dundee, then Swanage, and in 1942 it went to Malvern for safety from air-raids and to avoid espionage.

Malvern College

Temporary huts were built on the junior cricket fields of Malvern College, hence the saying that the war was won on the playing fields of Malvern. By the time the TRE reached Malvern a chain of radar stations had been set up around the coast and the TRE was responsible for both Ground and Airborne Radar to both the RAF and the Fleet Air Arm. Defford Airfield was used as an experimental base.

The Germans also knew about radar and could detect our planes. It was often a case of outwitting the enemy with new wavelengths. One of the first of the many successes of Malvern TRE was finding a way to jam the enemy radar. TRE was also able to feed false information – for example, leading the enemy to believe that they had found a large number of planes and not just a single aircraft. One of the leading scientists was A. P. Rowe. There is a blue plaque on number 9, Malvern College, the house where he lived from 1942 to 1945, and a laboratory has been named after him in the college.

By the end of 1945, 3,000 staff were working there. It is now part of the global QinetiQ group in Malvern's Science Park. Our lives have been affected by radar signals in many ways. They have given us the means by which a light is turned on when we enter a room or walk past a house at night. TV weather forecasts rely on radar, so do hospitals for their advanced equipment such as thermal imaging. One of the latest applications is in the field of radio astronomy.

VULNERABLE POINTS AND THE HOME GUARD

In May 1940 all men between the ages of seventeen and sixty-five who were not on active service were asked to sign up for a voluntary part-time organization. The choice was wide – for example, a man could become an ARP (Air Raid Precaution) warden, NFS volunteer (National Fire Service), train for the St John's Ambulance Brigade or he could become an LDV (Local Defence Volunteer). The majority of men became LDVs, known locally as 'Look, Duck and Vanish'. They were given an allowance of 1/6d for twelve hours' duty. Shortly afterwards, the name was changed to Home Guard. This is now referred to as 'Dad's Army', but its role was a serious one – that of protecting Worcestershire and its many vulnerable points that were vital to the war effort.

At first, the LDVs were poorly equipped. Headless Cross C Company was expected to defend the county with an American P17 rifle and a bayonet, both of First World War vintage. Bill Hay remembers going on duty with a chair leg tied to his wrist by a piece of string! However, uniforms and equipment began arriving bit by bit. Large factories established their own platoons and the Home Guard was joined, in 1943, by the Women's Defence Corps.

One worker remarked: 'During the war, life on the factory floor was extremely dull. We ordinary people just did what we were told, we got our heads down and worked. Everybody worked long hours. I worked from eight in the morning until seven at night every weekday, then on Saturdays I worked until four-thirty or five. By the end of the day we were just glad to fall out of the factory and on to our bus.'

Local author Mike Johnson writes:

What is not realized is that these part-time soldiers, unlike the Regular Army, seldom rested. They were all involved with essential war work, working twelve-hour shifts in the factory or working on farms, and then turning out two or three nights a week for drill, or to mount guard on vulnerable points in the town. It is no wonder some of them have said that they were constantly tired. After being on duty, they had to be at work next morning but were allowed to be up to half of an hour late. Most Sunday mornings were taken up with training exercises.

The principal responsibility of the local Home Guard Battalions was to create and man the Stop Lines at Vulnerable Points which included all towns, villages, river crossings and road bridges. The 'Stop Line' was basically an anti-tank ditch with concrete road blocks but anything could be added, such as a fallen tree. It was designed, in the case of invasion, to delay the armoured columns for as long as possible to give the mobile troops (held in reserve) time to mount a counter attack. The idea was that the advancing enemy would have to bypass the Stop Line. In larger towns there were designated anti-tank islands which were, again, the principal responsibility of the local Home Guard.

The late Albert Wharrad was leader of the Redditch Conservative Party and he often told the tale:

One of our exercises was carried out on the Evesham Road where the mini-island is at Headless Cross. There are shops on the right-hand side, and a member of the Home Guard lived over one of these shops. We had to run a clothes line from the bedroom window of his house to the house opposite, to which we attached a runner line. Attached to the runner was an old blanket soaked in paraffin. We had to set fire to the blanket then suspend it over the middle of the road. The idea was to drop it on a German tank. It was a serious business. People really thought the Germans were going to invade. They were only 22 miles away across the Channel.

By the end of the war, Worcester had 2,000 Home Guard in twelve Battalions. Mike Johnson adds: 'With the threat of invasion receding, the Home Guard took on additional responsibilities such as manning the anti-aircraft guns and defending the local factories, thus releasing regular troops for other duties. There can be no doubt that from humble beginnings in 1940 to the time of stand-down, the Home Guard, now nearly two million strong, was a highly trained and motivated group of men, a force to be reckoned with.'

A few Worcestershire men would put on their Home Guard uniform and disappear into the night at regular intervals. Their wives assumed they were attending a Home Guard meeting, but in fact they were on a highly secret mission. These were the members of a Resistance Group, trained to carry out acts of sabotage in the case of invasion. They were told when they were sworn in that if invasion took place, their life expectancy was only two weeks. Captain John Todd was the Intelligence Officer responsible for recruiting in Worcestershire and three other counties. The training and meeting centre for Worcestershire was at Overbury Court, south-east of Bredon Hill. Among those recruited were two Dutch diamond merchants, the van Moppes brothers, who had escaped with their stock of industrial diamonds from Amsterdam and continued their diamond processing operation at Wolverton Hall, near Pershore. They lived at Yewtree House, Ombersley.

The following Vulnerable Points in Worcestershire were of such importance

Overbury Court

that the Home Guard shared responsibility with the army and special police:

The railways and Worcester

Worcester was the centre of a national railway network, with lines going to Kidderminster, Birmingham, Wales and London. At Honeybourne and Long Marston miles of additional track were laid down to facilitate the loading of military supplies. The old railway tunnel at Colwall (Malvern), which runs alongside the present tunnel, was used as a major store for bombs, shells and mines.

The Rivers Severn, Teme and Avon and the network of canals

There were RAF Aviation Fuel Reserve Depots at Upton-upon-Severn and Stourport-on-Severn, together with the RAF Cased Fuel Depot at Hinton on the Green (south of Evesham) and the Petroleum Board Reserve Storage Depot at Stourport-on-Severn. In his book *Severn Tanking*, B. A. Lane writes, 'During the war years the number of craft working on the Severn was great. At the height of this period, there were four depots at Stourport, and one at Worcester, War Ministry depots at other places on the river, and five at Gloucester. Being war time, these craft were vital to the depots full of the grades of oil … we were given our orders and we had to sail in fog, wind or whatever weather, to ensure our cargoes got through.'

Factories

At the beginning of the war it was thought that German bombers were unable to fly as far as Worcestershire and many armament factories were moved here – for example, part of the Imperial Chemical Industries (Metals Division) moved from Witton in Birmingham to Kidderminster. High Duty Alloys in Redditch, producing forges and castings for military aircraft, were moved from the south of England to Redditch and many folk remember the reverberations across the town as the Chambersbury drop hammer stamped out the crank cases for the Rolls-Royce engines. In addition, many new factories were built.

Factories across Worcestershire, except those providing essential supplies, switched to the manufacture of military equipment. In Kidderminster, Wilton looms wove the webbing for haversacks, gun covers and tenting. The Metal Box Company in Worcester was making parts for Hurricane and Spitfire fighter planes, ammunition boxes, ration packs, parts for Churchill tanks, food dehydration plants, etc. The Foundry in Gilgal at Stourport-on-Severn was producing hand grenades while Anglo-Enamelware supplied the army with enamelware ranging from water bottles to grenades and bombs. Terry's Springs in Redditch were making shell holders for Bofors guns and a special Anglepoise lamp for the navigator's table in a plane. Even part of the old county gaol was taken over

During the Second World War, Royal Enfield had five factories.
The largest was the 31-acre site in Redditch, the smallest was this house in Feckenham

by Rackstraws, producing components for the Mosquito fighter, while, next door, Vickers Armstrong made guns for Spitfires. Royal Enfield expanded into seven factories across England; one of them was a converted underground mine at Westwood, about 5 miles south-east of Bath.

The Bond Worth carpet factory was making grenades and anti-tank bombs, but down at the far end of the factory were two large rooms securely locked. They held a tragic secret. This is where all the personal items from the battlefield or from civil victims were sent – watches, rings, etc. They arrived, tagged, in sealed metal boxes. The workers sorted them out and sent them on to relatives.

The electricity power station

Worcestershire had an enormous power station at Stourport-on-Severn. It covered 32 acres between Severnside and the Worcester Road, with an additional 20 acres linking it to the Staffordshire and Worcestershire canal and the Great Western Railway. It was opened before the war, in 1927, by the Prime Minister, Stanley Baldwin. Arthur Mee, in his series 'The King's England', describes it as follows: 'From the bridge over the Severn is seen one of the two important buildings of the town. It is a station giving 100,000 horse power to supply the needs of most of three counties. To it come the pylons marching from every quarter across the countryside, meeting and merging in a gigantic medley of wires, insulators and girders.'

The power station began with two 18,000 kw turbo-alternators, but it rapidly expanded, and a second power station was started in 1943. More extensions were added in 1953. Had it been damaged, many of the factories in three counties would have come to a halt. It was a beautiful Art Deco building. The Luftwaffe never managed to destroy it, but the council did it for them. The power station was demolished in 1980 when the national grid went nuclear.

Wood Norton and Wychbold

Worcestershire was at the centre of a communications network. In 1939, with great secrecy, the BBC was moved to the old home of the Duc d'Orleans at Wood Norton just outside Evesham, and an emergency broadcasting centre was hastily erected. It was christened 'Hogs Norton' by the staff after a popular wartime comedy programme. By 1940 it had become the largest broadcasting centre in Europe, sending out about 1,300 programmes every week! Many famous writers lived and worked there during the war. It was also a monitoring station where foreign language experts listened to enemy broadcasts. After the war it became a BBC training department and still has a Technical and Operational Training Centre in the grounds. In the late 1960s, when the Cold War was at its height, an underground nuclear bunker, 175 feet long, was built in the grounds.

The radio was the backbone of the nation – it was never switched off in some households! The transmitters at Wychbold near Droitwich are a well-known landmark, the two tallest being 700 feet tall. During the war there were only a few transmitters in England capable of broadcasting to radios right across Europe and they were therefore of great importance. They played a part in the D-Day landings on 6 June 1944; the date was broadcast in code as part of a poem. The day before, messages were sent out to the resistance to carry out acts of sabotage.

The Wychbold transmitters

In recent years a young lady from Wychbold went on holiday to Germany. When she was asked where she lived, she said shyly, 'Oh, you won't know it, it's a tiny village in Worcestershire, Wychbold.' 'Wychbold!' exclaimed her hosts, 'Of course we know it. We used to listen to the broadcasts from there during the war. It was the only way we could get reliable information.'

The Germans were listening to the messages right through the war, struggling to unravel the codes. They even managed to use the apparatus themselves and send their own messages from the transmitter! When the war was over, photographs of the transmitters taken from the ground were found in a German airfield. They could only have been taken by a spy.

Worcestershire airfields

Most of Worcestershire was farmland, which meant that airfields could be hidden in the countryside. There were airfields at Pershore, Perdiswell, Berrow (a landing ground), Littleworth, Tilesford, Defford, Honeybourne, and Weston Subedge. Hedges and crop patterns were painted on the ground so that they looked like farmland from the air. At one point a herd of cows was manoeuvred on to an airfield between flights, but they ate the painted grass and died from the poison.

The large number of local airfields meant that there were, unfortunately, many serious crashes in Worcestershire. Fifty-seven airmen from the Commonwealth and Britain are buried in Pershore cemetery, most having served at RAF Pershore, with other fatalities scattered in churchyards throughout the county.

A commemorative tree was planted in Rowney Green in October 2007 to commemorate the five members of the Royal Canadian Air Force killed in November 1943 in the Wellington X3932. Forty minutes from Pershore airfield it developed a problem in the port engine. Sgt Long decided to take the aircraft back to Pershore, but overshot the runway and continued in a north-easterly direction. He was too low for anyone to bale out and without the power to gain height. The plane crashed near Rowney Green, just over a mile south-east of Alvechurch. On board were flying officer Hugh Barton, pilot officer Gordon Gallagher, wireless operator/airgunner Harold Magnes, the pilot Charles Long, and air gunner sergeant O'Neil. All were promising young men in their late twenties.

In 1943–4 a Wellington bomber was flying low over Pershore. No one knows why it was down to 50 or 60 feet. Engine failure has been suggested; but also it was carnival day and perhaps the pilot wanted to get a better look at the carnival – or perhaps he attempted a flypast. Anyway, the plane clipped the trees round the abbey and crashed into the garden of The Brandy Cask public house in Bridge Street, taking off the roof and killing all five airmen on board. They were, again, five Canadians from RAF Tilesford in Pershore. Technically they

The Brandy Cask

were only trainees, but during the war a shortage of airmen meant that most of them flew before they had completed their training. The ground staff from Tiles-ford station marched with the funeral cortège from the airfield to the Pershore cemetery, a distance of about 2 miles.

The occasional German parachutist would create a stir. When it was reported in June 1940 that German parachutists had been seen in or near Bewdley, crowds of spectators came out to watch the action, ignoring advice to stay indoors in the event of an invasion. At Stourport-on-Severn one night a parachutist was seen coming down over Wilden. All the men rushed out with shovels and pitch-forks. Locals say that Pop Millward was a big strapping man and he had got a pitchfork – 'He was a terrible sight'. Apparently, the parachutist wasn't found, because another resident tells the tale that her aunt was going down Mill Lane very early one morning when she met a tiny, terrified man who didn't speak a word of English. He was a pilot who had come down and he was far more fright-ened than she was. She ran for help – to the local pub.

Barracks and hospitals

The geographical position of England made it very convenient for the Ameri-cans to use as a base, where troops could wait before being sent to the Front Line. Injured troops could be flown to Worcestershire quickly from the Front Line; consequently, hospitals for American troops were scattered across the county. Ronkswood was a military hospital and there were at least two at Malvern, one at Wolverley, and another two as described below:

Stourport-on-Severn Hospital

At Burlish, between Stourport-on-Severn and Kidderminster (east of Ribbesford Woods), was an American Command post with an upper camp on higher ground and a lower camp below. By May 1944, 4,000 combat troops were billeted there prior to D-Day. The famous General 'Blood and Guts' Patton visited the camp as some of the troops were under his command. After D-Day both the upper and lower camps were converted into an army hospital with a capacity of about 3,000. Both camps were lavishly equipped and even had a theatre that seated 500, with dressing rooms and a projection room. The Americans brought their injured personnel straight from the battlefield in special trains which were unloaded at goods sidings at the eastern end of Minster Road. Each train used to bring in about 300 patients and there were six or seven trains a day.

Terry Mann was seventeen in 1944 and worked at the hospital while he was waiting to go into the army. He said that the patients wore a denim-type maroon uniform and added, 'The GIs were very generous to the locals. Every year they gave a party for all the Stourport children and provided sweets, some chocolate or cocoa, an orange and a banana. They were able to get hold of luxuries which had disappeared from British shelves during the war like soap and stockings and they passed them on to the local population.' Local girls met the Americans in churches and dance halls, and several young women became GI brides and went off to America. Terry has a heartwarming tale to tell:

> There was one big black lad, a good six-footer, an impressive guy especially when he was wearing his maroon-coloured combat suit. He had badly lacerated wrists from when he had been thrown through a windscreen in France. I was walking down the High Street at about 5.30 one afternoon when I met him and we got chatting. I said to him, 'Are you off on the town?' and he said, 'Yep'. I told him that he was a little bit early for that. I went on, 'This is only a small town and things don't start to happen until 7.30 or 8.00. Why don't you come to my house and have a cup of tea?' and I took him home. When my dear old mother saw him she nearly dropped on the floor. It was the first black man she had seen and she was barely four feet ten inches. But he was very polite and had a cup of tea and a couple of cookies. He only stopped for an hour or so. When my father came home from work he was taken aback to see this big black guy sitting there. Looking back, I was always pleased that I had extended the hand of friendship.

Bromsgrove Hospital

In Bromsgrove there were two hospitals on adjacent sites and between them they could accommodate 500 patients. The first site was behind the old Work-house which had been built in 1836 on farmland off the Bromsgrove Road. In 1878, a hospital was set up behind it. When war broke out, temporary hospital huts were erected in the grounds as a neurological unit for British soldiers suffering from nervous disorders and head injuries. The Americans arrived in 1943, took over the hospital, and the neurological unit was transferred to the second hospital, Barnsley Hall.

The original Barnsley Hall had been demolished in 1850 when the 324-acre site was bought by Bromsgrove Council. Bromsgrove Lunatic Asylum, always referred to as 'Barnsley Hall', opened in 1907. At the outbreak of war, thirty new wards were erected in the grounds. Barnsley Hall became one of the largest emergency hospitals in the county, taking a variety of casualties including air-raid victims and men from the Front.

Americans from all the hospitals flooded into the nearest town each evening, despite the blackout. Most evenings during the war, towns and even villages were buzzing with activity. In every town and sometimes in a village there was at least one cinema showing such delights as Laurel & Hardy and Cary Grant. People would queue for hours to see a good film. A dance would

This converted workhouse was an administration block for Bromsgrove Hospital

An American jeep – exhibited at a re-enactment at the Forge Mill Needle Museum in Redditch

be held in a local hall every Saturday and sometimes during the week. Nearly every association had a social committee to organize events – there were fancy dress parties, whist drives, amateur dramatics, choirs and concerts, all in order to raise funds for the war effort from the two or three shillings charged for admission.

A retired police officer remembers, 'The Americans were everywhere in the war. They used to come down in lorries to go to the cinema or the dances. The town was full of them. They were billeted everywhere … They had a smart uniform and an American accent and plenty of money. The girls loved them and some became GI brides. A few returned, disillusioned, from America. They went over expecting Hollywood and all they got was a tin shack.' One hundred and thirty-one Worcester girls became GI brides.

The Americans were not always impeccably behaved. In the evening, the Military Police, known as 'The Snowdrops', drove round collecting up those who had drunk too much. They were banged over the head with a truncheon and thrown into the back of the jeep. Some of the young GIs found themselves suffering from a venereal disease. They were asked which pub had played host to their assignations and it was put out of bounds.

Worcestershire's stately homes

Large houses were requisitioned as hospitals, convalescence homes, prisoner of war camps, and so on. Hewell Grange, situated between Bromsgrove and Redditch, had been the home of the Windsors since 1542 but was up for sale because it was subject to heavy death duties. In 1939, Alan Wright was a junior officer in a Territorial Army unit (Royal Field Artillery) based in Redditch. He remembers:

The Redditch 267th Field Battery R.A.T.A. mobilised on September 1st at Easemore Road. There being no proper billets or living facilities at Easemore Road Drill Hall, we were ordered, after about ten days, to take over and move into Bentley Manor, about three miles to the South of Redditch. Bentley Manor was an old manor house of, I guess, the late eigheenth or early nineteenth century. It had stabling and outhouses but was not really suitable for housing a Battery of some two hundred men. Very little equipment was available and our armament consisted of a few rifles and about two Lewis Guns. It did, however, provide an opportunity to teach all personnel the rudiments of gunnery.

In about early January 1940 the Battery was ordered to move to take over and occupy Hewell Grange [the house is now a remand centre]. This was a much more suitable building and could well accommodate all our personnel. We were the first to occupy the building after it had been a private residence of the Earl of Plymouth. When we moved in we were not permitted to use certain of the main rooms including the Great Hall. The spacious grounds and larger building were much more suitable for training and military exercises although we were still virtually unarmed.

In the early spring of 1940 it was thought by our Regimental Headquarters that it would be nice to try, in some measure, to thank the very many people who had helped and supported the two Batteries and Headquarters of the 119th Field Regiment. As 267 Battery was occupying Hewell Grange it was considered that a Dinner Dance and Ball in the Great Hall would be an appropriate way to mark this occasion. Accordingly a Committee was set up. Although only a junior officer, I had been with the Regiment since its formation and was appointed a member of the Committee. The Earl of Plymouth was approached and, very kindly, allowed us to have the use of the Great Hall for this special occasion. The date of the Ball was set for May 10th, food and drink was ordered from London suppliers, and a Section of the Royal Artillery Band was booked to play for us. I think the original number expected was around four hundred.

May 10th duly arrived when, to our consternation, Hitler ordered the invasion of the Low Countries. Suddenly the war had moved from 'phoney' to deadly serious. All leave was cancelled and officers were forbidden to leave their units. The Committee decided that, as all the food and drink had been delivered, the band was able to be present, and most of the civilian guests would be able to attend, we should go ahead. In the event it was a most successful occasion enjoyed by all who were able to be present and marred only by our concern for our colleagues who were now engaged in a fight which was to end up at Dunkerque.

I wonder if our Ball was the last occasion of that kind in the Great Hall.

————————————

ON THE HOMEFRONT

This was the first war in England in which every man, woman and child was involved. An hour after the Declaration of War, the air-raid sirens sounded (a false alarm) and barrage balloons were raised on the south side of Birmingham. Over the next twelve months, young men were called up, ration books were issued, and air-raid shelters built.

Employees of Woolworth's and Marks and Spencer's in Worcester had already been assembling gas masks in St Andrews Church and now these were distributed. Schools and public buildings were sandbagged, and all signposts

At the beginning of World War II a huge variety of bomb shelters were constructed. Usually they were sunk below ground level. This shelter can be seen at Avoncroft Museum of Historic Buildings

taken down. At night, there was a complete blackout. Not the slightest chink showed in any window. Only tiny dipped torches and dipped car headlights were permitted. The favoured transport of the day was a bicycle, and manoeuvring along rural roads in total darkness with only a tiny headlamp was an acquired art. The late Arthur Newbould, in his book *Not Just Bricks and Mortar,* tells of the time in the blackout when an army driver crashed into the night soil cart which had just finished collecting the contents of the lavatories. He notes, 'I remember, by the light of the policeman's lamp, seeing a triangular bit of the *Birmingham Post* caught on the door handle of one front door.'

Everybody was involved in the war effort, perhaps collecting National Savings or making up parcels for troops or knitting socks for the forces. Even children collected waste paper or milk bottle tops. There was a community spirit that postwar planners have never managed to revive.

With so many men away, the role of women changed dramatically, as it did in the First World War. They took over work that was considered to be a man's job, teaching older children, driving cars and tractors and manning heavy presses.

Rationing came in at the beginning of the war. Margaret Robins worked at a branch of Lipton's grocery stores and remembers:

You had to cut the coupons out, they were tiny little things. I had to sit with a needle and thread and sew all these coupons on a thread. When I reached a hundred I would thread a piece of paper in between so they were easy to count. Then I had to take them to the local Food Office. You had to fill in a form saying which shop you were and you were allocated your rations for the following month. Each customer had to register with you and get their rations from you. Each person was allowed 2 ounces [about 60g] butter, 4 oz [about 120g] margarine, half a pound of sugar and 2 ounces of tea. The cheese ration varied from a quarter of a pound [about 120g] to 6 ounces [about 180g]. Then you were allowed two eggs a week. We each had our own customers. We knew our customers by name, it was a family affair. One lady had fifteen children and she didn't have an awful lot of money. When she was in bed with her latest baby, she sent an order by one of her little girls. The Manager asked the staff if somebody could deliver it and he said, if he paid my bus fare, could I take the groceries? I knocked on the door but there was no reply. The door was open and I heard her calling me upstairs. I took the groceries up and there she was, sitting up in bed, doing her washing in a bucket at the side of the bed. She asked me if I could wring the washing out and hang it up. Those were the kinds of things you willingly did in those days.

A pensioner in Stourport-on-Severn remarks:

> You had to queue for everything. You would stand in a long queue at Marsh and Baxters for three sausages. If they had all gone by the time you reached the front, that was just your hard luck. I had two small children and found it difficult to queue. There was a terrible cold winter in 1947. I had no food and no coal and the children had whooping cough. The lady next door looked after the children for me while I went to fetch some coke from the gas works. You had to queue for that. I brought it home on my bicycle, balancing it between myself and the handlebars.

People were constantly coming across new ideas, experiences, situations and nationalities. There was a tremendous movement of people. At Worcester, workers could find themselves working alongside a Ukranian, a Pole, an Italian, a Lithuanian or a Czech. By 1941, 4,000 workers had been transported to Redditch to work in factories or on farms. Old houses were hastily converted into shared flats. Where Sainsburys now stands on the A441 Redditch to Birmingham Road was the Abbey Hostel, a large complex of single- and two-storey flats and apartments.

One morning, the staff of Stourport-on-Severn High School arrived to find that the army had occupied the whole school overnight! The headmaster, Mr E. J. Jones, insisted that the army moved into the quadrangle; desks and chairs were replaced, and morning assembly was only fifteen minutes late!

Prisoners of war

Sometimes, especially on the land, local people would find themselves working alongside a prisoner of war. Just across the border in Ledbury was a 5-acre camp of 2,000 German prisoners of war. A prison was built next to the American camp in Burlish to hold 200 Italian prisoners of war. They were put to good use in the American camp, gardening, painting, cleaning and so on. Four of the Italians worked at a timber yard in Stourport where a lorry dropped them off every morning. In charge of the four was fourteen-year-old Ron Hughes, who had only just left school. He says that the prisoners were no trouble. Every lunchtime, one of the workers gave the prisoners a pint of beer and a packet of cigarettes.

Ron Tongue managed the 200-acre Lane House Farm, at Bentley, near Bromsgrove. He was helped by prisoners of war, sometimes as many as twenty. He says:

> I had all nationalities at different times. They started off with Poles and then they were mixed up with a few Italians and so forth and there were one or two

Russians amongst them. I had a good cross-section. Then when they got withdrawn, I had German prisoners. I liked those a lot, they were good workers.
Lane House farm had got servants' quarters on the side of it, separate to the
rest of the building ... I had two, occasionally three, Germans living in there.
They used to get up at seven o'clock in the morning and took on a lot of responsibility. In the evening they came down to have their dinner with us and loved
that ... We had rabbits then, my mother was a marvellous cook and she looked
after them, and they thought the world of her.

Some prisoners of war married local girls and stayed on. For many years, the
author's next-door neighbour was a kind, elderly German ex-prisoner who,
years before, had married an English girl. He kept a photograph of himself in SS
uniform on the piano, and played loud patriotic German marches in his garden
on his record player every Sunday afternoon throughout the summer for years.

Evacuees

In the sixteenth and seventeenth centuries Worcestershire was a refuge for those
Catholics who refused to convert to Henry VIII's new religion. In 1939 it became
a refuge again when it was designated by the government as an evacuation area.
The first evacuees arrived in Worcester on 1 September, and the following day
106 mothers and infants arrived, followed by 184 mothers and 193 infants, chiefly
newborn, from the Birmingham maternity centre. That same year 500 children
were evacuated to Stourport-on-Severn, despite it being a potential target for
German bombers.

The editor lived in Hockley, Birmingham, in 1940. The whole school was to
be evacuated. We had to march down to the local train station and wait, but the
designated train shot by, filled to capacity. This happened twice, so my mother
decided to answer an advert for private evacuation. That is how, at a tender age,
I was whisked from the chaos of a family business into the ordered life of two
gracious and aristocratic ladies in Chapel Street, West Hagley, the Misses
Stevens and Horton, known to us as 'Steve' and 'Hort'. They had been teachers,
probably governesses, until Hort became stone deaf and Steve was stabbed by
a pupil. My name was actually Margaret, but as there was already another
Margaret staying there the Misses Stevens and Horton used my second name,
Anne. My parents were not very pleased when they visited and discovered that
their daughter had been renamed. The two ladies were very eccentric. They were
great animal lovers and had innumerable cats. They didn't believe in British
summertime, nor school, so I didn't go to school until the war was over. These
two ladies should be remembered as the kind benefactors who bought the
playing fields near Chapel Street next to the allotments and donated them to the

council. What had happened was that they heard, with horror, that the field next to their house was to be developed, which meant their view would be spoiled. So they bought the field and gave it to the council on the condition that it would be used as a playing field, but unfortunately the council's first action was to build a large red-brick toilet block right in front of their window. After that, the two ladies gave up protesting and were eventually surrounded by houses on three sides. When I returned to Birmingham, my classmates complained that I 'talked posh' – but I soon acquired a Birmingham accent again!

Issue number 21 of the *Clent Clarion* tells how Violet Portman, who in 1941 lived in Shady Rock cottages, heard a faltering knock at her door one night and opened it to see a little old lady huddled there with a stool under her arm. The old dear asked if she could come in and sit down for half an hour. She stayed for three years! Violet also describes how, during the blitz, charabancs would arrive from the city and park in Violet Lane (which at that time was like a tunnel through the elms, and blue with violets in the spring). She says: 'The Brummies brought their suppers with them and would eat them at the Fountain Inn. Then, after a few bevvies, they would return to their coaches and sleep the night away,

The Transport Museum, Wythall

The charabanc was most probably a single decker bus. Charabancs died out in the 1930s but the name lived on in general use for any kind of single-decker bus or coach. It was customary for Midland Red to disperse the fleet at night to avoid disaster in the event of a direct hit on a garage. The driver probably lived in the vicinity

returning to Birmingham at dawn. This started off with just one charabanc but the word got around – eventually there were as many as six or seven of them parked the length of the lane!'

The day the bomb fell

Despite its importance, Worcestershire escaped lightly from the bombing as the Luftwaffe was more interested in the industrial Midlands. Most of the bombs that fell were jettisoned spares and landed in fields or back gardens.

Forty evacuees at Clent were staying in the Foresters Home. Unfortunately, it was hit by a bomb in 1940 but no one was hurt and the children were moved to Field House for a week until they were found new homes. In the summer of 1942 a Heinkel 111 dropped a bomb on Stourport-on-Severn boys' school. Fortunately, it was a Sunday afternoon and the school was empty. The building was wrecked but, strangely, the huge dome on the top dropped to the ground intact. The question was, where could the boys continue their education? It was decided that the boys should share the girls' school up the road. One week the boys used the school in the morning and the girls used it in the afternoon, then the next week the situation would be reversed. Eventually it was decided to use an old chapel along the Lickhill Road.

A wartime fire engine at Wythall Transport Museum. It would have been used in the worst of the air raids

The two worst bombing raids with fatalities came in 1940 – one in Worcester and the other in Redditch. The day of 3 October was grey with heavy clouds, when suddenly, at about midday, out of the clouds above St John's in Worcester, came a German Junkers 88. Two bombs were released, falling on the Mining Engineering Company Works. The first fell at an angle so that, although it dropped into the machine shop, it went through an outside wall before exploding. The blast ripped out a huge hole in the factory, demolishing the canteen and the clocking-in area. Seven employees were killed and about seventy were injured, including the canteen lady who lost the sight of an eye. The second bomb missed the works, but damaged several houses, inappropriately named 'Happy Land'.

A few days before Christmas in 1940, three high explosive bombs were dropped in Redditch, on Evesham Road, Orchard Street and Glover Street. Six or seven people were killed, twelve were seriously injured, and eight houses were demolished. Charlie Stallard was living nearby in Mount Street with his parents, his wife and ten-day-old son and he was working nights at the BSA. The foreman rushed in and said, 'Quick, Charlie, you had better get home. A bomb has dropped on your street.' Charlie says that as he ran home, the glass crunched under his feet. 'Our front door was hanging on one hinge and the windows had been smashed in … Dad was sitting on the stairs with his head in his hands. He said, "They're all in the cellar [mother, wife and baby]." We called it the cellar, but it was the space under the stairwell … I stood there at three o'clock in the morning and you could have read a newspaper, the moon was so bright. They were digging in the debris to try and find anybody who was still alive. Seven people had been killed, one of them a babe in arms. The mother had been sitting with the baby on the rug in front of the fire when the bomb had hit the house. The family were the only people in the street with a proper air-raid shelter … but they hadn't been in it.'

Those were the days of toilets down the garden. The father of the baby, Harold, had been in the garden shouting a conversation to his next-door neighbour, Bill, who was on the toilet. Bill had his head blown off, and Harold was thrown down the garden and his sight was damaged. He lost everything he possessed – his home, his wife and his baby. Even the clothes were blown off him.

One young lady was going out and had reached the bottom of Orchard Street when she realized she didn't have a clean hanky, so she went back and got to her home just as the bomb hit the houses opposite! The roof of her house fell in. Fortunately, the family were safe but the bottom was torn off her wedding dress. The wedding was due the next week and the dress had been bought through all the family donating their precious clothing coupons. It was repaired by a friend just in time for the wedding.

Spies

Worcestershire had its fair share of spies, and the photograph of the Wychbold transmitter station taken from the ground has already been mentioned. A teenage Arthur Newbould worked on maps for the central control room in Redditch, but accidentally dropped a blot on one of the maps. He tried frantically to scratch it out, but it was an impossible task and it remained clearly visible. In 1947 he was employed by the council and it so happened that he was sent German air navigation maps including those of Redditch. And there was his map, complete with scratchings! They must have been sent by a spy in the office.

When John H. Smith moved into his house in Barnt Green, a passer-by said to him, 'Did you know that a famous spy was associated with your house?' This turned out to be Alan Nunn May, educated at Cambridge where he became a member of the Communist Party in the ring that included Philby, Maclean, Burgess and Blunt. In 1939 Nunn May worked on a secret radar project, and then on the possibility of making an atomic bomb. In 1944 he went to Canada to work on the Atomic Energy Project at Montreal. By 1945 he had supplied the Russians with a sample of Uranium 233 and information on the first atomic test. Nunn May would never have been caught, but in September 1945 Igor Gouzenko, a cipher clerk working in Canada, defected with a number of secret files that included the spy's activities. Nunn May returned to England where MI5 kept him under surveillance, then arrested him in 1946. He was sentenced to ten years but released after six.

THE END OF THE WAR

The war ended in 1945. First came victory over Europe on 8 May (VE Day), then the atom bombs fell on Hiroshima and Nagasaki, bringing victory over Japan on 15 August (VJ Day). Peace at last. Church bells rang and housewives ran in and out of each other's houses with excitement. Most roads held a street party for the children – there were no concerns about insurance in those days. Despite the rationing (which continued for months), there was plenty of jelly and cupcakes and jam sandwiches. Tables and benches were erected from old doors and planks of wood, and no one bothered about 'Health and Safety'. Soldiers returned to their families but, for engaged couples, sex was risky as there was little in the way of contraception and to have an illegitimate baby was a terrible disgrace. Bonfires were lit on scraps of waste ground, probably fuelled by many a valuable antique – the nation wanted to forget the past. Everyone wanted the new – the

In 1944 Churchill mentioned easing the acute housing shortage by means of prefabricated homes. One of the original designs, shown here, has been preserved at Avoncroft Museum of Historic Buildings

Avoncroft's prefab contains fittings and furnishings from the mid 1940s

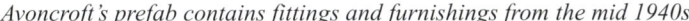

A few prefabs are still in existence, such as this one in Mill Lane, Stourport

contemporary. A great wave of euphoria hit the nation. The country was under new leadership: Winston Churchill was out, and Labour under Clement Attlee was in.

We end with a conversation that took place towards the end of the war between two Royal Enfield workers, Vic Bott and Wally Powell, who were with a group of firemen on the roof of the factory. They were all watching a lone enemy plane high above them, and as it neared the moon, it seemed to disappear. Wally exclaimed, 'The b——'s gone behind the moon.' They all laughed, but Vic remarked that technology was advancing so rapidly that if the plane had gone behind the moon, they wouldn't have been at all surprised.

APPENDIX

In the early 1960s the residents of Redditch learned, to their horror, that they were being designated a new town.

Birmingham was overcrowded and needed to expand, but the city had run out of spare land. The solution was, the government decided, to persuade hundreds of businesses and thousands of people to move out of the city to a new site a few miles away. The location they chose was Redditch, which was surrounded by farmland.

Redditch was a quiet little country town about 15 miles from the centre of Birmingham with a population of approximately 32,000. Basically it was where the road from Birmingham to Evesham was crossed by the road from Studley to Bromsgrove. At the centre of these crossroads was a market place and a large Victorian church. Redditch had been famous for its needles, springs and fish-hooks, but unfortunately foreign competition had affected the trade, many companies were struggling, and some had closed. The town had expanded rapidly in the early nineteenth century so that there were several pockets of slums in the town centre. When you walked down the High Street with its Victorian shops these were just frontages with old property behind. One senior citizen remembers that as a schoolboy he had a part-time job in the basement of a grocer's shop, weighing unwrapped food, where cobwebs and strands of dry rot were hanging down all round him and he had no access to running water. It was a town that needed regenerating.

A sad fact was that Redditch was already starting on a programme of slum clearance under the guidance of Councillor Walter Stranz. Part of Unicorn Hill had already been cleared and he had plans for the rest of the town. In 1939, at the age of fifteen, Walter had come to England as a refugee from Nazi Germany because of his Jewish grandparents; he then moved to Redditch in 1948 when he was offered a post at the County High School. He threw himself into the political life of the town with great enthusiasm and by 1962 he was assistant chief finance officer. He tells the story of how the town clerk tricked him into buying the Bordesley Abbey meadows for the town. The chief finance officer was on holiday when the town clerk sent for him and said that the meadows had just come on the market for a mere £5,000. After purchase they could be licensed for building at great profit. A lot of people were after them and the purchase had to be done quickly, so Walter signed the papers. In actual fact, there was no hurry because the rest of the meadows were not sold for some months, and then soon after they were acquired they were registered as a public amenity so that they could never be built on.

Walter rose to become head of the School of Planning at Birmingham Polytechnic and was leader of the council (equivalent to mayor) three times. It is an indication of the respect and debt the town owes him that the area in front of the council house, Walter Stranz Square, is named after him.

Redditch was finally designated a new town in 1964 and the Redditch Development Corporation arrived. All Walter's plans were now irrelevant. He was not even asked to join any of their committees as the corporation was an independent body, state owned and state run. No Redditch councillors were invited to join.

To achieve their housing brief, the corporation had to build accommodation for between forty and seventy persons per acre, then work to about 2.5 children per family household. It was planned that the population of Redditch should rise to 70,000 by 1980. In actual fact, it has remained fairly static at about 79,000.

'Walkwood' is named after the local farm. The farm buildings still exist but the land is now covered by a school, a fast road and a housing estate

No new towns had been built since 1947; therefore there was no master plan to follow. The corporation had to start from scratch and it was an enormous task. About 10 or 11 square miles of farmland was to be turned into housing estates and industrial sites, and a network of roads was to be created. A consultant planner was called in, Hugh Wilson, who had been responsible for Cumbernauld, a new town in Scotland.

Redditch was the first town in England to be built with a road plan catering for cars. It was decided to keep the people and the traffic separate as far as possible, and the bus-only lanes were a new concept. One of the leading members of the corporation was Norman More FRICS from East Kilbride Development Corporation. He was appointed as chief estates officer and became general manager in 1979. He explains, 'There were a lot of criticisms because people didn't understand the road system. It's really quite simple, from the two main highways you move on to district distributor roads, through estate roads then you reach the housing areas.'

Encircling the town were seven new housing estates: Greenlands, Woodrow, Lodge Park, Oakenshaw, Winyates, Matchborough, and Church Hill. Each one was a satellite village, designed with all the shops necessary for day-to-day living so that there was no need for the elderly or disabled to travel into Redditch. If they did need to visit the town centre, a bus service was (in theory) very good and could do the circuit in about thirty minutes along the dedicated bus lanes, providing a service for some 30,000 people.

Norman Moore says that in the 1960s new towns were not known for encouraging owner occupation, so he gathered about a dozen property developers round the table, told them what he was prepared to do, and asked if they would help. At first they were a bit wary, then one of them said, 'OK, I'll have a go but it will have to be a very small development.' They began on a small site near Winyates. When other developers saw the scheme was a success they moved in.

One of the early problems was persuading landowners to sell their land, particularly if they were farmers. The compensation the Corporation was allowed to pay was minimal. Philip Terry of Terry's Springs says that from his house his entire view was of company land. He thought that nobody could creep up on him and build houses without his consent and then the Redditch Development Corporation came along. 'You either negotiated or had a compulsory purchase slapped on you', he said.

The financial situation was always difficult. Norman More says, 'We were not allowed to borrow from the private sector and I knew how difficult it was to get money from the Treasury. I therefore used a new fund-raising scheme known as the lease and lease-back. Broadly speaking, this is a property deal in which there are two partners; one partner – that is, the Redditch Development Corporation

– provides the development experience and the other partner provides the money upfront for the development to go ahead.

THE GREEN TOWN

Right at the start it was realized that Redditch had a natural asset with all its greenery. The roads were designed to run along the edges of fields so that the natural hedges could be preserved. Hedges and established trees were all part of the planning process. All large trees had a preservation order on them where each tree was earmarked and described. In addition, over five million new trees were planted, together with huge numbers of the daffodils on the main roads and masses of other wildflowers dotted about.

The chief landscape architect was Roy Winter, a qualified landscape architect who had been working on the Birmingham city centre. He has received a number of awards for his work in Redditch, and says, 'I wanted to make the new town a decent place in which to live. We decided that we should only build on lower-lying land and leave the higher ground with open space or woodland, so that the view across Redditch would be a green one. We also wanted to make sure that everybody who lived in the town had immediate access to a feeling of the countryside with its trees, shrubs and water courses.'

Arrow Valley Lake

The 3 miles of the Arrow Valley Park runs through Redditch from north to south with a triangular-shaped lake in the centre. Roy continues, 'The River Arrow used to flood quite regularly and so weirs were introduced to control the flow and the lake could be used to abstract excess water before it was released into the river. The Corporation ran out of money to build the Coventry highway, which needed to be on a raised bed, but I was able to provide them with the excavated soil from Arrow Valley Lake. I was left with a huge hole in the ground; however, it was fed by a natural stream and over a number of weeks it filled up.'

THE KINGFISHER CENTRE

The whole of the centre of Redditch was demolished; entire streets were flattened. George Street, Walford Street, New Street, Littleworth, and part of Evesham Street were all buried beneath the Kingfisher Shopping Centre.

Many Redditch people felt that the destruction of their town was a great tragedy. John Lewis of the police 'Specials' kept an eye on the demolition work for one night each week and he expresses the feelings of many when he says: 'To clamber over piles of rubble and walk past the shells of well-known buildings was quite upsetting. I remembered the shops and the shop owners, the pubs and pub landlords, and the young people who used to flirt in the street at night. As I walked away, I turned around and had a look at the depressing scene which was all that remained of old Redditch.'

Norman More says, 'If you think back to the 1960s and 1970s you will remember that a covered shopping centre was a completely new concept for the Midlands. The question was, where should it be sited? I felt that St Stephens and the Church Green was the focal point of the town and it seemed wrong to create one centre away from another … We wanted the name of the centre to have some sort of significance and so we named it after a boat which had been adopted by Redditch during World War II.'

The centre has two unusual features. Roy Winter felt that there was a need to provide some sort of spectacular feature in the Kingfisher Centre. He says, 'We wanted something different and it was suggested by Sir Edward Thompson, chairman of the Board of the Corporation, that we might like using date palms. They were ordered from Spain and arrived on huge lorries. They did give us concern a couple of years after they were planted when they started to show signs of yellowing of the foliage, so we had a lot of the roof panels taken out to let more light in.'

The second unusual feature is the Paolozzi mosaics, situated in Milward Square, between Marks and Spencer's and British Home Stores. Paolozzi has become one of the most sought-after artists of the last few decades, and a gallery solely for his work has opened in Edinburgh. Norman More says that he was recommended by Sir Hugh Casson. 'The theme is that of needles, and the mosaic had to be put together on the wall. Each of the 12 panels is 21 feet x 10 feet. It was the largest publicly commissioned work of art in Britain in the twentieth century … We were very fortunate in getting the Queen on a visit to formally open Milward Square in 1983.'

INDUSTRY AND INDUSTRIAL SITES

To quote Norman More, 'The health of any town revolves around its Industrial Development Policy. It was no use providing houses without employment … also the guarantee of housing was an important factor in persuading industry to move to Redditch.'

In 1975 James Thacker FRICS arrived from Tarmac in Wolverhampton, where he had been a quantity surveyor, to develop the industrial estates and take charge of the letting of factories. He explains:

> We had basically two different ways of developing the larger purpose-built units (over 50,000 square feet). Either we built the factories and rented them out, or we leased out the land and they built their own premises. Halfords, for example, took a ground lease and built their own property.
>
> The RDC industrial philosophy was to operate a 'ladder system' where people would start off in a chosen size and if and when they wanted to expand they would come to us. We would 'tear up' the old lease and they would move into another larger factory on the same site or another site in the town on a new lease within a few days. A number of firms began in a small way with us and then became large companies – for example, Cirrus Technology.
>
> In times of industrial growth we could have, say, five people after each small unit and we had to choose the best potential tenant … The classic tenant who did well was someone who had been employed by, say, Herbert's or Terry's or Hymatic and had bought a couple of machine tools to set up on their own. They knew the trade and the customers and they would pay the rent regularly. Around about the mid-1980s the biggest employer in the town was AT & T Istel, the ex-Rover computer systems company. They employed between 15,000 and 20,000 people.

Newspaper reports reveal that although all the applications were carefully vetted, the Corporation managed to install the biggest conman in the Midlands. Basil Wainwright claimed to have invented an engine that could do at least 100 miles to the gallon. He offered to build Noel Edmonds, of the television programme *Deal or No Deal* fame, the fastest ever speedboat for the annual Cowes offshore powerboat race. Edmonds gave him £70,000. A model of the boat was built and that was as far as it got. The money disappeared and there was no speedboat. Wainwright was found guilty of fraud and jailed for eighteen months. The last anyone heard of him was that he was in prison in America for fraud, having sold what he claimed to be a cure for cancer.

THE PALACE THEATRE, FORGE MILL AND MORTON STANLEY PARK

Were it not for the Corporation, Redditch would be without three of its major leisure attractions.

The Palace Theatre in the town centre, built in 1913, is one of the few remaining cinemas in the country designed by Bertie Crewe.

It was acquired under a compulsory purchase by the Redditch Development Corporation. According to Walter Stranz:

The Palace Theatre

They fell in love with it, refurbished it at a cost of £120,000 and gave it to the town as a gift. The council rejected the gift because the corporation wanted it to be run by a Trust and they did not believe that Redditch was the kind of place where you could find millionaires to finance a Trust to run the theatre. In 1970 the council accepted the gift on condition that it was run by them. The Corporation could have arranged for a well-known personality in the theatrical world to open the theatre, but instead they arranged for it to be done by Peter Walker, a prominent Tory politician, which upset the Labour Council.

FORGE MILL

It is said that when Walter Stranz signed the cheque for the Bordesley Abbey Meadows in 1962 he had also, inadvertently, bought an old scouring mill. It was probably originally an iron refinery mill converted for needlework in the eighteenth century and was still working as late as 1958 when the last of needles were scoured. Major Rollins worked for the council and took a liking to the ancient mill. He gathered together a group of a dozen or so enthusiasts who began clearing up the mill and repairing the water courses. The Redditch Development Corporation arrived to begin knocking down the town centre and there was a lot of old machinery lying around that nobody wanted. They were able to borrow a lorry from Darvill and Bakers, the mineral water people, drag the machines down to the mill, and put them into storage. It took them eight years to get organized, starting in 1971, and they began to turn it into a museum in 1979. They tried to get the money together to get the waterwheel working but nobody wanted to know. Then the Redditch Development Corporation arrived and agreed to fund it completely. When the Queen visited the town in 1983 she opened Forge Mill. One of the volunteers remarked, 'Then everyone wanted to know. It was unbelievable.'

Forge Mill is the only museum in the world dedicated to needles. Packed with information about needle-making, it includes a dark, dungeon-like scouring shop. Next to the mill is the rebuilt barn from Marlfield farm, moved here by the Corporation, and now extended and converted into a Visitors' Centre that gives the history of the abbey.

MORTON STANLEY PARK

Mr W. Morton Stanley was a needle and fishing tackle manufacturer in George Street in the 1880s. He probably lived in Hillview on the Bromsgrove Road, now a doctor's surgery. The Stanleys owned a great deal of land and property in the district, including Upper Grinsty Farm. His wife, Jane, had no children and so in 1955 Morton Stanley, in his will, gave the farm to the people of Redditch, on the condition that the council turned it into a public park. However, instead of converting it into a park, they used the western portion of the land as a council tip. The solicitor overseeing the transaction, Mr Thomas, was also a relative of the Morton Stanleys. He served the council with a notice saying that this was not the use envisaged by the Morton Stanleys and if the land was not made into a public park immediately, it would be sold. At that point the Redditch Development Corporation arrived and saved the day.

THE NEW ARRIVALS

As for those who came to live in the new town, Josie was the first to move into a Corporation house with her husband and three children. She says:

> We had come from a flat in Kings Norton. It was cold, draughty, damp and hard to heat. When we moved here it seemed like paradise. If I took the children out for a walk they could play in the brook, the woods and the fields. When we were at home, they could play on a patch of green opposite and I could watch them out of the kitchen window.
>
> It was quite a culture shock coming here. It was so quiet that we couldn't sleep at night and it was very dark when we went out at night, there were no street lamps. Everything was laid back and slow. When you travelled on a Corporation bus in Birmingham, as soon as you passed the stop before your destination you had to get up and dash to the front. We started to do the same here. The locals waited for the bus to stop before getting up. They used to look at us as if we had gone mad.
>
> A lot of people got into debt. When we lived in the flat the rent was £3.10s and when we came here it suddenly doubled to £6.14s. Then there were the electricity and gas bills. It took us a long time to adjust.

THE REDDITCH DEVELOPMENT
CORPORATION DRAWS TO A CLOSE

When the Redditch Development Corporation handed over to the Commission for New Towns in 1985 they had been in Redditch for twenty-one years. Norman More remarks: 'No doubt there are lots of areas where we could be criticized, we don't pretend that we have got it right all the time. But we have never forced people to come here. The fact that we have attracted so many people to live here, to set up industry here and to work here, shows that we must have done some things right.'

BIBLIOGRAPHY

Domesday Book, various editions

Florence of Worcester's Chronicle, English translation by Thomas Forrester (Archive No. RR942.01), Bohn's Antiquarian Library

The Victoria History of the Counties of England – A History of the County of Worcester, St Catherine Press, 1926

Albutt, Roy, *A. E. Lemmon* (stained glass windows), published privately, 2008

Albutt, Roy, *A. J. Davies of the Bromsgrove Guild,* published privately, 2005

Albutt, Roy, *Stained Glass Windows of Bromsgrove & Redditch,* published privately, 2002

Amphlett, John, *A Short History of Clent,* Ashgate, 1991, republished by Clent History Society, 2004

Atkin, Malcolm, *Worcester 1651,* Pen & Sword, 2008

Atkins, Elizabeth, *The Knights Templars in Feckenham,* published privately, 2006

Avery, William, *Old Redditch, being an early history of the town 1800–1850,* Hunt End Books, 1999

Baker, Nigel and Holt, Richard, *Urban Growth and the Medieval Church: Gloucester and Worcester,* Ashgate, 2004

Baring-Gould, Sabine, *Nebo the Nailer,* Cassell & Company, 1902, copy in Worcestershire Record Office

Billington, Neville, *Flint and Steel: The Story of the founding of the Institution of Mechanical Engineers,* Came Hundred Publishing, 2010

Bradford, Anne, *Ghosts, Murders & Scandals of Worcestershire II,* Hunt End Books, 2009

Bradford, Anne, *Old Redditch Voices,* Hunt End Books, 2005

Bradford, Anne, *Royal Enfield from the Bicycle to the Bullet,* Hunt End Books, 1996

Bradford, Anne, *Stourport-on-Severn, A history of the town and the area,* Hunt End Books, 2002

Bradford, Anne & Johnson, Mike, booklet on Ron Tongue (prisoners of war) from *Memories of Old Redditch* series, Hunt End Books, 1999

Bradford, John, *River Avon, from Tewkesbury to its source,* Hunt End Books, 2006

Bradford, John, *River Teme, from Worcester to its source*, Hunt End Books, 2008

Bradford, John, *Severn's Southern Hills,* Hunt End Books, 2011

Bradford, John, *The River Severn, from the Estuary to its source*, Hunt End Books, 2004

Brassington, Salt W., *Historic Worcestershire*, Midland Educational Co., 1894

Bridges, Tim, *Churches of Worcestershire,* Logaston Press, 2000

Bund Willis, J. W., *The Civil War in Worcestershire 1642–1646 and the Scotch Invasion of 1651*, Alan Sutton, 1979

Burton, Rev. John Richard, *Kidderminster 1890*, Family History Centre, RR942.441

Campbell, James, *The Anglo Saxons*, Phaidon Press, 1982

Carpenter, Jeff and Owen, Brian, *Worcester at War,* published privately, 2000

Castor, Helen, *She-Wolves, the Women who ruled England before Elizabeth*, Faber & Faber, 2010

Chaucer, Geoffrey, *Canterbury Tales*, various editions

Dalwood, Hal and Edwards, Rachel, *Excavations at Deansway: Worcester, 1988 to 1989,* Council for British Archaeology, 2004

Dyer, Christopher, *Bromsgrove: a Small Town in Worcestershire in the Middle Ages,* Worcestershire Historical Society, 2000

Flanders, Judith, *A Circle of Sisters,* Viking, 2001

Fraser, Antonia, *The Gunpowder Plot,* Weidenfeld & Nicholson, 1996

Freeman, Marion, *Ancient Crosses of the Three Choirs Counties*, The History Press, 2009

Freeman-Greville, G. S. P., *The Book of Kings & Queens of Britain,* Wordsworth Reference Series, 1997

Freeman, Marion and Daniels, Janet, *Pershore Places,* Aspect Design, 2009

Grierson, Janet, *Dr Wilson and His Malvern Hydro,* C. Weaver, 1998

Grundy, Michael, *Worcester at Work, Portrait of a Victorian City,* Osborne Heritage, 1997

Gwilliam, H. W., *Old Worcester People and Places,* Rose Hill Teachers Centre, 1977

Harding, Paul, *The Worcester Story: A brief history of an ancient city,* Discover History, 2003

Haughton, Brian, *Coaching Days in the Midlands*, Quercus, 1997

Haughton, Brian, *Haunted Spaces, Sacred Places: A Field guide to Stone Circles, Crop Circles, Ancient Tombs and Supernatural Landscapes,* The Career Press, 2008

Haydon, Peter, *The English Pub: A History,* Robert Hale, 1994

Hodges, John, *Chateau Impney: The Story of a Victorian Country House,* published privately, 2010

Hodgson, Carol, *Clent Clarion No 21,* Clent History Society

Holder, Len, *River Severn Passenger Steamers 1956–1986*, published privately, 2006

Hoskins, W. G., *The Making of the English Landscape,* Hodder and Stoughton, 1955

Hunt, Tristram, *The English Civil War at First Hand,* Weidenfeld & Nicolson, 2002

Hurst, J. D., *Savouring the Past: The Droitwich Salt Industry,* Droitwich Town Development Committee, 1992

Johnson, Mike, *The Redditch Home Guard, 1940–1945,* published privately, 2009

Jones, Rev., *Porcelain in Worcester 1751–1951: An Illustrated Social History,* Parkbarn, 1993

Jusserand, J. J., *English Wayfaring Life in the Middle Ages,* Kessinger Publishing Co., 2003

Kissack, Keith, *The River Severn,* Terence Dalton, 1982

Lack, Katherine, *The Cockleshell Pilgrim,* Society for Promoting Christian Knowledge, 2003

Lane, B. A., *Severn Tanking,* Douglas McLean, 1991

Langland, William, *Piers Plowman,* various editions

Lloyd, David, *A History of Worcestershire,* Phillimore, 1993

Malmsbury, William, *Life of St Wulstan,* translated by J. H. F. Peile in 1934, reprinted by Lanerch Publishers, 1996

Mayby, Margaret, *A Thousand Years of Tardebigge,* Cornish Brothers, 1931

Nabarro, Gerald, *Severn Valley Steam,* Routledge & Kegan Paul, 1971

Newbould, Arthur, *Not Just Bricks and Mortar,* published privately, 1999

Palmer, Roy, *The Folklore of Worcestershire,* Logaston Press, 2005

Park, Betty I., *Brinton Park & the Sutton Common Area,* Kidderminster Civic Society, 2008

Pevsner, Nikolaus, *Worcestershire,* Buildings of England series, Yale University Press, revised edn, 2007

Poultney, Bernard & Richards, Olive and Alan, *The Lost World of Hanbury,* Poultney & Richards, 2000

Putley, Ernest, *Science Comes to Malvern: The Story of Radar,* Aspect Design, 2009

Rackham, Oliver, *The Illustrated History of the Countryside,* Weidenfeld & Nicolson, 1994

Royle, Trevor, *The Wars of the Three Kingdoms 1638–1660,* Abacus, 2007

Sage, Lorna and Davies, Pat, *Alvechurch Past & Present,* BPL Publishing, 2002

Savage, Anne, (trs.), *The Anglo Saxon Chronicles,* Bramley Books, 1997

Scaplehorn, Alan and Swan, Connie, *Worcestershire Turnpikes, Trusts and Tollhouses,* The Milestone Society, 2010

Shaw, Robin, *Housman's Places,* Housman Society, 1995

Sinclair, Max, *Droitwich Salt & James Brindley,* Droitwich Canals Trust, 2002

Thompson, Melvyn, *Woven in Kidderminster,* David Voice Associates, 2002

Thurlby, Malcolm, *The Herefordshire School of Romanesque Sculpture,* Logaston Press, 1999

Tuberville, T. C., *Worcestershire in the 19th Century* (archives) L9424407

Waters, M. Charlotte, *An Economic History of England 1066–1874,* Oxford University Press, 1925

Watt, Quentin, *The Bromsgrove Guild,* The Bromsgrove Society, 1999

Weaver, Cora, *A Short Guide to Malvern as a Spa Town,* published privately, 1996

Weaver, Cora, *Short Guides to Edward Elgar* (1997) *Charles Darwin & Evelyn Waugh* (1991), *Elizabeth Barrett and George Bernard Shaw* (1992), all published privately

Weaver Cora, *The Priory Gatehouse at Great Malvern,* published privately, 1993

Weaver, Cora, *Florence Nightingale and the Water Cure,* published privately, 2010

Weaver, Cora & Osborne, Bruce, *Aquae Malvernsis, The Springs and Fountains of the Malvern Hills,* published privately, 1994

White, Alan, *Worcestershire Salt, A History of Stoke Prior Salt Works,* Halfshire Books, 1996

Whitehouse, D. B., *The Roman Road between Bromsgrove and the Lickey Hills,* A paper presented to the Birmingham Archaeological Society, 1959

Wilks, Mick, *The Defence of Worcestershire and the southern approaches to Birmingham in World War II,* Logaston Press, 2007

Wood, Michael, *Domesday: A Search for the Roots of England,* Guild Publishing, 1986

_____

OTHER SOURCES

Evesham library has information on Saint Egwin and the persecution of the Quakers.

Bromsgrove library has information on the Chartists and local hospitals.

The Bromsgrove Society magazine, *The Rousler,* is a mine of historical information.

The Almonry museum in Evesham has plenty of information on the Battle of Evesham.

Forge Mill in Redditch has the history of Bordesley Abbey and information on needlemaking.

Information on Pitchcroft, the Foley family and Worcester porcelain came from the archives in Worcester Record Office.

INDEX